A Constitutional History
of Australia

A Constitutional History of Australia

W.G. McMINN

Associate Professor of History
UNIVERSITY OF NEWCASTLE

Melbourne
OXFORD UNIVERSITY PRESS
Oxford   Wellington   New York

Oxford University Press

OXFORD LONDON GLASGOW
NEW YORK TORONTO MELBOURNE WELLINGTON
NAIROBI DAR ES SALAAM CAPE TOWN
KUALA LUMPUR SINGAPORE JAKARTA HONG KONG TOKYO
DELHI BOMBAY CALCUTTA MADRAS KARACHI

First published 1979

NATIONAL LIBRARY OF AUSTRALIA CATALOGUING IN
PUBLICATION DATA

*McMinn, Winston Gregory, 1930–
A constitutional history of Australia*

*Index
Bibliography*
ISBN 0 19 550562 x

*1. Australia—Politics and government—1788–1978.
I. Title.*
3~~54~~42 .94

TYPESET BY ASCO TRADE TYPESETTING LIMITED, HONG KONG
PRINTED IN HONG KONG BY BRIGHT SUN PRINTING PRESS CO., LTD.
PUBLISHED BY OXFORD UNIVERSITY PRESS, 7 BOWEN CRESCENT, MELBOURNE

Preface

Forty years ago, when he published what became the classic *Constitutional History of Modern Britain*, Sir David Lindsay Keir defined his task as twofold: 'to describe the structure and working of the main organs of government during successive stages of their growth' and to make some effort towards 'interpreting their evolution with reference to the political and social conditions and the currents of thought and opinion by which it has been determined'. I seek, in a much narrower field, and without presuming comparison in performance, to share his aims. Keir's implied definition of 'constitutional history', a broad definition, not limited to the consideration of powers encoded in written documents but extending to cover at least some of the socio-political factors which form the context of these documents and condition their interpretation, is the definition accepted in this work.

In other words, this book attempts to explain the enormous changes which have taken place in Australian governmental institutions since the first necessarily autocratic régime came into existence in January 1788, in the light of the British traditions from which they developed and the peculiar economic and social conditions in which they evolved. While it is intended to be of use not only to students of history, but also to students of law and political science—and to those who are simply anxious to understand the workings of the Australian political system— its emphasis is historical. It is concerned more with the working and evolution of the Australian system of government than with the strict law of the constitution or with the minutiae of colonial, state or federal politics. Obviously consideration of neither can be avoided completely, but the approach attempted is essentially that which Justice Oliver Wendell Holmes had in mind when he said that in discussing the problems of government a page of history is worth a volume of logic.

As one of the functions of such a book is to introduce readers to specialized monographs and periodical articles, I have provided, instead of a full apparatus of footnotes and citations, a 'Bibliographical Note' covering the books and articles and some of the published documents which might form a reasonable second stage for anyone anxious to pursue further the study of Australian constitutional development.

In the preparation of this book I have been particularly encouraged by the interest of the Head of the Department of History in the University of Newcastle, Professor John Bach, his predecessor, Professor Geoffrey Cranfield, and the former Vice-Chancellor, Professor James Auchmuty C.B.E., F.A.H.A. I am also indebted to Mrs Robyn Gay for her quick and efficient typing and to two of my colleagues in particular for their assistance, Dr. D.I. Wright of the History Department and Mr.

C.S. Enright of Legal Studies. Naturally the reputations of these gentlemen are not committed in the use I have made of their researches.

W.G.M.

Contents

The British Background

'Continuity has been the dominant characteristic in the development of English government. Its institutions, though unprotected by the fundamental or organic laws which safeguard the 'rigid' constitutions of most other States, have preserved the same general appearance throughout their history, and have been regulated in their working by principles which can be regarded as constant. . . . Neither in its formal and legal, nor in its informal and practical aspect, has English government at any stage of its history violently and permanently repudiated its own tradition.'

SIR DAVID LINDSAY KEIR

Australian government, federal and state, is 'Westminster government'. It is based, in its essentials, on the system of government which had developed over a period of a thousand years in England and, by the time the first European settlement was made in this country, had come to be understood as government by 'King, Lords and Commons'—a system under which a bicameral parliament, meeting at Westminster, made the laws while the King's ministers controlled the day-to-day administration of those laws and an independent judiciary enforced them. Any attempt to understand the history of Australian constitutional development must start from this point: it must make clear how the Westminster system evolved before 1788 and note that it continued to evolve during the formative years of the Australian colonies.

It originated, as did all western European systems of government, in the synthesis which emerged from a collision between the folk traditions of Germanic tribes and the highly developed legal principles of the Roman Empire, but its lines of development began to diverge from those of continental systems soon after, if not indeed before, the conquest of England by William of Normandy in 1066. By the early fourteenth century there had developed in England a Parliament which, while in some ways similar to the 'Estates' of other European countries, was eventually to attain a position *vis-à-vis* the Crown that they were never to gain. It began, as G.M. Trevelyan once wrote, as 'oil for the machinery of government'; almost accidentally it divided itself into two 'Houses', Lords and Commons; and it developed two functions. From the King's point of view the more important of these was the provision of financial assistance; as an assembly of men of property, Parliament, and more particularly the House of Commons, could advise the King on what help he could expect from his subjects when his own revenues were inadequate; its advice became his authority to tax those subjects. Its other function was as a 'court of petitions': from this developed, very slowly, the idea of Parliament as a legislature.

The modern idea of Parliament is that it is a body which makes laws, but the medieval view was that law was not 'made' at all. The 'Law' was something which existed naturally and it was interpreted by the King's judges or, in the most important cases, by the King himself. The King's assent to a petition or 'Bill' presented to him by his Parliament would make the Bill a 'Statute'—in theory a definite statement of what the law was in this case, but often, in practice, a new law.

Neither as a means of registering consent to taxation nor as a 'court of petitions' did the medieval English Parliament play a central part in the governance of the kingdom. Except in times of crisis the King was expected to 'live of his own'—to raise sufficient revenue for the purposes of government from his own estates and his feudal dues—and very few Statutes were passed. In normal times there was little need for the King to call Parliament together at all. In the course of the sixteenth century, however, the situation changed considerably. As the tasks of government became more complex the Crown was forced to have more recourse to Parliament for finance. Henry VIII, moreover, felt the need for the support of Parliament in his quarrel with the Pope: the principal changes made by the Reformation were made by Statute. So when James I came to the throne in 1603 Parliament was playing a much more significant role than it had played a century before.

As yet, however, it was neither independent nor sovereign. Its members' freedom to criticize the Crown's policies was subject to very strict limits, and the King's Council was able both to issue proclamations with something like the force of law and to raise money in various ways without parliamentary sanction.

The roles of the Crown and the Parliament in the English constitution were anything but distinct, and the confusion was made greater by the existence of two different sets of courts. During the middle ages the powers which the feudal aristocracy had exercised in the period immediately after the Norman conquest gradually passed into the hands of judges appointed by the King. The 'common-law courts' over which these judges presided dispensed justice in the King's name, but since the law they administered was traditional and unwritten, the judges' knowledge of this 'common law' gave these courts some degree of independence from the King's government. Their freedom was increased by the fact that while the judges presided and interpreted the law, verdicts were brought in by juries of ordinary citizens. From the late fifteenth century, however, there had existed also a number of 'prerogative' courts, staffed by the King's councillors and charged with enforcing his proclamations. The functions of these two sets of courts in the enforcement of the laws were as confused as those of the Parliament and the Crown were in their making. In 1603 the constitution was in a state of balance, with the powers of Parliament matched by those of the King's council, and the jurisdiction of the common-law courts overlapping that of the prerogative courts. But the balance was too delicate to be stable. In the 1620s it began to shift under pressure applied by Parliament, and in the early 1640s it collapsed completely in the crisis which produced the Civil War.

In a vain attempt to stave off the rebellion which was ultimately to overthrow him, Charles surrendered many of his financial powers and also the right to decide when Parliament should be called together; most importantly, he acquiesced in the destruction of the main prerogative courts. This effectively deprived the Crown of the right to issue proclamations with the force of law, for without the prerogative courts proclamations could not be enforced. So when Charles II came to the throne in 1660, after the Civil War and the interregnum, the constitutional balance was very different from that of 1603. The King could no longer make laws or impose taxation without the consent of Parliament; the common-law courts had a virtual monopoly of jurisdiction, and the idea of a royal prerogative which could not be called into question had been destroyed. The King did not become a mere figurehead. He chose his own ministers; he alone could appoint and dismiss judges; he controlled the army and navy. But he could not prevent Parliament from discussing his policies and he relied on Parliament for the money necessary to carry them out. The King's ministers had to be able to come to terms with Parliament if his government was to be carried on at all.

The years from the restoration of Charles II to the second great revolution of the seventeenth century in 1688–89 showed how difficult this could be. That revolution made two significant changes: after 1688 the King could not maintain an army without the formal consent of Parliament, and all his official acts had to be countersigned by a minister, whom Parliament might call to account. Then in 1701 the Act of Settlement, which provided for the Crown to pass to the House of Hanover after the death of Queen Anne, made another important alteration: it laid down that henceforth the King might not dismiss judges; they might only be removed for proven misbehaviour and on an address from both houses of Parliament. By the beginning of the eighteenth century, therefore, the principle that the judiciary should be independent of the executive government had become part of the constitution.

The problem of relations between the executive government and the Parliament had, however, not been solved. It was the King's duty, not Parliament's, to govern the kingdom, but his policies could easily be wrecked by parliamentary opposition: the contradiction which had led to a complete breakdown in the system of government in 1640 and again in 1688 apparently remained. But, as has often occurred in English history, forces were working beneath the surface of strict constitutional law which were to alter the 'working constitution' fundamentally. In the years after 1714 it became normal for the King's ministers to make some attempt to influence the composition and behaviour of the House by pressure, patronage and bribery. Between 1721 and 1742 Sir Robert Walpole developed these tentative efforts into a great system. While direct bribery was seldom used, appointment to every position in the gift of the Crown, from great offices in the royal household and bishoprics to minor posts in the customs service, was made conditional on support for the government. In this way Walpole was able to build up in Parliament a party which, though not a majority government party in the modern sense, enabled him to get parliamentary support for most of the policies he, as the King's minister, wished to further.

The use of the Crown's patronage forged a link between legislature and executive and so resolved the constitutional conflict which made the seventeenth century 'the century of revolution'. Though hardly attractive to the modern mind, the Walpole System laid the foundations of Westminster government as we now know it. Out of it there slowly emerged, in the years which followed, the ideas of government and opposition groups in Parliament, and of a cabinet which took collective responsibility for the King's actions. These ideas were in turn to evolve into a system under which the Sovereign should reign but not rule, while the cabinet became responsible to Parliament. The process that produced the modern system of 'responsible government', under which the party winning a majority in a general election forms an executive, was far from complete at the end of the eighteenth century, but the influences which were to produce it were already being felt. The eighteenth-century 'enlightenment' and the industrial revolution were producing a new society, one which emphasized individual rights and believed in 'the career open to talent'. In this new society the methods whereby elections had been influenced came to be regarded as abuses: ultimately they were to be swept away by the 1832 Reform Act, and the King's ministers were in the long run to sustain their position by making their policies attractive rather than by exercising electoral influence. When this happened, what emerged was responsible government in its modern sense, which was defined by the third Earl Grey in 1858 as requiring that

> the powers belonging to the Crown be exercised through Ministers, who are held responsible for the manner in which they are used, who are expected to be members of the two Houses of Parliament, the proceedings of which they must generally be able to guide, and who are considered entitled to hold their offices only while they possess the confidence of Parliament.

When the First Fleet arrived in New South Wales in 1788 the emergence of this system was still more than a generation in the future, but the two most fundamental principles of the Westminster system, judicial independence and parliamentary control over finance, had already become so firmly established that Englishmen had come to consider them the distinguishing features of free government. That no Englishman could be condemned but by a jury of his peers, or be constrained to pay taxes but by the consent of Parliament, were the basic and unshakeable assumptions of the nation from which Australian political institutions were to be derived.

CHAPTER ONE

Autocracy and Prerogative

'The form of government employed in New South Wales between
1788 and 1823 was altogether unique; never before had the Crown
withheld legislative institutions from colonies governed by English
law and assumed to itself of delegated to colonial Governors the
authority to make laws for the colony which would otherwise have
been entrusted to a colonial legislature.'

ENID CAMPBELL

European Australia began as a gaol. In the early eighteenth century
transportation of felons beyond the seas, which had originated earlier as
a commutation of the death penalty, became also a punishment
prescribed by law, and for many years large numbers of criminals were
sent as virtually slave labour to the plantation colonies of North
America. After 1776, when the revolt of the thirteen American colonies
closed the ports of Georgia and the Carolinas to the surplus felonry of
England, a number of temporary Acts of Parliament provided that those
sentenced to transportation might be held in hulks and employed on
river maintenance works; and in 1784 the Crown was authorized to
nominate 'parts beyond the seas' to which such criminals might be sent.
After more or less desultory enquiries and a humanitarian outcry
against a proposal to use the fever-ridden coasts of West Africa, the
government issued, in December 1786, Orders-in-Council naming New
South Wales.

A purely convict colony, as opposed to a colony of settlement or a
garrison post to which convicts might be sent incidentally, was an
innovation. There was no precedent for its government. At first sight this
hardly seemed to matter, for what institutions of government are needed
in a gaol? A governor with autocratic authority would be enough, and
commissions issued to Captain Arthur Phillip early in 1787 certainly
gave him that.

But there was a problem. A gaol New South Wales was to be, but
something else as well. Phillip's commissions involved the annexation of
half a continent—all Australia east of the 135th meridian, with the
'adjacent' islands. This was far more territory than would be needed for
a prison. Subsequent instructions to him concerning the alienation of
land were designed to provide for emancipists and expirees, for members
of the forces who might wish to settle, and for free immigrants—the first
of whom arrived within five years. Clearly the gaol was to evolve into a
settlement colony, and was to have some of the elements of such from the

I

beginning: indeed, some historians have contended that the disposal of convicts was not the primary purpose of the establishment of New South Wales at all. Now, while a ceded territory could retain its existing laws and institutions, and a colony of conquest, being legally at the King's mercy, could be governed 'by prerogative', as the King saw fit, the people of a colony of settlement were usually regarded as taking with them from England their rights and liberties, including the benefits of government according to the British constitution. It was generally held that the Crown was bound to provide a newly established colony with legislative institutions in the tradition of those of Britain: to do otherwise required an Act of Parliament. But New South Wales was established during a period of transition in the history of the British Empire, a period which the American historian Helen Taft Manning has called the 'age of the strategic post', when ministers, preoccupied with matters of strategy, tended to look upon the niceties of colonial government as secondary. Although a Statute was passed to authorize the establishment of a criminal court, the Crown founded the colony and conferred power on the Governor to administer it by commissions 'issued under the great seal', that is, by executive action alone. This was unfortunate: clearly no legislature could be established in the early years of settlement, but much trouble would have been avoided if the great powers given to the Governor had had a statutory basis.

Phillip's two commissions, one military, the other of a type normally issued to colonial governors, and his instructions, did confer great powers upon him—and, since they were to receive similar commissions and instructions, upon his successors. He was authorized to appoint justices of the peace and other necessary officers, to pardon convicts, to remit punishments for all crimes committed in the colony except murder and treason (in which he might reprieve), to regulate trade, to make (or at his discretion withhold) grants of land, to proclaim and execute martial law. And all these powers he was to exercise alone. He was given a civil staff to help with administrative work; a force of marines, which was later replaced by a specially raised military corps, to defend the colony and maintain order; and an extraordinary judicial system, but in his rule he was limited by no executive Council. His subordinate officers were ordered to obey him 'according to the rules and discipline of war'. He had wide powers over even the courts. The Court of Criminal Jurisdiction, which was to punish crime 'according to the laws of England as nearly as may be, considering and allowing for the circumstances and situation of the place and ... the inhabitants', was composed of his subordinates, the Judge-Advocate and six other military or naval officers rostered to the duty; and no death sentence could be imposed without his consent. A civil court was composed of the Judge-Advocate and 'two fit and proper persons', again appointed by the Governor, and appeals from this court were to go to the Governor himself, with a right of further appeal to the Crown-in-Council where more than £300 was involved.

The courts were, indeed, in their composition and practice, as anomalous as the Governor's powers, though, it is perhaps fair to remark, not more strange than the institutions which passed for courts in some of the West Indian islands at the time. The criminal court, which resembled a court martial rather than a regular British court, was in fact extraordinary even by that standard: the accused did not have the right of challenge which he would have enjoyed before a court martial; and the Judge-Advocate, who in a court martial would have been confined to prosecuting and advising on points of law, had, in this court, also a voice in determining the verdict. The civil court, set up under an act which really authorized only the establishment of a criminal court, was later claimed by the philosopher and critic of British government policy, Jeremy Bentham, to be illegal (though a precedent for the establishment of such a court without specific legislation existed in the Court of Judicature at Gibraltar).

In the penal settlement established when Phillip's commissions were read on the shores of Sydney Cove on 26 January 1788, therefore, a system of government was founded which was foreign to British practice. The Governor was not an oriental despot: for all his wide powers he was expected to refer important questions, and in particular matters involving expenditure, to England. Was he, then, the satrap of a distant despotism? He was not, for British liberties still existed in Britain, and the Governor could not have pleaded either his commissions or his instructions as a defence if, upon his return, he had been prosecuted for acting illegally. Indeed, as will be seen, indemnity Acts had to be obtained to protect one of his successors. Moreover he was subject to an intangible but very real restriction in the attitude of mind of the men subordinate to him. The thousand convicts he brought with him and the tens of thousands who were to come in the years that followed had, as felons, forfeited their rights. But the free settlers (who, though few in the early years were to be joined by many more later), were very conscious of theirs, as were the native-born, the pardoned, those whose sentences had expired, and, indeed, the very officers upon whom he relied to put his commands into action. In a convict colony they knew that they had to submit to an extraordinary form of rule, but, brought up in a tradition of almost superstititious devotion to 'the rights of Englishmen', they were temperamentally unable to accept the implications of the fact. From the first, Phillip's orders were frustrated by the commander of the marines. After he left at the end of 1792, the officers of the newly-arrived New South Wales Corps, who in turn administered the colony, Francis Grose and William Paterson, avoided trouble only by avoiding positive action. The next two governors, John Hunter (1795–1800) and P.G. King (1800–06), fought a series of running battles with the colony's gentry; William Bligh's rule (1806–08) ended with a rebellion which its leaders, who were the leaders of the colony's society, justified in terms which might have been used by the great defender of the 1688 revolution, John Locke. Lachlan Macquarie, who took over the governorship in 1810, was seldom accorded cheerful obedience, and after a quiet start his period of office degenerated into a chain of crises. It is wrong to put this down to sheer factiousness, to see the whole of early Australian history (as it is sometimes seen) as the story of the attempts of governors to suppress the activities of officers who were making fortunes by corrupting small emancipist freeholders with liquor. The real trouble was the obvious, even the predictable attitude of Englishmen to a power situation which was foreign to them.

When all this is said, the fact remains that Australia's first system of government can best be described as an autocracy. There was always a problem of authority, but the governors were forced to govern: which meant, in this extraordinary and new colony, that they often ignored nice points of law. Indeed, at times they could not avoid taking actions which might seem quite arbitrary. They were handicapped by a situation so isolated that, at least until economic development produced a better shipping service after about 1816, two years might elapse before an answer would be received to any question referred home. They were further handicapped by the fact that, even after the establishment of the Office of War and the Colonies in 1801, nearly a dozen departments of the home government had a hand in instructing them. They were encouraged to answer the questions which arose in their own way and, as they were serving officers of the forces, they normally sought to answer them by the direct method of a command. Macquarie, by whose time the development of the colony was pushing the problem of its government to a climax, was particularly inclined by temperament to follow his own judgment, even in cases where the wide terms of commission and instructions did not apply.

Some of his actions clearly went beyond his authority. Faced with a shortage of currency and attendant economic problems, he struck a local coinage, having a quantity of Spanish dollars defaced by the removal of the centre, to which he gave the arbitrary value of 1s. 3d. while decreeing that the 'holey dollar' should retain the conventional value of 5s. When this did not solve the problem he issued a charter to a joint stock bank and, when the Crown law officers at home advised that the charter was illegal, successfully resisted orders to withdraw it. Earlier he had granted a three-year monopoly of spirit sales to a consortium which agreed to build a hospital, though he had no more right to grant a monopoly than to issue a charter. He was later to get into serious difficulties by permitting an American vessel to land goods in breach of the Navigation Acts, which prohibited trade between foreign ships and British colonies. On two occasions, neither without grave provocation certainly, he assumed an illegal power to deport. And, as Marion Phillips has pointed out, 'he exercised a complete control over all public discussion', controlling the only printing press and insisting that no public meeting should be held without his consent, and without one of his officials, the provost marshal, in the chair.

The Problem of Authority

Once this peculiarly authoritarian system had been established, it became very difficult to draw a line between what a governor might and might not do. This was particularly so in matters concerning the judiciary. As has been seen, the letters patent which established the colony's courts, the 'first charter of justice', provided that the principal judicial officer should be the Judge-Advocate, who held a military commission and was thus directly under the Governor's orders. Except for two years, 1798–1800, when Richard Dore was Judge-Advocate, the office was held until 1810 by men with no legal training whatever. Dore's brief incumbency was marked by clashes with Governor Hunter over the Judge-Advocate's insistence on his independence. When another lawyer, Ellis Bent, came to take up the office in 1810 its anomalous position, which had not worried his untrained predecessor, was bound to cause him concern. At first he accepted the situation, perhaps because he was for a time on very good terms with Macquarie. But a crisis had to come. A second 'charter of justice' issued in 1814 made some changes in the judicial system. The Judge-Advocate was relieved of part of his responsibility for civil jurisdiction. The old civil court was replaced by a 'Supreme Court of Civil Judicature' to be composed of a new judge and two justices of the peace. There was established an inferior civil court (with the very inapt name of Governor's Court) presided over by the Judge-Advocate, to hear suits concerning amounts less than £50, and in the sub-colony of Van Diemen's Land, which had been established in 1803, a similar court, presided over by a deputy Judge-Advocate, was set up. The Judge-Advocate was also to advise the Governor on appeals from the Supreme Court, the lower limit on further appeal to the Crown-in-Council being raised to £3,000. But the criminal court was unaltered, the Judge-Advocate remained subject to the Governor's orders and the new Supreme Court judge was placed in the same position.

Ellis Bent's brother, Jeffery Hart Bent, was appointed to the new judgeship, and shortly after his arrival in the colony the long-postponed crisis came. The personalities of the men involved played a part in causing it, but the basic problem was that men were sworn to administer the law and at the same time ordered to obey a governor whose position forced him to take, at times, a very elastic view of it. The problem had two aspects.

The first concerned the Governor's power to make regulations, which is discussed in more detail below (pp. 7–11). At the end of 1814 Ellis Bent refused a request by Macquarie that he should put into legal language a draft revision of the colony's port regulations which, he claimed, involved deviations from British law so extensive as to 'set the Governor of New South Wales above the Legislature of Great Britain'. It has been suggested by Macquarie's biographer, M.H. Ellis, that Bent had interested motives, a desire to cast doubt on colonial regulations generally because others the Governor had made, concerning currency, might have seriously embarrassed the Judge-Advocate personally; but, whether this is the case or not, Bent was placed by Macquarie's request in a position where his judicial oath might be in conflict with his duty of obedience.

The second concerned emancipist lawyers. When Jeffery Bent had been appointed, two London solicitors had been given a government subsidy to set up practice in New South Wales. One of them arrived in Sydney with Bent in July 1814; the other was travelling in a ship which was captured by an American privateer and did not land in New South Wales for another fourteen months. Bent was at first unwilling to convene the Supreme Court, since with only one legally qualified solicitor in the colony one litigant in any suit would be at a disadvantage. There were in the colony, however, three emancipists, George Crossley, Edward Eagar and George Chartres, who had formerly been lawyers and had been permitted *de facto* right to practise in the old civil court. Macquarie suggested to Bent that he should allow these men to appear, at least temporarily, and get the court open; and when they petitioned him he told the judge that he was 'decidedly of opinion that it would be fair and reasonable' to admit them. Bent objected to the Governor's intervention, as undue influence by the executive on the judiciary. By convening the court and refusing to hear the petitioners, and abusing the two magistrates who sat with him when they suggested that the men should at least be heard, he publicly announced his disobedience. He refused to sit with the two magistrates; the court remained effectively closed. When the Governor asked for a report on proceedings Bent declined to acknowledge any duty to give it, and added: 'Feeling it to be inconsistent with my dignity and independence, as a judge, to submit to any interference or investigation into my judicial conduct on the part of the Executive Government of the Colony, I shall decline entering into any further discussion with Your Excellency on this subject, except on terms of equality and independence.' After this there was nothing for Macquarie to do but refer the whole issue to Earl Bathurst, the Secretary of State for War and the Colonies, particularly as Ellis Bent openly supported his brother.

The Secretary of State came down on the side of the Governor. He made clear that he considered the Bents wrong in claiming independence, and drove the point home by removing them from office—though Ellis Bent had, in fact, died before he wrote. Macquarie was informed that his superiors had 'every reason to be satisfied' with his conduct in the affair. Legally, of course, the Bents had been substantially in the right. Bathurst was aware of this: he was putting the good order and discipline of what he never forgot was a convict colony before the considerations of strict law. But he and his colleagues in the government took no action to rectify the anomalous arrangements of the colony: they merely replaced the Bents with two men whom they thought more likely to come to terms with the situation. The administrative system of New South Wales remained at best extra-legal.

And what was true of administration was, by definition, true of the Governor's legislative activities. English law came to the colony with the first fleet, but, while the government recognized that the circumstances of the colony would make many detailed modifications necessary, no machinery was provided. No legislature was established; nor was there any warrant in the form of Phillip's commissions for his assuming the legislative authority which might be conferred on the governor of a conquered territory. But, faced by the necessity to rule, he instituted the practice of issuing what he called, by adapting a familiar term in military law, 'government and general orders'. His successors followed the same procedure but, largely because the matters dealt with by such orders covered subjects ranging from the grave to the trivial, not all of them were reported to London until after 1800. From 1803 all government and general orders were published in the *Sydney Gazette*, which was established in that year, and in this form were transmitted to London; but by this time so many orders had been issued that they constituted an almost impenetrable tangle of local law.

For eighteen years no one in the colony challenged the validity of the Governor's frequently-pronounced fiat. Then at the end of 1805 Governor King was alarmed when the colony's most formidable citizen, John Macarthur ('the Perturbator' as King called him), quoted to the Governor 'some counsel's opinion of the illegality of all local regulations'. Behind the challenge lay Jeremy Bentham's pamphlet, *A Plea for the Constitution of New South Wales*, published in 1802, which attacked the government's policy—or lack of policy—towards the colony. Bentham contended that, as no prerogative power existed, and no statutory power had been conferred to allow the Crown to legislate for the colony, the Crown could not validly delegate legislative authority to the Governor. In substance he was probably right. It could be argued that the absence of any reference to legislative authority in the Governor's commissions was unimportant, that such authority could be inferred from the fact that the commissions imposed on him duties which might necessarily involve him in making regulations—if the Crown had the power to legislate itself. But since the Crown's independent legislative authority in England had disappeared in the middle of the seventeenth century there was room for considerable doubt about its right to make laws for settlement colonies. There was a body of legal opinion that until such time as legislative institutions were established in a colony the Crown could legislate for it, provided that the laws made were not repugnant to the laws of England insofar as they could be applied in the colony; but in the absence of precedent (and hitherto all colonies had been given legislatures at their foundation) this was only opinion; and in any case the question of how much variation to suit local circumstances might be allowed was a difficult one. Governor King thought that almost no limits could be drawn in a colony where 'three-fourths of the inhabitants [had] been spared from an ignominious death by the humanity of the laws of England', and the home government, by virtually ignoring the problem, agreed with him. The next Governor, Bligh, issued orders just as his predecessors had.

When Macquarie was appointed he was aware that a problem existed, and that it had been complicated by the rebellion against Bligh. But he was unable to get any more guidance from Downing Street than King had been given. In 1812 the House of Commons select committee on transportation had recommended that an executive council should be appointed, to share with the Governor 'the Responsibility of the Measures they may think necessary for the Security and Prosperity of the colony', but the government had rejected the idea, and Macquarie had concurred. He sought to give his legislation a less haphazard flavour by drawing a distinction between orders, which dealt with the petty issues of day-to-day administration, and 'proclamations', which he was careful to have framed in lawyers' language; but the difference was in form rather than substance. The Governor continued to legislate. The extent of the authority which he claimed is shown clearly by one of his first proclamations. Designed to help heal the breach in society left by the rebellion, this purported to give magistrates and constables who had acted under the authority of the rebels indemnity from prosecution: it threatened those who brought prosecutions or suits against such officers with the Governor's 'grave displeasure' and instructed the Judge-Advocate 'to enter a verdict of not guilty or a verdict for the Defendant . . . in such prosecutions or suits at Law, with full costs of suit'. A governor who could thus penalize persons for asserting what were, in strict law, their rights was indeed a powerful man. But, unlike his predecessors, Macquarie had in Ellis Bent a Judge-Advocate with a totally different conception of gubernatorial authority from that which circumstances and the tacit support of the home government had inculcated in all the governors. Bent, as has been seen, was complaisant for a time, but when a conflict came over the port regulations he protested to London that the Governor 'claim[ed] and exercise[d] a power to make . . . not merely bye-laws . . . but general laws upon all subjects . . . in many instances directly contrary to the spirit and principles of the laws of England'. His brother Jeffery, who after his own clash with the Governor saw the assumption of legislative authority as the Achilles' heel of Macquarie's position, was more vehement: 'I am required', he complained to the Governor himself, 'to acknowledge that Your Excellency's will, expressed by proclamation ... has the force and validity of law, a proposition so startling that I cannot conceive any person in England ... could have the slightest notion that it would be maintained even in argument, far otherwise that it would be carried out to its fullest extent in practice.' Bathurst, in reply to Ellis Bent, was a model of a politician avoiding the real question: he had 'only to observe that the Power of the Governor ... rest[ed] now on the same Foundation on which it ha[d] ever stood'. That bland refusal to discuss what the 'Foundation' was, and the dismissal of the brothers, closed their case.

But it did not solve the problem. Of this fact, if not of a solution, Bathurst seemed to be aware. He told Macquarie that all regulations dealing with trade (he was thinking particularly of the port regulations) 'must derive their Justification from the necessity of the case, from their expediency with a view to the Security of the Convicts, or the maintenance of public Tranquility' and that other proclamations 'must equally be guided by the English Laws, modified by the Usages which [had] always subsisted'. These vague phrases side-stepped the issue, and the Bents' successors, John Wylde as Judge-Advocate and Barron Field as judge of the Supreme Court, were uneasy, particularly about orders and proclamations imposing taxes. Before Jeffery Bent left the colony he drew spectacular attention to this aspect of the problem of the governor's powers: he refused to pay toll on the turnpike road between Sydney and Parramatta, on the ground that, since the charge was paid into general revenue ('the police fund') instead of a special road-maintenance account, it was not a toll legally exactable by the Crown but a tax. Bent was principally concerned to embarrass the Governor, so his objection might have been dismissed as a vexatious quibble, but there had existed in the colony from the beginning small imposts which were indisputably taxes, as opposed to port or market dues of a kind which the Crown might legally impose by prerogative in England, and which the Governor as its representative might, therefore, impose in the colony. They caused no problem until early in 1818, when Macquarie, proposing to raise some of the duties, decided also to issue process against defaulters, who up to this time had generally escaped scot-free. Mr Justice Field, alarmed that the defendants might plead the invalidity of the taxes and thus put him in the position of having to apply the maxim 'that no subject of England can be constrained to pay any aids or taxes but such as are imposed by [parliamentary] consent', dissuaded the Governor from proceeding until parliamentary sanction for the charges had been obtained. The British government failed to seek such sanction until one of its most redoubtable opponents in the House of Commons, Henry Brougham, inspired by a long list of criticisms of Macquarie brought home by Jeffery Bent, drew the attention of the House to the fact that 'taxes to the amount of £24,000 a year were imposed by the Governor without his having any warrant in his commission'. Then it put through an Act to indemnify Macquarie and his officers, to legalize existing duties, initially for one year, and to give the Governor specific authority to levy an import duty on spirits. This act was periodically renewed until the government of the colony was put on a statutory basis in 1823.

The Governor's proclamations in other fields continued to give trouble. In 1819 the Colonial Office counsel, James Stephen, in giving an opinion on port regulations promulgated for Van Diemen's Land, argued that the Governor had no right to impose fines, as he sought to do in these regulations. In the same year the Judge-Advocate gave a decision which seemed to imply that a proclamation giving magistrates power to enforce wage rates fixed by the Governor was invalid; when this matter was referred home, Stephen took an even stronger line, holding that to allow the Governor to issue proclamations with the force of law was in effect 'to deprive the colonists of the constitution and laws which, it is admitted, they ... carr[ied] with them' to the colony. Two years later he gave the same sort of opinion when Macquarie's successor, Sir Thomas Brisbane, sought to hold a census and impose penalties for non-co-operation.

The legislative activity of the Governor thus became something of an embarrassment; but if, twenty years after Bentham had fulminated against government and general orders as 'original acts of legislation, forbidding, and thereby converting into misbehaviours, a variety of acts, such as if performed in [England] ... would not have been misbehaviours', nothing had been done to rectify this anomalous situation, the explanation was that there was no deep and conscious sense of grievance in the colony. There was the vague uneasiness of Englishmen who genuinely cherished English constitutional traditions; there were sporadic appeals to principle when Macquarie's policies (particularly his policy of encouraging emancipist small-holders) touched the special interests of leading free settlers; but there was no concerted movement of protest.

Another deviation from the fundamental canons of British law was more striking—the absence of trial by jury. Juries could hardly have been used if the colony had remained purely a convict station; but, as has been remarked, it inevitably developed some of the elements of an ordinary settlement colony. When the first charter of justice was being drafted, Lord Chief Justice Camden had recommended to the Prime Minister, William Pitt, that trial by jury should be established as soon as reasonably possible, but to judge when this might be was difficult. For many years there was no serious pressure in the colony for the reform:

the first significant mention came in a memorial largely concerned with other matters presented to Governor Bligh at the beginning of 1808. But as the free and freed population grew the military flavour of the criminal court became more offensive to men who thought in such terms as 'the imprescriptible rights of Englishmen'. Two former governors, Hunter and Bligh, spoke in favour of trial by jury before the 1812 committee on transportation and the committee recommended it. Macquarie asked the Secretary of State, who at this time was working on the second charter of justice, to consider the use of juries in both civil and criminal cases where the presiding judge considered it to be in the interests of justice. Ellis Bent supported him, at least as regards criminal trials, and further suggested that the duties of the Judge-Advocate, who was both prosecutor and presiding judge in such cases, should be divided. The acquittal of murder by a court of their brother officers, of two officers who in 1813 killed a man while endeavouring to force entry to his house strengthened Macquarie's desire for regular jury trials.

Bathurst would not agree: the new charter of justice affected the civil jurisdiction only, leaving the criminal court unaltered. The Secretary of State explained the refusal of trial by jury in terms of the colony's social composition:

> The great principle of that excellent Institution is that men should be tried by their Peers. Would that principle be fairly acted upon if Free Settlers were to sit in Judgment on Convicts . . .? Would it be prudent to allow Convicts to act as Jurymen? Would their admission satisfy Free Settlers? Would not their exclusion . . . be considered as an invidious mark, and be at variance with the great Principle upon which the Institution itself is founded?

The objection here raised was not generally seen in the colony at the time; Bent believed that satisfactory criminal-court juries could be empanelled from among the free immigrants and the emancipists of long standing and respectable conduct; many free colonists agreed with him. But the social division between 'emancipist' and 'exclusive' was at this time being sharpened by the tendency for the Governor's opponents to find a rallying point in his policy of trying to have selected emancipists accepted in respectable society. Bathurst's opinion that 'in a society so constituted as that of New South Wales' jurymen might have 'passions and prejudices ill-fitted for the discharge of their Duty' was better grounded than it appeared to be.

The Background to the Bigge Inquiry

Bathurst's opinion was given at the end of 1815. After this time all the problems of government in New South Wales, administrative, legislative and judicial, intensified greatly. Inevitably they forced themselves on the attention of people in England who hitherto had not taken very seriously the affairs of a tiny prison camp on the other side of the world. The Colonial Office despatches to New South Wales, which in 1806 had taken up twenty-nine pages in the letter book, occupied 320 pages in 1816 and 729 in 1824. With the Napoleonic War over Parliament began to take an interest. Macquarie had made many enemies, and after the dismissal of the Bents the volume of complaint against him led to several debates in the Commons, initiated by radical members who were probably as much concerned to attack the government's policy of employing soldiers in colonial governorships as to reform New South Wales. In March 1817 one such member, Henry Grey Bennet, presented a petition on behalf of two officers whom Macquarie had disciplined for conduct which he considered subversive of his authority. The ministers, though they disapproved of Macquarie's action in this matter and privately censured him for it, (more particularly for withdrawing privileges from people who had supported the men by endorsing their petition) defended him warmly in the House. But in February 1819 Bennet returned to the attack. Armed with highly-coloured accounts of further apparently arbitrary exercises of power by the Governor, which had been supplied by a person with whom Macquarie was on very bad terms, the senior chaplain Samuel Marsden, Bennet moved for a committee of inquiry. A month later, in the course of presenting a petition from two more victims of Macquarie's irritability, Brougham made his attack on the Governor's taxing power. Meanwhile the government had sidetracked Bennet's motion by agreeing to the establishment of a select committee on gaols and transportation which made very little reference to the constitutional problems of New South Wales, though it did hear evidence from the prominent former colonist Alexander Riley and suggest that the Governor of New South Wales needed a Council.

By this time, however, the Secretary of State had decided that something would have to be done to put the affairs of the colony in order. Apart from the grievances of individual colonists which Bennet and Brougham had been bringing to light, there were wider issues. Since 1788 ministers had been defending transportation as a punishment which was feared by criminals and was thus an effective deterrent, and had been stressing the incentives for reform which the colony provided. Macquarie had made a particular point of encouraging reform by rewards and favour, and had been thoroughly supported in his policy. But as the sharp increase in the British crime rate after 1815 became a cause for concern there developed a tendency to exaggerate Macquarie's leniency and to relate the two. Moreover the free population of the colony was growing steadily. Already, when Macquarie arrived, free immigrants made up ten per cent of the population; emancipists and expirees added to their number and by 1819 large numbers of the first generation of the native born had reached adulthood. In that year fewer than forty per cent of the people of New South Wales were convicts. It was becoming necessary to decide whether the colony could continue as a penal settlement. Bathurst had come to the conclusion as early as mid-1817 that New South Wales would have to be 'placed on a footing that [would] render it possible to enforce ... strict Discipline, Regular Labour and constant Superintendence', or convicts would have to cease being sent there.

An essential preliminary to a decision on this question, and the related one of the colony's future government, was a full inquiry. Bathurst, after considering the choice of a suitable man for fifteen months, decided to entrust the investigation to John Thomas Bigge, former Chief Justice of Trinidad and a man who, he had concluded, would be sufficiently detached from the quarrels of New South Wales to give a detailed and balanced picture of its problems and needs.

The government's view of what these problems were was made clear in instructions issued to Bigge in the first days of 1819. He was enjoined to 'bear in mind that transportation to New South Wales was intended as a severe Punishment', that it had to be 'rendered an object of real Terror to all Classes'. But he was also told that, although the colony had been established to receive convicts, not 'with a view to Territorial or Commercial Advantages', the government might decide, at some time in the future, to end transportation there and to Van Diemen's Land; so he was to report upon 'a variety of topics which [had] more or less Reference to the Advancement of those Settlements as Colonies of the British Empire'. Bigge, therefore, had to make two inquiries, one concerning the efficacy of transportation to New South Wales as a punishment, the other concerning possible future developments. Among the 'variety of topics' on which he was to report in his second inquiry were several of an economic nature. As regards constitutional problems, he was to investigate how objections which had been raised to the judicial system could be met and to obtain information on the division between 'emancipists' (former convicts and their sympathizers) and 'exclusives' (the wealthier free settlers) which would obviously complicate any plan for constitutional reform. He was, however, not specifically directed to report on the possibility of establishing a Council to share the Governor's legislative authority.

It should be noticed that the real initiative of the Bigge inquiry came from England. It was encouraged by personally dissident elements in the colony, coalescing around Jeffery Bent, and by a general subconscious uneasiness about deviations from normal British governmental practice, but here was no case of colonists struggling against an unjust and tyrannous home government. In fact the clearest uneasiness was among the officials in the colony, people like Wylde and Field. It was inevitable that the anomalies of the colony's position should become more obvious as its convict and military origins became submerged in a rising free population. But although there were 16,000 free people in New South Wales in 1819 their division into two classes, almost two castes, prevented them from speaking with a united voice.

It was not, indeed, until March 1819 (after Bigge's appointment, but before his arrival in the colony) that the many small irritations to which colonists were subject drew from them any kind of representative protest. This took the form of a petition to the Crown bearing 1,260 signatures. The names, Macquarie reported, of 'all the men of Wealth, Rank and Intelligence' in the colony, except a few officials who felt disqualified by their office, and John Macarthur, who had given a pledge (when he was allowed to return after seven years' post-rebellion exile) to keep out of politics. But even this protest, concentrating on such economic grievances as restraints on colonial trade, showed little consciousness of united interest in political reform. It asked for one constitutional change only, the introduction of trial by jury, contending that there were now in the colony 'a great number of free, respectable inhabitants sufficient and competent for Jurymen'. Interest in this reform was growing, partly, as Judge-Advocate Wylde pointed out, because the officers on the criminal bench, anxious not to exacerbate their unpopularity with civilians, were becoming rather lenient, but there must be some doubt whether the petitioners took their own statement very seriously. They must have known that, even if emancipists were to be included, the number of people available for jury service would have been so small as to make it an intolerable burden. The possession of freehold property was a normal qualification for inclusion on jury lists at home, and there were only some six hundred freeholders in the colony. This number included perhaps fifty holders of Crown offices, several more who were magistrates, and a significant number of very small settlers for whom frequent jury service would have involved ruinous neglect of their farms. Like the terms of reference of the Bigge enquiry, the 1819 petition envisaged only very modest changes in the administration of New South Wales.

But less than a year later there arose an issue which had considerable incidental effect on the attitude of many colonists; an issue, moreover, which brought the emancipist-exclusive split to the surface. In 1817 the English Court of King's Bench, in the case *Bullock* v. *Dodds*, had ruled that the legal disabilities consequent on conviction of felony were not removed by any pardon unless issued under the great seal, which meant, in effect, issued on the direct authority of the British government. This seemed to throw doubt on the right of emancipists holding governor's pardons to sue in the courts, but there was little trouble at first because Field required anyone who raised 'the objection of attaint' in the Supreme Court to produce an office copy of the record of conviction, which was not available in the colony. Field's complaisance in this matter was of particular benefit to Edward Eagar, one of the emancipist 'attorneys' who had been excluded from court practice after 1814. Since then Eagar had supplemented his large-scale trading interests from the proceeds of informer's actions to such an extent that he had become a professional vexatious litigant. In January 1820 Field made, from the Bench, some savage comments on Eagar's activities, and Eagar responded by actions in the Governor's Court for slander and illegal exaction of fees. In defence Field chose to use the objection of attaint, which up to this time he had rather discouraged, claiming that Eagar's name had never been inserted in a pardon issued under the great seal, and obtained an adjournment to enable him to get a copy of the conviction record from England. When Eagar's next action came before the Supreme Court the defendant, Prosper de Mestre, raised the same objection and obtained an adjournment from Field for the same reason. No one could have much sympathy for Eagar, but the application of the rule that unless subsequently 'passed under the great seal', in other words specifically confirmed by the Lord Chancellor in England, a governor's pardon did not remove the disqualifications of attaint cast grave doubt on the civil rights of large numbers of emancipists.

At the beginning of 1821, therefore, a new petition was drawn up, a petition signed only by emancipists and taken home by two of their number, Eagar and the much respected Dr Redfern, with the Governor's blessing. It claimed, with reasonable accuracy, that the emancipist community (including the children of emancipists) outnumbered free settlers and their children by 13,000 to 2,300. It made reference to their wealth and the value of their past labours to the colony. It prayed that they be freed from the disability to acquire, hold or transfer property and to sue or to give evidence under which they now found themselves. Although the petitioners made much of the fact that the failure to insert their names in a great seal pardon was not a consequence of unworthiness but rather an oversight by the British government, and insisted that their disabilities should be removed to avoid 'introducing and perpetuating party distinctions, unpleasant discussions, irritable feelings and Jealousies, heats, Animosities and diversions' in the colony, the effect of the petition was to entangle constitutional issues in the colony's class struggle. They were to remain so entangled for two decades.

Wentworth and Bigge

This connection between emancipist-exclusive hostility and the emerging problems of constitutional development was underlined by the entry on the scene of a man who was to remain at the centre of New South Wales politics for forty years, William Charles Wentworth. Being a member of the 'emancipist' class almost by choice, he had his views much more highly-coloured by his membership than did many real emancipists. It has been suggested, indeed, by A.C.V. Melbourne, the great authority on early New South Welsh constitutional development, that the direction of his political career was determined by a desire to destroy the power and pretensions of exclusives who had imposed slights on him and his family.

In 1819, while he was in England reading for the bar, Wentworth published *A Statistical, Historical and Political Description of the Colony of New South Wales*. This contained a considerable amount of factual material and advocated a number of changes in economic policy, but its primary purpose was to advocate constitutional reform. Wentworth was prepared to admit that an authoritarian system was necessary at first, but argued that it had become out-of-date by 1804, when the colony had first become self-sufficient in grain. He claimed that the rebellion of 1808 should have convinced the government of the need for change, and that to continue the old system under a new governor, without even the addition of an executive council, was foolish. The book contained a good deal of rhetoric to the effect that New South Wales could not be expected to submit indefinitely to 'tyranny', that the alternative to a radical constitutional reform was a rebellion, in which the colonists might well appeal to the United States. The exaggeration was obvious, but the appeal by a young colonist to British traditions of free government had a certain impact on public opinion.

The weakest part of Wentworth's case was in the reforms he actually proposed. These went too far to be taken seriously by even the most sincere liberal in England. Basing his argument principally on the illegality of local taxes, Wentworth claimed that nothing short of a bicameral legislature with the Lower House fully elective, a legislature patterned on those established in the two colonies of Canada in 1791, would satisfy New South Wales. The size of the colony's population, greater than that of 'several of our West Indian islands, where Houses of Assembly [had] been long established', amply justified the erection of such a legislature—provided that ex-convicts were not automatically excluded from the franchise. This was the crux of the argument: emancipists should not be excluded. The behaviour of transportees after their arrival 'should be subjected to the *severest tests*, to the *most rigorous scrutiny* [,and] *Conviction* . . . for any *offence* of a *criminal nature* should be a *bar* to their pretensions *for ever*'; but a man who had earned his freedom by good behaviour after his arrival should have the same privileges as a man who had never lost it. Wentworth argued that the exclusives were trying to keep subordinate not only emancipists but also the children of emancipists, 'to convert the ignominy of the great body of the people into an hereditary deformity'. The only way to defeat them was to provide for uniform qualifications—the possession of five hundred acres of freehold property for a member of the legislature, of twenty acres freehold, a £5 leasehold or a £10 occupancy for an elector.

Ministers in England, considering the nature of New South Wales, were hardly likely to be impressed. Wentworth was not quite alone in believing that the convict colony was ready for representative government. Edward Eagar claimed in a letter to Bigge, before he had seen the book, that 'a Government similar to that of every other British Colony, Consisting of a Governor and a Legislative Council, the members to be appointed by the Crown, and a House of Assembly, to be elected by competent Electors qualified as in other Colonies' was 'the plain and obvious system' for the colony. But if Wentworth's views were not quite unique they certainly seemed eccentric. And his reference to the West Indian assemblies, notoriously close little corporations which were under heavy criticism from anti-slavery interests in England, hardly strengthened his position. In any case there was no question of his having an influence on Lord Bathurst. *He* was waiting for Bigge's opinions.

Bigge spent eighteen months in New South Wales and Van Diemen's Land. He wrote three voluminous official reports and two confidential supplementary ones. These took up many matters, only four of which need be considered here.

First, there was the question of the validity of government orders. Though Bigge was not instructed to inquire whether a legislative or executive council might be necessary, he inevitably became concerned with the Governor's legislative powers. He was very critical of some of Macquarie's actions, so critical, indeed, that his reports might not unreasonably have been interpreted as implying a condemnation of the autocratic power which Macquarie wielded; but in fact he recognized that in such a colony as New South Wales the Governor needed power to promulgate regulations. He suggested that a codification of existing orders be made, that in future a regulation should make clear its relationship to those already in existence and, most importantly, that the Governor should consult the magistrates before issuing an order, and go ahead only if a majority agreed. But subject to these rules, and of course to veto from London, he recommended that the Governor's power to make regulations which involved variation from British law reasonable in the circumstances be established by Statute.

Secondly, Bigge considered objections to the judicial system and advised various modifications. One serious objection concerned the position of the Judge-Advocate. Bigge recommended that his office be abolished and his functions be divided between the judge of the Supreme Court, who henceforth should preside in both civil and criminal jurisdictions, and an attorney-general, who should file criminal indictments and act as the Governor's legal adviser. The commissioner also turned his lawyer's eye on the strange composition of the courts. He thought that the two magistrates who sat with the judge in the civil jurisdiction should have only the function of assessors concerned with matters of fact and that the judge alone should rule on questions of law. In the criminal jurisdiction, likewise, the judge should be distinguished from the officers who made up the court, these (increased in number to seven) performing the duties of a jury. Bigge was prepared to allow a right of challenge against an officer where an interest seemed to be involved, but he would not recommend the use of civilian juries until the distinction between emancipist and exclusive should die out. Then jury trials might be introduced in stages—first in civil suits where both parties consented.

Thirdly there was the question of the civil rights of emancipists. Bigge did not like what he considered the Governor's policy of forcing emancipists on the free settlers as social equals, but he was urgent in his recommendation that the civil disabilities of emancipists should be removed. He pointed out that the right to use the civil courts was a corollary of the right to hold property; since emancipists had been allowed to acquire property—since they had, in fact, right from Phillip's time been granted land—to deny them audience in the courts was absurd. He argued that legal doubts about the effect of Governor's pardons should be put beyond doubt by retrospective legislation.

Finally there was the minor question of judicial appeals. Bigge believed these to impose too heavy a responsibility on the Governor. The reports considered the possibility of establishing a Council to assist him in this matter (as opposed to his executive and legislative functions) but Bigge came to the conclusion that people capable of forming such a body were not available in the colony, so he recommended that whenever the Governor reversed a decision of the Supreme Court a further appeal to the Crown-in-Council should be possible—even in the case of an amount less than £3,000.

Bigge's reports heralded the end of prerogative rule in New South Wales, not that either he or the ministers to whom he reported envisaged more than an adjustment, a removal of anomalies. Neither Bathurst in his instructions to Bigge, nor Bigge in his reports, took seriously even the idea of a nominated Council. In the colony there was nothing remotely resembling a popular demand for the establishment of a legislature. The exclusives would have suspected the introduction of representative institutions as likely to give power to the emancipists, who were absorbed in the question of legal status. In agitating for radical constitutional reform Wentworth was almost alone. But he provided both a nucleus around which an emancipist reform movement could grow in the future and an irritant to which the exclusives might react, and in reacting find themselves forced to support a positive reform movement of their own. In a very real sense Macquarie, who left the colony early in 1822, was the last of the autocrats.

CHAPTER TWO

Governors and Councils

'It is difficult to understand how any English statesman could have
imagined that representative and irresponsible government could
be successfully combined. There seems ... to be an idea, that the
character of representative institutions ought to be thus modified
in the colonies; that it is an incident of colonial dependence that
the officers of government should be nominated by the Crown
without any reference to the wishes of the community, whose interests are trusted to their keeping.... But if there be such a necessity, it is quite clear that a representative government in a colony
must be a mockery, and a source of confusion.'

LORD DURHAM (1838)

Order and Formality: the Act of 1823

For the first thirty years of British rule in Australia the problems of
government had been virtually brushed aside, naturally enough since
the over-riding problem of any colony in its early years, survival, was in
New South Wales complicated by the colony's penal function. The
institution of the Bigge inquiry was a recognition that these problems
must be faced, and for the next thirty years the history of New South
Wales, and of the other colonies which came into existence during the
period, was a history of constitutional evolution.

Bigge's reports were immensely valuable to the Secretary of State.
They gave him a clear picture of the context in which he and his office
would have to work: of the contradiction which had arisen between the
colony's penal nature and its socio-economic development, of the class
animosities which were latent and were about to open up seriously, of
the opinions of the colonists themselves on what their constitutional
needs were. Bigge did not make up the minister's mind on the necessity
to legislate for the government of New South Wales; Bathurst was keenly
aware that further delay, particularly as regards the Governor's legislative power and the validity of pardons, was out of the question; but the
reports put in perspective the demands which Wentworth claimed to be
voicing. Bigge, therefore, influenced profoundly the shape of the Bill 'for
the better Administration of Justice in New South Wales and Van
Diemen's Land, and for the more effectual Government thereof' which
was brought down in June 1823.

Not that Bathurst, who was aptly described by the Privy Council clerk
Charles Greville as 'a regular Tory of the old school', was the man to
take Wentworth seriously. The Bill, drafted under his instructions partly
by Francis Forbes, the former Chief Justice of Newfoundland who had

been promised the new post of Chief Justice of New South Wales, and partly by the Colonial Office counsel James Stephen, did not even provide for an appointed Council. Instead, it sought to solve the problem of colonial law-making by providing that the laws of England should apply, as far as possible, and that the Governor, after consulting the magistrates, might make regulations, not repugnant to those laws, on a number of listed subjects. The question of whether English law could be applied in a particular case, or of whether a particular regulation was compatible with it, was to be decided by the Chief Justice. However the task of listing all the matters on which local legislation might be necessary proved extremely difficult; and both Forbes and Stephen opposed giving the Governor unrestricted legislative authority. Consequently a provision for a nominated Legislative Council was written into the Bill at the last moment. When this was done the various clauses intended to impose restrictions on the Governor's legislative power were not removed, though the limitation imposed by the existence of the Council made them redundant.

The Act received the royal assent on 19 July. As the need for the legislation arose directly out of the legal problems of administering the colony, it is not surprising that the emphasis was placed heavily on an overhaul of the judicial system. The first section authorized the Crown to set up separate Supreme Courts in New South Wales and Van Diemen's Land, each to be presided over by a Chief Justice, whose duties might be shared by one or two puisne judges, and each to have both criminal and civil jurisdiction. The office of Judge-Advocate was abolished: an attorney-general was to be appointed in each colony to take over the duty of filing prosecutions. In the criminal jurisdiction trial was to be by judge and a seven-man military jury; in the civil jurisdiction by judge and two justices of the peace. In both cases there was to be a right of challenge where interest was involved, and in civil trials a jury of twelve civilians might be used if both parties agreed. Courts of Requests and Quarter Sessions were to deal with minor matters, and machinery was provided for appeals. The Act fixed substantial property qualifications for jurors where they might be used, and a Colonial Office ruling in 1824 excluded emancipists from service. Edward Eagar had lobbied hard for unrestricted trial by jury, but without success. The Crown was authorized, however, to keep the matter under review and to extend the use of juries if it thought fit, and juries were actually used, contrary to the intentions of the Act, in the New South Wales Quarter Sessions right from their institution. Moreover, though the emancipist spokesman lost on this point he was successful on others. Governor's pardons were confirmed retrospectively; all future pardons were to be sent home for ratification or disallowance; and a clause in the Bill giving the Governor power to deport emancipists and expirees under certain circumstances was struck out in committee. It is also possible that his efforts led to a decision to limit the operation of the Act so that Parliament would have an opportunity to consider its working after five years.

The Legislative Council established by the Act of 1823 was clearly intended to legitimize, rather than to restrict, the Governor's actions. It was to consist of men nominated by the Secretary of State (or, in the case of vacancy and subject to ratification, by the Governor). The first nominees were five officials, and although in 1825 the number of officials was reduced to four and three non-official members were appointed, these latter were in no sense representatives. The Council met in camera and its members were bound by an oath of secrecy. The Governor was required to lay his legislative proposals before the Council, which was entitled to discuss and vote on them; but members who opposed his Bills were required to record their reasons and, although this was not laid down in the Act, a majority were in practice his subordinates. Moreover, while he normally required a majority to put a proposal into law, he was empowered to act in serious cases with only one concurrent vote (provided he was prepared to accept responsibility and write his reasons into the minutes), and in case of insurrection or its immediate danger he could act alone. Since Acts had to be reported to Parliament and could be disallowed by the Crown, and since the Crown was specifically empowered to put into force Bills which the Council might previously have rejected, the legislative devolution involved was obviously minor. But, as Melbourne has pointed out, the British government did not intend to interfere in day-to-day problems any more than absolutely necessary; and the 1823 Act did allow most of the colony's affairs to be settled in the colony. This was true even of its financial affairs. Existing taxes, continued since 1819 by the annual Indemnity Act, were made permanent, the Governor being thereby given a revenue which he could expend at his own discretion; but no new tax could be imposed without the consent of the Council, which would also have the right to 'appropriate' the proceeds (that is to decide in detail how they should be expended).

The real restriction lay in the power of the Chief Justice. He was required to certify, before submission to the Legislative Council, that any proposal by the Governor was compatible with the laws of England 'as far as the circumstances of the ... colony [would] admit'. The difficulty lay in the quoted clause. The question whether or not circumstances might warrant a deviation from English law to the extent the Governor suggested was a political question, but it had to be asked, in every case, of a judicial officer. The Chief Justice was in effect, as Forbes himself was to point out, being saddled with the functions of a house of review. This provision, like various others left in the Bill after the decision to establish the Council had made them unnecessary, was to be a cause of considerable trouble.

The Council was to be 'legislative': the Act made no provision for an executive council. But the growth of the colony meant the growth of its bureaucracy. The sixth Governor, Sir Thomas Brisbane, could not successfully hold all the reins Macquarie had held, and his successor, Darling, was too wise to try. New senior officers had to be appointed: a colonial secretary in 1821, a colonial treasurer in 1823 and an attorney-general under the terms of the act. Definition of function became difficult: Brisbane and the colonial secretary, Frederick Goulburn, took different sides in the widening factional quarrel; the colonial treasurer, Saxe Bannister, claimed a right to influence policy which the Governor would not concede. In an effort to meet these problems the Secretary of State, when he appointed Darling, decided to bring together the Governor's chief advisers in an Executive Council. The Governor was to 'remain exclusively responsible for every act', but the Executive Council provided an opportunity for heads of departments to influence his decisions, and, as W.A. Townsley has pointed out, its very existence modified the position by giving an impression of shared authority. So the Governor's executive authority, as well as his legislative power was put in commission. The extent to which the situation had been changed since Macquarie's time was made very clear in 1828, when the Colonial Office forbad Darling to continue his practice of making known his personal pleasure, or displeasure, on any matter, and instructed him to have all orders and statements framed by the attorney-general. However minor the specific changes provided by the Act of 1823 may appear to be, the Act revolutionized the colony's government by substituting order and formality for a system which had been haphazard and charismatic.

The operation of the new Constitution was profoundly influenced by the existence of the two groups, emancipists and exclusives, and by relations between W.C. Wentworth, who returned to lead the emancipists in 1824, and Governor Darling, who arrived at the end of 1825. Darling was a man with a soldier's mind and, though it is possible to exaggerate the contrast between his conservatism and the 'liberalism' of his successor Sir Richard Bourke, and although he at first tried to avoid siding with either 'party', his sympathies were essentially with the exclusives. A clash between the Governor and the young aspirant to popular leadership was inevitable, particularly as Wentworth had issued a third edition of his book, with a supplement on the Act of 1823 which described the Legislative Council as 'a wretched mongrel substitute' for a representative assembly, and had, in October 1824, helped his Cambridge friend Robert Wardell to establish an opposition newspaper, the *Australian*.

Wentworth, indeed, fired his first shot before Darling arrived, when he and his supporters captured a public meeting called to draw up a farewell address to Brisbane and added to the address a request that Brisbane should use his influence in Britain to obtain for the colony an elected legislature and trial by jury. The effect of this was to enlarge the political dimension of the emancipist-exclusive split which, as Brisbane pointed out in a gracious reply to the address, was the thing most likely to hinder the granting of such a request. One exclusive sympathizer wrote sourly of the address's being 'couched in language as equivocal as ... fulsome and disgusting'; in London John Macarthur Junior, on behalf of the 'respectable inhabitants', wrote to the Colonial Office to dissociate his class from it and to characterize its supporters as the 'republican party'. Macarthur also asked for trial by jury (though he envisaged juries without emancipists) and suggested that the colony needed not an elected legislature but an enlargement of its nominated Council to fifteen members, chosen from 'the most respectable landholders and merchants'.

Though Wentworth repeated the tactic when an address of welcome to Darling was being written in January 1826, this time getting in a statement that the colony would be satisfied with nothing less than 'taxation by representation' and 'representation by election', he was hampered by the fact that most emancipists were much less interested in constitutional abstractions than he wanted them to be: for them the 1823 Act had removed the great grievances by validating governor's pardons. For the first twelve months of Darling's rule, therefore, the campaign was conducted in a minor key; but at the end of 1826 Wentworth got his opportunity in the death of a soldier, Joseph Sudds, a few days after he and a comrade named Patrick Thompson had been drummed out of their regiment and into an iron gang for an offence which they hoped would earn them only a short prison term—and a discharge. As Forbes, no friend of Darling, pointed out later, Wentworth sought to use this excessive punishment, which was inflicted illegally on the personal orders of the Governor (who was naturally anxious to prevent soldiers from winning by petty crime what they could otherwise win only by desertion), to 'bring the people together' against the Governor or perhaps to serve as 'some pretext for contending for popular checks upon the abuses of power' in the colony.

Wentworth made good use of the chance. A threat to impeach Darling, although it had in it a touch of the ridiculous, served to keep alive for years an issue which might otherwise have died in weeks. Moreover an opportunity was provided to promote a petition to the Crown in Parliament emphasizing the fact that New South Wales was not 'on the same footing as all other His Majesty's Plantations settled by British Subjects', asking for those 'imprescriptible rights of Englishmen, Trial by Jury and Taxation by Representation', and putting the emancipist view that a legislature given to the colony should be large enough, and elected on a wide enough franchise (by the occupiers of houses worth £10 per annum) to counteract the influence of 'certain private families'. This was a skilfully drawn up petition. It was based on the idea, so evocative of the 1688 revolution, of 'imprescriptible rights', and the suggestion that the proposed franchise would minimize 'influence' was designed to appeal to the supporters of Parliamentary reform in England, who often used the word as a synonym for 'corruption'.

But the real significance of poor Sudds' death was that it enabled Wentworth and his supporters to provoke Darling into treading on another susceptibility of the Englishman, the right of a free press. Up to October 1824 the only newspaper in New South Wales had been the *Sydney Gazette*. Though privately owned, it served the purpose of a government circular and was subject to official censorship. When Wardell and Wentworth founded the *Australian*, they assumed freedom to publish as a right and did not submit their copy to the colonial secretary before printing. Governor Brisbane, rather nonplussed, decided to free the *Gazette* from censorship; subsequently two more uncensored papers, the *Sydney Monitor* and the *Gleaner* appeared. Bathurst did not approve: when Darling became Governor he was told that the press needed more, not less, regulation in New South Wales than in England, where, although publication was free and licensing unknown, a stamp tax put a brake on the radical papers. Darling had not yet carried out his instructions to put before the Legislative Council a Bill for a stamp tax and some other regulation when the Sudds outcry began. Then, when he was attacked in the most scurrilous terms, particularly by the *Monitor*, he brought in two Bills. The first was a Newspaper Regulating Bill which sought to license the press, to require the lodging of a bond which would ensure payment of libel fines, and to allow repeated offenders against the libel law to be deported. Chief Justice Forbes refused his certificate of compatibility with English law until the licensing clauses were removed. They were excised and the Bill was passed. At the same time another Bill, imposing a tax, went through, but after this was published Forbes announced that it was not covered by his certificate and that he considered it repugnant. This exercise of the Chief Justice's function of review (an extraordinarily 'political' exercise of it, since he suggested that his objection was to the level, rather than to the existence of the proposed tax) forced the Governor to withdraw the Act and seriously weakened his prestige.

Adjustment: the Development of Emancipist Agitation

By this time it had become necessary for the British government to review the working of the Act of 1823. It drafted a new Bill, embodying amendments which were based largely on the ideas of Forbes. These amendments went little beyond removing the redundant sections of the earlier Act and abrogating the Governor's extraordinary and emergency legislative powers, but they sought to add a degree of flexibility by authorizing the Crown to extend the right of trial by jury and even, though the clause was vague, apparently to establish an elected legislature, if it might think fit, before Parliament should consider the matter again. This willingness on the part of the Colonial Office to administer flexibly, though its existence was not recognized in the colony, was to be the principal feature of policy for the next twenty years. To a very large extent it was the achievement of James Stephen, who in 1824 had relinquished private practice to become full-time counsel to the Colonial Office and who, after serving as assistant under-secretary from 1834 to 1836, was to spend the next eleven years as its permanent under-secretary. The 'real founder of Colonial Office methods and traditions', he held the Office together from the resignation of the experienced Bathurst in April 1827 to the advent of the strong-willed Grey in July 1846. Stephen's sense of responsibility was too well developed to allow him to condone a weak colonial policy, and he was particularly determined not to allow comparatively small numbers of colonists unrestricted control over the resources (and the native peoples) of vast territories; but under his influence the Colonial Office was never insensitive to local desires.

The government's unwillingness to foist its own solutions of colonial problems on the colonies was clearly demonstrated by the events of 1827. The new Bill had been introduced late in the session; before it had been dealt with the ministers became aware that there were likely to be objections to it so, rather than push it through, they withdrew it, had the 1823 Act extended for one year, and gave those objections a chance to be heard. In the next few months they received the petition drawn up by Wentworth, some vehement but idiosyncratic counter-proposals from old John Macarthur, and recommendations and comments from Darling. Stephen considered all these carefully in drafting a new Bill which was passed during the 1828 session.

The Act was intended, as the Secretary of State, William Huskisson, pointed out when he brought the Bill into the House of Commons, as a step towards 'the establishment of institutions ... similar to those of the people from whom the inhabitants have sprung'. To critics like Wentworth it seemed a derisively small step, but it was, in fact, of considerable significance. Trial by jury was considered by Stephen, but rejected as an immediate reform because the existence of the colony's factional divisions would make 'every law suit, and almost every criminal trial ... assume the character of a party quarrel'; indeed, the use of juries in the New South Wales Quarter Sessions was abolished.

A jury might, however, be allowed in a civil case before the Supreme Court, at the discretion of the presiding judge, where one party requested it. More importantly the Act, like the Act of 1823, recognized that trial by jury would have to come eventually and, unlike the earlier

Act, opened the way for the Legislative Council to have a share in deciding when and how. The reform would require an imperial Order-in-Council, but such order would take the form of an authorization to the Legislative Council to extend the use of juries. Immediately after the Act was put into effect Huskisson's successor, Sir George Murray, instructed the Governor to have the Council inquire and report on the matter. In the meantime it was to have power to fix the qualifications of jurors in the limited range of cases where juries were as yet allowed.

The establishment of an elective assembly was not considered, but changes were made in the size and position of the Legislative Council which involved a significant transfer of authority. It was enlarged to between ten and fifteen members, nominated by the Crown. The Act did not apportion the places between officials and others, but the Council actually appointed had seven of each. As the Governor was to attend, and to have a deliberative and, where necessary, also a casting vote, the government intended him to be able to command a majority; but on the other hand the new Council, in contrast to the old, was to have a representative function. The non-official members were in no sense a cross-section of colonial society; not for eight years did they include even one man of emancipist sympathies; but they were to be free to canvass opinion outside their chamber; and the Governor was required, as a normal procedure, to advertise his legislative proposals in the press eight days before presenting them to the Council. Public discussion of proposed laws was, therefore, not only allowed but encouraged. Moreover the Governor lost his power to over-ride the Council, and the Crown its power to enact directly Bills which the Council had previously rejected, though the power to disallow ordinances was, of course, retained. Initiative in legislation remained exclusively the Governor's as it had been under the 1823 Act, but any councillor could request him to introduce a measure and if he refused he was required to record his reasons for perusal by the Colonial Office. And the financial authority of the Council was greatly increased: it was given power to appropriate all taxation revenue; the Governor had left at his uncontrolled disposal only such casual revenues as fees and fines and the revenue from the sale and rental of Crown lands (which was, as yet, insignificant).

The Act made another change in the government of the colony. The power of the Chief Justice to forbid the enactment of Bills was replaced by a device less likely to cause friction. All Acts of the Legislative Council were to be recorded by the Supreme Court *after* their enactment. The three judges who now constituted the Bench were given the right to protest if they felt an Act to be seriously repugnant to English law; if they did so it was to be reconsidered by the Council, which could over-rule the protest by passing the Act again, thus putting it into force temporarily pending a decision on the matter by the Crown. Other changes of a minor nature were made in judicial procedure.

The Act of 1828 was not received with any great enthusiasm in New South Wales. It satisfied the exclusives, but was hardly a satisfactory response to the petition sent home after the Sudds case. Two things might be said in defence of Downing Street, however. First, the Act did open the way for reform in the matter which was of greatest interest to the colonists, the system of trial in the courts. The importance which general colonial opinion placed on the idea of 'representation by election' at this stage should not be exaggerated: few colonists would have enjoyed that right if they had remained in England. Secondly, the colony was an extraordinary one. Forty-six per cent of the population in 1828 was convict; there was no immediate prospect that transportation would end; and free immigration was still insignificant. Among the free the distinction between emancipist and exclusive seemed, if anything, to be growing more bitter. The Act was far from perfect, but in circumstances of the time and place it was reasonably designed to serve the purpose Huskisson had ascribed to it.

The fact remained, however, that there were West Indian colonies with large slave populations and only one quarter of the free population of New South Wales which enjoyed representative government and trial by jury, and the small group of emancipist politicians who had fought Darling to the point of seeking to impeach him could not in logic be satisfied with less. This group gradually stepped up its campaign. A petition for which it was responsible was presented to Parliament in 1832 and, although this was rejected by the government on the ground of the existence of the factions, the passage of the great Reform Act encouraged the signing of another, which was presented in 1835. Again the government would not promise representative institutions. The group was not without support. Governor Bourke, who succeeded Darling at the end of 1831, rapidly became convinced that a majority (he suggested two-thirds) of the Legislative Council should be elected on a franchise which would embrace emancipists—though he felt that they should be excluded from membership. But the Governor's liberal sentiments, and his Whig abhorrence of the imposition of taxes by a nonrepresentative body, could not obscure the fact which most impressed the British government, that the leaders of colonial society, the Crown's natural allies, were opposed to his idea.

The Colonial Office was in an unenviable position, and its difficulties were increased as lobbying became more intense. Henry Lytton Bulwer, the emancipists' unofficial parliamentary representative, who presented their petitions in 1832 and 1835, persuaded them that their campaign for reform should be more organized and less sporadic; at his suggestion they organized in May 1835 a permanent body called the Australian Patriotic Association which was to raise funds, mobilize public opinion, and retain and instruct a permanent agent in the House of Commons. Bulwer himself accepted this brief temporarily. The Association acted immediately to increase the pressure on Downing Street, and, though it was by no means a radical body, being dominated by men of wealth, its existence as an essentially emancipist organization provoked the exclusives into strong resistance to the programmes it advocated.

The Association began by endorsing, and laying before the government, two alternative outline drafts of a bill to reform the colony's Constitution which were drawn up by Wentworth. One of these proposed a bicameral legislature to include an elective Lower House; the other a mixed legislature with a large majority of its members elected; both provided for property franchises and qualifications which made no distinction between emancipist and free settler. The exclusives responded, in mid-1836, with a petition which elaborated on a remark by Judge Burton of the Supreme Court that the level of crime in the colony made it unfit for 'those free institutions which are the pride and boast of the parent country'; asked for a non-official nominated majority in the Legislative Council with members having the right to initiate legislation; and even hinted that when election was ultimately introduced emancipists should be excluded from the franchise. The emancipist rejoinder was a counter-petition which expressed a rhetorical preference for 'the old despotic form of government' over an exclusive-dominated Council. So when the British government came to consider replacing the Act of 1828, which was due to expire at the end of 1836, it had a most confused situation to deal with.

Meanwhile Bourke had his views developed into a full constitutional scheme. When this arrived the government took refuge in the necessity to study it, the Wentworth bills and the exclusive petition, and extended the 1828 Act for one year. Before this time had expired there were more things to consider: 1837 saw the publication of four books on the colony, James Macarthur's *New South Wales, Its Present State and Future Prospects*, James Mudie's savage *Felonry of New South Wales*, and two works by the indefatigable clerical publicist J.D. Lang. More importantly, the House of Commons had appointed a select committee under the chairmanship of the colonial reformer Sir William Molesworth to enquire into the transportation system, which was coming under heavy fire from humanitarians at home: a further extension of the existing Act became necessary because the Molesworth committee went into considerable detail about the general affairs of the colony, and because it was widely recognized that the committee's report was likely to alter the situation.

Emancipist-Exclusive Rapprochement and the Acts of 1842

The report of the Molesworth committee was hostile to the whole transportation system, and its tabling in Parliament was followed by the indefinite suspension of transportation to New South Wales. This contributed greatly towards bringing together the factions whose mutual hostility had been the principal obstacle to reform of the colony's government. Indeed, while that hostility was at its height there had been operating beneath the surface certain forces which tended in the long run to damp it down. The most important of these was a slight easing of friction over the question of trial by jury.

The rules framed by the Council to regulate the restricted use of juries authorized in 1828 limited jury service to substantial property holders who were free of attaint. The holders of free pardons were eligible, unless twice convicted, but the rules were at first interpreted in such a way as to exclude those who were free by expiry of sentence. In 1830 the British government decided to make mandatory the use of juries in cases where high officials were involved, and the Order-in-Council which implemented this decision also gave the Governor discretionary authority to ask the Legislative Council to introduce jury trials generally. Bourke investigated the matter thoroughly; in 1832 he had some minor adjustments made, in particular to allow expirees to be empanelled in cases where juries were used; and in 1833 he pushed through the Council, on his casting vote, an Act to allow an accused person the right to demand trial by a twelve-man civilian jury. There were very strong protests. Bourke had been forced, to get even the official members of the Council to agree, to retain the seven-officer jury as an alternative which the accused could accept, and there was much subsequent criticism of the operation of the Act: Judge Burton's strictures on the criminality of the colony are a case in point. Moreover, accused persons tended for some years to prefer the jury of officers. But the exclusives learnt to live with the *fait accompli*, and this inevitably took some of the heat out of the factional quarrel.

At the same time issues arose in which the interests of exclusives and emancipists were almost identical, and these were handled in such a way as to lead the two groups to make common cause against Downing Street. As has been pointed out, the Legislative Council had been given the right to appropriate all revenue from taxation, but the land and casual revenues were not put under Council control. When the estimates were brought before the Council in 1832 they included a small sum for the colonial secretary, Alexander McLeay, over and above his salary, as a pension in recognition of services to the Crown prior to his arrival in Australia. There was an outcry in the press, partly at least inspired by McLeay's unpopularity with the emancipists, an outcry which forced even the Council, which approved his exclusive sentiments, to protest. The Secretary of State responded by instructing the Governor to withdraw the item and pay the pension out of the casual revenues. This, rather than solving the problem, raised the wider constitutional issue, whether any New South Wales revenues should be reserved from control by the Council and be thus available to circumvent its attempts to

influence the budget. Clumsy handling of this petty matter by the
Secretary of State thus led to a demand that the colony should have full
authority over its finances, a demand in which exclusives and
emancipists were inclined to join, even if they had different views on the
question of what sort of legislature should exercise this authority.

Such a demand was bound to intensify as land revenues increased. In
the 1820s these, though legally distinct, had, because they were small,
never been carefully separated in the colony's accounts; so their omission
from the estimates in the 1830s, just when rapid economic expansion
was combining with the new policy of land sales laid down in the 1831
'Ripon Regulations' to make them more valuable, appeared to involve
an actual diminution of the Council's control over finance. The Ripon
Regulations provided that henceforth colonial land would not be
alienated except by auction sale with a reserve price of five shillings per
acre: the proceeds were to be treated as a capital fund for the colony, to
be expended on such things as immigration. The graziers of New South
Wales, hindered in their efforts to exploit the pastoral boom by a
shortage of labour, which was bound to be aggravated if convicts
became unavailable, were anxious to have all the land fund spent on
immigration. They were, therefore, even more sensitive than they
otherwise would have been to the fact that the colony was not allowed to
control this money. Again there was little difference of opinion between
the factions, the leaders of both being heavily involved in the pastoral
advance.

Then, in 1834, the British government announced that the full cost of
police and gaols in the colony, hitherto largely met by the British
Treasury, was to be transferred to the colonial accounts. The Council
protested strongly, arguing that the colony should not be expected to
find all the money needed to prevent and punish crime, the high level of
which was due to the transportation of large numbers of the British
criminal class. Once again clumsy handling in London converted a
purely financial squabble, though this time one of some magnitude, into
an issue of constitutional principle, for the Secretary of State suggested
that, if the Council failed to appropriate funds for police and gaols, these
services would be made a charge on the land revenue. This was resented,
partly as a threat to immigration, but principally as an open exercise of
suzerainty and a reminder of the colony's subordinate status. Every year
from 1834 to 1842 the Council protested; every year public meetings did
the same. At first the strongest protests came from the more liberal
members of the Council, but by 1840 even the exclusive leader James
Macarthur was joining in. The issue became one of 'taxation without
representation', one in which emancipist and exclusive united against
Downing Street, and one which was exacerbated by a rise in the reserve
price of land to twelve shillings per acre in 1839 and an attempt in 1840
to institute a system of local government, this being seen by many

colonists as a disguised measure of taxation. The alliance was cemented by a change of governor. Bourke was sympathetic to the colonists' complaints; Sir George Gipps, who succeeded him in 1838 and rapidly became embroiled with the squatters, was impatient. With a common enemy on the spot rather than on the other side of the world the factional division in the colony disappeared.

Before the reconciliation which had been promoted by the solution of the jury problem, by the development of common interests and by the suspension of transportation, was thus completed (and solemnized by James Macarthur's public withdrawal, in February 1841, of his opposition to giving emancipists the franchise) the Constitution of the colony had again come under review in London. Discussions had been held during 1837 and 1838 between James Stephen and such people as Francis Forbes, James Macarthur, Bulwer and his successor as the agent of the Australian Patriotic Association, Charles Buller. In these discussions various ideas for reforms which fell short of representative government were canvassed by Stephen, partly, perhaps, because the rebellions which had occurred in Canada in 1837 had produced something of a reaction against the idea of giving colonies representative institutions; but he became convinced that such proposals were no answer. Further work was done in 1839, and the Colonial Office reverted to the idea of a mixed Council, partly elected and partly nominated, which Gipps, like his predecessor, favoured. However the Chartist crisis, the beginning of serious agitation against the Corn Laws, and the acute problems of the North American and West Indian colonies, forced the government to put the matter aside. The 1828 Act was again, as in the previous three years, extended for another year. By 1840, however, the Secretary of State, Lord John Russell, was ready to proceed.

He introduced a Bill to give New South Wales a Council two-thirds of the members of which would be elected on a £10 property franchise extending to both free and freed, the other third to be Crown nominees. The Bill provided for the reservation of land revenues to the Crown and for the separation from New South Wales of the newly-settled Port Phillip and Moreton Bay districts. The colonial agents in London protested against these provisions, the more vehemently because it was proposed that the northern boundary of the Port Phillip district would be the Murrumbidgee River and this would cut off from New South Wales one of the most promising areas of pastoral expansion. In the face of these protests Russell took refuge in another extension Act and withdrew the Bill while he waited for comments upon it from the colony.

The outstanding feature of the comments which came was the unanimity among the leaders of the old factions. They were not averse to a mixed Council, though some of them, observing signs of a new and more radical group forming on their left, felt that in the colony, where almost any house was worth £10 per annum, the franchise was too low. They were thoroughly hostile to the dismemberment proposals and the re-servation of the land revenue. At this point the complexity of the whole land problem became a gravely complicating factor. In London a board of Colonial Land and Emigration Commissioners had been set up to assist the government re-settle surplus population on the abundant lands of the Empire. The Commissioners were more or less under the influence of the theorist E.G. Wakefield, who argued that colonial land should be disposed of at a substantial fixed price and the proceeds devoted to emigration, in order to produce in the colonies a (rather idealized) reflection of English rural society, and they were pressing Downing Street to apply the Wakefield theory to New South Wales. In the colony the graziers, already coming into conflict with a Governor who thought that they should pay more for the use of the Crown land which was supporting their great prosperity (though he considered the Wakefield idea nonsense) were urging that complete control of lands should be transferred to the colony. Torn between a desire to treat colonial lands as a 'trust for the Empire and for posterity' (rather than a resource to be exploited by a small number of colonists) and the desire to find a sol-ution to the colony's constitutional problems, and hampered by the weak parliamentary position of the government to which he belonged, Russell had done nothing when he left office in September 1841.

But the government of Sir Robert Peel, backed as it was by a healthy Commons majority, was in a position to cut Gordian knots which the previous Administration had struggled vainly to unravel: in 1842 the new Secretary of State, Lord Stanley, put through Parliament, after the most perfunctory consultations with the colonial agents, both a Government Act and a Sale of Waste Lands Act.

The Government Act set up a Legislative Council similar to that proposed by the 1840 Bill. The colony was not partitioned, though the Port Phillip district, with its border pushed back to the Murray, was made a separate unit for representation and the Crown was given the power to subdivide later if this seemed necessary. The Council was to consist initially of twelve nominees, not more than six of whom might be officials, and twenty-four members to be elected from men with freehold property worth £2,000, or an annual income of £100, by those who held a £200 freehold, or occupied a house with an annual value of £20; six of the elected councillors were to represent Port Phillip. Provision was made for the possible enlargement of the Council in the future, but there were always to be twice as many elected as nominated members. The Governor was to have, as well as the normal prerogative power to give or withhold assent to bills, or to reserve them for consideration at home, the power normally associated with an Upper House of referring Bills back with proposals for amendment; but he lost the exclusive power to initiate legislation, though the practice normal in British government of requiring an executive message to initiate a money Bill was, of course, retained. Subject to the need for such a vice-regal message, the Legislative Council was to have a general right to appropriate revenue from taxation, except for an amount of £81,600, the expenditure of which was to be in accordance with 'three schedules' to the Act; £33,000 for the salaries of the Governor, the superintendent of Port Phillip and the judges and other law officers and for the expenses of administering justice; £18,600 for the chief civil officers and their departments, for pensions and for the expenses of the Council; and £30,000 for the maintenance of public worship. Land and casual revenues were also reserved.

The Sale of Waste Lands Act raised the minimum reserve price of land to one pound per acre, except that large remote areas might be sold at a lower price, and established a formula for the use of the land revenue: fifty per cent was to be spent on immigration, the rest was to be expended by the Governor in accordance with instructions to be given him from time to time. The Governor was to continue to have power to issue de-pasturing licences and to make regulations for the use and occupancy of unsold lands, but the existence of the Sale of Waste Lands Act placed an important restriction on the colony by implying a prohibition against the Council's legislating on these matters. The first instructions on the expenditure of the second half of the land fund enjoined the Governor to spend a proportion on Aboriginal protection and another on the roads; he was left free to hand any surplus over to the Council for appropriation; but it was made clear that the whole of the fifty per cent was to be considered as an emergency reserve available if the Council proved difficult.

The Smaller Settlements

Up to this point it has been possible to discuss Australian constitutional development almost entirely in terms of New South Wales, but by 1842 the problems of three other colonies, Van Diemen's Land, Western Australia and South Australia, and of the Port Phillip district, were influencing Colonial Office policy. Some consideration is necessary, therefore, of the ways in which these problems differed from those of New South Wales.

Van Diemen's Land remained part of the colony of New South Wales for over twenty years after the establishment of settlement there. The two Lieutenant-Governors, one at Hobart and one at Port Dalrymple, who between them governed the island from 1803 to 1810 were subordinates of the Governor, as was the single Lieutenant-Governor who was responsible from 1810 to 1825; and there was no system of courts (though after 1814 the colony had a minor civil court and in 1819 and 1821 Barron Field held sittings of the Supreme Court at Hobart) most matters having to be dealt with in Sydney. The Act of 1823 established a separate Supreme Court in Van Diemen's Land and authorized the Crown to set up a separate government in the future. In June 1825 an Order-in-Council separated Van Diemen's Land from New South Wales and gave it a nominated Legislative Council with the same authority as that of the parent colony. The Act of 1828 applied to Van Diemen's Land and made the same changes there as in New South Wales. By this time a petition had already been made for 'the pride and birthright ... of every Briton—Trial by Jury and Legislation by Representation', and throughout the 1830s the islanders tended to show interest in the same constitutional issues as the mainlanders. But transportation to Van Diemen's Land was not suspended in 1839 and the colony did not share in the wave of prosperity which New South Wales enjoyed during the period. The Act of 1842, therefore, made no substantial changes in the government of Van Diemen's Land. It continued to be ruled under the terms of the 1828 Act.

In the free colony established on the Swan River in 1829 the Governor ruled alone for three years over a handful of settlers too busy struggling against starvation to worry about his constitutional status. In 1832 small Executive and Legislative Councils were appointed: at first they were composed of the same officials, but in 1839 an equal number of non-official nominees was added to the Legislative Council and it was given powers essentially the same as those of the councils then existing in the older colonies. Small size, and financial difficulties, provided an even more effective brake on constitutional development than did convictism in Van Diemen's Land until 1849, when the settlers, feeling their economic progress, which was stultified by chronic labour shortages, to be more immediately important than progress towards self-government, petitioned for convicts and so added another obstacle. No further change was to be made in the colony's constitution until after transportation was abolished in 1865.

The plan for the foundation of South Australia was supposed to save the colony from the pitfalls into which Western Australia had fallen, but within a few years of the first settlement in 1835, it, too, was in difficulties which inhibited constitutional growth. The Foundation Act contained what was virtually a promise of representative government when the population should have reached 50,000; there were to be no convicts; the settlers, proud of their freedom from the 'convict taint' were even more insistent on 'the rights of Englishmen' than were those of New South Wales. But the Act also provided a peculiar system of divided control: land sales and the expenditure of land revenue on immigration (the shibboleth of the foundation plan) were the responsibility of a 'Resident Commissioner', who was independent of the Governor and his small nominated Council. The collapse of this system in a series of disputes between Governor and Commissioner, defects in the original plan and the sudden reversal under the third Governor, Sir George Grey, of the imaginative if inflationary works policy of his immediate predecessor, left the colony financially weak. At the end of 1839 (before the financial crisis had been precipitated by Grey) about 400 of the colony's 10,000 inhabitants petitioned for the addition to the Legislative Council of a number of elected members, with the power to force reference of any legislative proposal to London by opposing it unanimously. Governor Gawler did not object to the election of some members, but described the idea of a suspensive veto as likely to lead to 'systematic party opposition ... altogether at variance with the constitution of the Council'; the petition was rejected. Three years later another petition, asking simply for some elected members, was drawn up: it also failed. But the Government of South Australia Act, already passed when the second petition was received, made possible the establishment in June 1843 of a new Council consisting of the Governor, three officials and four non-official nominees, the Governor to have both deliberative and casting votes and the sole power to initiate (though other councillors could request the initiation of measures).

The Act made the granting of representative institutions in the future conditional upon the Crown's being satisfied of the colony's ability to provide an adequate 'civil list', that is, to make adequate provision for the ordinary expenses of government. When in 1844 government revenue first exceeded expenditure, a further petition was made for the election of members to the Council. It was rejected, partly on Grey's advice that the financial position of the colony was still dubious. In the years following there was some hostility to control from Downing Street, but this was due mainly to an attempt to exact Crown royalties on minerals. No further change in the constitutional position of the colony was to be made until 1850, by which time the population had reached 50,000 and the discovery of rich mineral lodes had put an end to financial problems.

The originally illegal settlement, by squatters from Van Diemen's Land, of the area around Port Phillip was recognized by Governor Bourke in September 1836 and constituted as a district under a superintendent in 1839. Its remoteness bred separatist sentiments which were encouraged by the still-born separation proposals of Russell. The guarantee of specific representation in the New South Wales Council after 1842 did nothing to satisfy the Port Phillipians: they considered representation in a legislature as remote from their homes (and, they claimed, as ignorant and careless of their interests) as that in Sydney to be a mockery. For the next eight years all their other political ideas were subordinate to their desire for separation.

Gipps, the Land Question and 'Responsible Government'

In New South Wales itself the Act of 1842 never really worked satisfactorily. Though the confrontation between Governor and public opinion was prevented from becoming absolute by the emergence of a radical element which distrusted such leaders as Wentworth sufficiently to provoke a serious riot in Sydney at the time of the first Legislative Council elections, it was too definite to allow such a compromise between representation and authority to function smoothly. This is obvious now: but it should be said in fairness to Stanley and his colleagues that it was not obvious then. Ultimately the conflict was to be resolved through the grant of responsible government, but that solution did not present itself to the Colonial Office in the 1840s as clearly as it presents itself to the historian.

It may perhaps be thought that some such solution should have presented itself. Lord Durham's famous report had suggested in 1838 that the answer to the problems of Canada lay in a willingness to 'administer the Government on those principles which have been found perfectly efficacious in Great Britain', and Durham's successors in the Governor-Generalship were already beginning, with at least the tacit approval of Downing Street, to feel their way in the direction he had pointed out. But they were moving slowly; in New South Wales the position was complicated greatly by the land question; and, most importantly, there was less agreement on what those 'perfectly efficacious' principles really were than some historians realize. Even in Britain responsible government as it is now understood was not so much established as in the process of being established. There, though its eventual establishment became inevitable when the great Reform Act made control of the House of Commons by the government more a matter of proposing acceptable policies than of exercising wide patronage, the true nature of executive responsibility was not always understood. The two-party system, the great lubricant of responsible government, was slow to emerge; and as late as 1846 the Duke of Wellington could vote for the repeal of the Corn Laws against his own convictions because he felt his vote to be necessary 'to enable Her Majesty to meet her Parliament and carry on the business of the country'. The ghost of the old idea that the government of England was the sovereign's government and should be independent of Parliament was not finally laid until Walter Bagehot published *The English Constitution* in 1867. While the Monarch continued to be regarded as more than what Bagehot called 'the dignified part' of the executive, the transplantation to the colonies of the system of relations between executive and legislature which existed in England was hard to envisage. Lacking the Monarch's mystique, a colonial governor could not easily sustain the position which the Crown sustained in Britain if his advisers were placed in the same relationship to a colonial legislature as a British cabinet occupied in relation to the House of Commons. British ministers tended to suspect that colonial responsible government would mean colonial republicanism. In this context the Act of 1842 seems less unreasonable.

But whatever may be said of its conception, it worked very ill. The elected members of the Legislative Council, led by Wentworth, almost automatically constituted themselves into an opposition, and the Council became less a legislative body than a forum of protest. Almost its first action was to object vehemently to the restrictions placed on its control over finance, and in particular to the three schedules which, theories of executive government apart, clearly put it in a weaker position *vis à vis* the Crown than was the House of Commons at home. The situation in the colony fell into a pattern closely paralleling that in England in the early seventeenth century. The Crown had an independent revenue, but, while this met a certain minimum need, it was not enough to make efficient government possible: the Governor had to ask for supplementary grants even for the services protected by the schedules, as James I and Charles I had had to ask their Parliaments for subsidies. Just as their Parliaments had replied with demands for control over expenditure, the New South Wales Legislative Council claimed the right to examine all the estimates for the protected services. When Gipps would not admit that the Council had such a right, the elected members forced a drastic reduction in the supplementary grants which the Governor sought. For good measure they refused to make any provision for the surveyor-general's department, on the ground that it should be supported from the land fund. In effect the Council, like the seventeenth-century Parliament, was challenging the Constitution under which it had been called into existence.

The challenge did not end with the matter of the schedules. The Council protested against sections 47–9 of the Act, which provided for the levying, by district councils which the Governor was to set up, of rates to cover half the cost of police and gaols. It was particularly aroused by S. 49, which provided that if any district council failed to pay its assessed share of this cost the amount could be recovered by distress and sale upon the goods of the council's treasurer, those of the members of the council, or even those of all the inhabitants of the district. This section was such an affront to the colonists' conception of British liberties that it was dubbed 'the Algerine Clause'—the Bey of Algiers being the contemporary epitome of the tyrant. As a gesture of protest the Legislative Council refused to provide the other half of the cost, as it was expected to do. The local government clauses could not be put into operation. By the end of the first session the Governor and the Council were in unresolved conflict over the central provisions of the Act.

At this point the land question, which had been smouldering for years, suddenly blew up. Gipps had become convinced that the 'squat-

ters', who were de-pasturing large flocks on Crown land outside the
settled districts for an almost nominal fee, should be required to pay a
reasonable rent for the land they used. He was seized also with the
necessity to define their rights to particular tracts, and the terms under
which these tracts were held, before long occupancy came to be regarded as conferring some mandatory title. He was not unsympathetic
towards their desire for fixity of tenure, or to the problems which a
collapse in the pastoral boom was forcing upon them, but he was anxious to prevent a comparatively small number of men from monopoliz-
ing control of pastoral resources which he, like his superiors, considered
the Crown to hold in trust for the Empire as a whole. On 2 April 1844 he
issued a set of regulations on the occupation of Crown lands which were
to replace others issued in 1836 and 1839. Under the 1836 regulations a
man who took out a de-pasturing licence, which cost £10 per annum,
might occupy an indefinite area; in 1839 he was made liable to the
additional payment of a small head tax on his stock. The new regulations required a separate licence for every 'station', which was defined in general as an area of not more than twenty square miles capable
of carrying 4,000 sheep or 500 cattle. They thus imposed a considerable
additional payment on the larger investors in squatting, a payment
which these people chose to call a tax. There was an immediate outcry.
The publication six weeks later of proposals which Gipps was putting to
the Colonial Office for amendments in the Sale of Waste Lands Act did
nothing to damp down this protest. In these Gipps was seeking to give
the graziers some security in their tenure of what he considered a reasonable proportion of their holdings, but he was proposing that this security
be given only on condition of regular purchase of definite areas. Such
compulsory purchases the squatters saw as another tax.

The pastoralists reacted strongly. In the Council, where the franchise
and property qualifications had conspired to give their supporters a
majority, they claimed, wrongly, that the action of the Governor in
using Acts of the Legislative Council to promulgate the earlier occupation regulations rendered unconstitutional Gipps's action in issuing
the new set on his own authority. Outside they established the Pastoral
Association of New South Wales to lobby the Colonial Office against
both Gipps's regulations and the Sale of Waste Lands Act: two-thirds of
the elected members of the Council were on the committee of this body.
The Council appointed a 'Committee on Crown Land Grievances' to
catalogue its complaints, and a dispute between Governor and Council
over a Bill to extend the franchise to certain large leaseholders, which he
saw as an attempt to enlarge the graziers' majority, further raised the
political temperature.

Then the Council turned back to the question of the schedules. All the
classical Whig doctrines about taxation by representation and the right
to appropriate revenue were canvassed. The Governor was attacked for

his alleged attachment to the high prerogative doctrines traditionally attributed to the Stuart kings. A second select committee, on 'General Grievances', summed up the Council's objections to the Act of 1842 and praised the Durham report. Wentworth suggested the possibility of impeaching the Governor's advisers. The Council refused to extend the operation of the Act which provided for the payment of the police in the outlying areas of the colony: Gipps retaliated by retrenching large numbers of troopers and thus threatening to withdraw protection from the squatters.

In this hysterical atmosphere, with the Council appealing to ancient doctrines and archaic remedies, and the Governor suspending the operation of normal services, there emerged from the Council, in a rather confused phrase in the report of its General Grievances committee, the first demand for responsible government. Whether the councillors meant, when they used this phrase, government by a cabinet or merely the transfer of full control over finance is a matter of some dispute; what is clear, however, is that what Michael Roe has called 'a loathing of taxation too absolute for the twentieth-century mind to comprehend', and a deep-seated hostility to officials just because they were officials, lay behind it. In a real sense the desire for responsible government was originally a constitutional embodiment of frustrations over the land laws and resentments about the cost of police and gaols.

In the request for responsible government the Council referred to Canada. Stanley replied, a little ponderously, that Canada was being governed in accordance with the Reunion Act of 1840 and New South Wales in accordance with the Government Act of 1842, and that in neither case had the Colonial Office 'entered into any statement of any Theory or abstract principles of Colonial Government'. This reply was hardly likely to satisfy Wentworth and his supporters, and before it arrived in the colony relations between the Governor and his Legislative Council had reached almost complete deadlock. The situation appeared impossible, but it was, in fact, about to improve. Another decade was to pass before Stanley's 'abstract principles' became the basis of government in New South Wales and its sister colonies.

CHAPTER THREE

The Coming of Responsible
Government

'The din of indignation against "Downing Street policy" is so bad
and so incessant that I cannot help thinking there must be something in it. People are apt to be riled at having their minutest
affairs ... settled for them ... by a staff of clerks who cannot have
the faintest notion of the questions they are handling. From the
Cape to New Zealand, from Bishop to pot-boy, the cry is every-
where the same. And the worst part of the policy is that we get
nothing by it.... We alienate the colonies and harass every
Ministry with a set of impossible problems.'

LORD ROBERT CECIL (1852)

Grey: Tentative Schemes and the Transportation Crisis

An historian tracing in the post-imperial world the constitutional
development of a British dependency can easily fall into the trap of
seeing it in terms of a 'struggle'—a series of hard-fought but almost
divinely ordained stages leading, despite stubborn opposition from
London, to either the formal independence epitomized by the United
States and India or the *de facto* independence of Canada and Australia.
The risk is particularly great for an Australian historian because the
leading participants in the 'struggle for self-government' drew much of
their rhetoric from the history of the American Revolution and of their
practical inspiration from Canadian experience. But such a view is both
over-simplified and distorted. The attitude of British governments,
whatever colonists may have thought, was never blindly negative; and
the Australian experience, despite superficial similarities to that of other
colonies, was fundamentally very different. Events in Australia were
always in a minor key; and, while attachment to the principle of representation was genuine, the pressures which developed into a demand for
responsible government had their origin not, as in the American colonies, in the abstract political theory of the eighteenth-century
'Enlightenment' or, as in Canada, in the tensions of rival nationalisms,
but in mundane administrative grievances spiced with personal ambitions and even with cupidity. This is why the demand seemed less
impressive to the Colonial Office than it can seem to the modern student, why the Colonial Office was, in fact, less obstinate and more
reasonable than is sometimes thought, and why also the system in which
a representative legislature confronted an independent executive, ap-

parently on the point of breaking down in 1845, was able to survive in New South Wales for ten more years.

So much was the truculence of the colony at this time a matter of personalities and specific economic grievances that some changes in personnel and two concessions (one small, the other more apparent than real) mollified it sufficiently to allow the government to analyse, and even experiment with, the colony's constitutional needs. In December 1845 Stanley, whose lofty evasiveness about the 'abstract principles of Colonial Government' was in itself an irritant, resigned; W.E. Gladstone held the Colonial Office seals until the following July when, on the fall of the Peel government, they passed to the third Earl Grey. In the same month Gipps retired: he was succeeded by Sir Charles FitzRoy. Grey was later to become bitterly unpopular in the colonies, but the immediate reactions to his appointment were favourable. He was the son of the Prime Minister who had been responsible for the great Reform Act; had served as parliamentary under-secretary to the Colonial Office in his father's government and was known as a liberal, at least in matters of trade. Moreover FitzRoy's charm (and indolence) provided a welcome contrast to the honest inflexibility of Gipps. Meanwhile James Stephen had seen one way in which the Legislative Council's sense of grievance could be weakened. He pointed out that, while the 'three schedules' might be important, the reservation from Council control of the trifling amounts involved in the casual revenues was simply giving Wentworth a stick with which to beat the Governor. He advised that they should be surrendered, and one of Grey's first actions as Secretary of State was to instruct FitzRoy accordingly. The result, as Stephen foresaw, was an easing of tension out of all proportion to the amounts involved. Then a new Sale of Waste Lands Act and Orders-in-Council under its authority, which seemed to involve a much more considerable retreat from the Gipps-Stanley position than they in fact did, relaxed tensions still further.

Grey proposed to use the opportunity thus offered to him to overhaul thoroughly the government of the Australian colonies. He thought that the mixed Council in New South Wales should be replaced by a bicameral legislature, because 'that ... more ancient System, in which every new Law was submitted to the separate consideration of two distinct Houses, and required their joint consent for its enactment, was the best calculated to ensure judicious and prudent Legislation'. When he expressed this opinion he had already agreed to the institution of responsible government in the North American colonies; but, as J.M. Ward has noted, he felt that the Australian settlements 'lacked the political maturity that he deemed essential for so advanced a ... system'. Moreover, having studied the situation conscientiously, he was aware of the peculiar problems of Australian government: the complexities of the land question, the difficulty of administering vast areas, the remarkable strength of separatist sentiment in the Port Phillip district, South Australia's sense of being different. And as a devoted freetrader he was anxious to prevent the erection of tariff barriers between the colonies in the future. He set himself the task of designing a form of government more representative than that then existing in New South Wales, one, however, which should maintain a degree of imperial control sufficient to prevent inexperienced legislatures from aggravating such problems and which should contribute positively towards their solution.

There was available to him what seemed like a model. Stephen had devised, and Grey on coming to office had himself adopted, a quasi-federal plan for the government of New Zealand. This provided for elective municipal corporations in each of the main centres of settlement, bicameral legislatures in each of the two provinces into which the colony was to be divided, and a 'General Assembly', also bicameral, to deal with a short list of matters of overall interest. The Lower House of each provincial legislature was to be elected by the local corporations of the province, and the Lower House of the federal legislature by the two provincial bodies; at both levels the Upper Houses were to be nominated. On 31 July 1847 Grey outlined in a despatch to FitzRoy a plan to provide the same kind of Constitution for the Australian colonies. He hoped that the separation of Port Phillip, which was part of the plan, and the institution of local government, would, in combination with a pyramidal federal structure, provide the answer he needed to the special problems of Australia and the guarantee he valued of inter-colonial free trade; the existence of nominated councils and the use of indirect election might be expected to offset the colonists' political immaturity.

It is perhaps not surprising that reactions to Grey's scheme in New South Wales were hostile: while the colonists were not necessarily more aware of the problems to be solved than Grey, they believed themselves, and perhaps they were, better able to appeciate the objections to Grey's proposed solutions. Local government, obviously desirable when one looked at a map on a wall in Downing Street, was equally obviously impracticable in the sparsely settled country areas of Australia; worse, it had become associated during the Gipps-Stanley period with the police-and-gaols grievance. When Wentworth characterized the proposal for indirect election as a breach of the Bill of Rights of 1688 he was indulging his taste for Whig hyperbole, but he was also articulating the obvious complaint that it implied a view of colonials as less capable of free government than Englishmen at home. As for the 'General Assembly', few people in New South Wales, and fewer in South Australia, were interested enough in the long-term advantages of federation to suppress objections which arose not just from petty jealousies but also from real economic and social differences. The colonial reaction to the Grey plan was complicated by the split which had begun to open in the New South Wales Legislative Council between the squatters and a group, led by

Robert Lowe and Charles Cowper, who believed that the government had given too much to the graziers; in the Port Phillip district the attraction of any scheme which promised a degree of independence from Sydney provided a further complication; but the protests which greeted the plan as a whole were broadly enough based to convince the Secretary of State that it needed serious modification.

Grey's original despatch had been, in fact, intended to sound out opinion, and within a fortnight of its receipt that opinion had been forcibly expressed, and embodied in a petition, by a public meeting in Sydney. Even before the petition reached England, Grey had decided to bow to objections to the New Zealand constitution on which it was based and had begun to reconsider the Australian position. The consequence of his reconsideration was a despatch, written exactly twelve months after his first, which was so conciliatory that it was greeted as 'the Golden Despatch'. This confirmed his intention of transforming the Port Phillip district into a separate colony, to be called Victoria, notified his abandonment of the ideas of local government and indirect election and, in deference to opposition (which was by no means unanimous) to the bicameral principle, announced that no alteration would be made to the constitution of the New South Wales Legislative Council when Port Phillip was separated. Instead he proposed to establish representative councils in Victoria, South Australia and also Van Diemen's Land, and to give the colonies themselves a direct voice in future development:

> ... as the Australian Communities are, in my opinion, fully competent to originate and to discuss for themselves any changes in this portion of their Institutions, I have it further in contemplation to recommend that their respective Legislative Councils should have power to make such alterations in their own Institutions as they may think expedient; subject, however, to the condition that no Ordinance which any such Legislative Council may pass for this purpose shall come into force until it shall have been specially confirmed by the Queen in Council, after having been laid for one month before both Houses of Parliament.

This intention of 'accommodating the constitutions of those thriving colonies to the wants and wishes of their inhabitants' seemed indeed golden: in such a context the colonists might well accept Grey's decision to 'reserve for more mature consideration' methods by which he might provide for uniformity in such matters as customs. But the despatch was by no means the final solution to the problems of government as the people of New South Wales saw them: the promise to consider proposals from the colonial councils for 'alterations in their own Institutions' was not by any means an unqualified promise of responsible government. And before Grey was ready to proceed with the first step of his reforms, the establishment of part-elective councils in Port Phillip, South Australia and Van Diemen's Land, another of his policies was to provoke a crisis which completely dissipated the goodwill the despatch had evoked. This was his convict policy.

When transportation to New South Wales was ended, the practice of assigning convicts to work for settlers was abolished both in that colony and in Van Diemen's Land, where the vast majority of convicts were in future to be sent. In 1842 Stanley and his colleagues worked out an elaborate plan of penal discipline. Convicts, the worst of them after an initial period of close confinement at Norfolk Island, were to be employed in government gangs and then, if showing evidence of reformed character, were to be given probation passes which would enable them to work for wages. The scheme broke down because the colonists objected to paying the costs of a system from which they did not receive the direct benefits which they considered assignment to have given them, and in 1846 transportation to Van Diemen's Land was suspended for two years. By this time experiments had begun with a new penal system: convicts were confined for a period in the new British 'reformatory' prisons (of which Pentonville was the model) as a preliminary to being sent to various colonies, not as prisoners but as 'exiles', with pardons conditional on their not returning home. One of the places to which it was proposed to send these 'Pentonvillains' was Port Phillip. The first batch arrived in 1845, to be greeted by some mild protests in Melbourne and an enthusiastic welcome from labour-hungry graziers. In the next four years some 1,700 exiles were absorbed by the district.

But this was not enough. Gladstone investigated various other means of disposing of convicts, including the establishment of a new colony in northern Australia; Grey, when he came to office, turned to a great expansion of the exile system. A committee of the New South Wales Legislative Council encouraged him to believe that convicts would be welcome to the graziers, not only of Port Phillip but of the colony as a whole, and so in September 1847 he proposed, if the Council approved, to send out convicts with tickets-of-leave, accompanied by an equal number of free settlers. The Council, though it had at first repudiated its committee's opinion, changed its mind and accepted the offer. Then Grey, finding the selection and financing of immigrants difficult, asked if the colony would accept exiles without free-settler dilution. Probably because FitzRoy had not informed him of the true position in the colony, where there was strong opposition to the Council's action, he anticipated a favourable reply by sending five shiploads.

By the time the first of the ships, the *Hashemy*, arrived at Sydney in June 1849 a considerable slackening in the demand for labour had made convicts seem less desirable, even to some of those who might earlier have accepted them on any terms, and the absence of immigrants led to Grey's being accused of a breach of faith. Though three-quarters of the men in the *Hashemy* were hired in Sydney and the rest at Moreton Bay, and though the 1,400 sent in the five ships were all absorbed in some part of the colony in due course, a quayside protest meeting led by Robert Lowe and two influential clerics, the Presbyterian Lang and the Roman Catholic McEncroe, was vehement enough to convince FitzRoy of the need to discourage Grey from repeating the experiment. A Legislative Council election had just been held, and the new Council added its protests. Grey continued to hope for a change of heart, but this was the effective end of transportation to New South Wales. The problem was not yet solved for Van Diemen's Land: the exiles whom the mainland would not accept were diverted thence until transportation to eastern Australia was abolished after Grey left office.

The Australian Colonies Government Act

The *Hashemy* crisis effectively destroyed Grey's image as a reformer and therefore complicated seriously the problems which faced him. These were complex enough already, for he had to consider the constitutional needs not only of New South Wales but also of Victoria, South Australia and Van Diemen's Land. Victoria was perhaps the least of his worries. When in July 1848 the colonists of Port Phillip turned the election of their representatives in the New South Wales Council into a mockery by choosing Grey himself as member for Melbourne, they were expressing their opinion of the futility of 'representation' in Sydney and their resentment at what they believed to be the spending of their land revenue for the benefit of other districts, but as far as Grey was concerned they were preaching to the converted. He had agreed in principle to separation. The other colonies worried him more. In South Australia he was faced by strong objections to any sort of federal system. In Van Diemen's Land pressure for self-government was at first not strong. In November 1845, however, six non-official members of the Legislative Council, incensed by the government's convict policy, had resigned to leave the Council without a quorum and thus prevent the Lieutenant-Governor, Eardley Wilmot, from forcing through an appropriation Bill on his casting vote. Although Wilmot succeeded, with some difficulty, in replacing them, and although Gladstone removed the specific grievance by agreeing to meet two-thirds of the cost of police and gaols, the 'Patriotic Six' had not only raised the issue of representative government but had also entangled it with the colony's grievances over convict administration. It remained so entangled from then until transportation was abolished in 1853.

When Grey wrote in July 1848 of his regard for 'the wants and wishes of [the] inhabitants' of the colonies, he was not, as some colonists thought, abdicating his authority to them. In particular, the vagueness of his reference to the 'mature consideration' he would give to the means of providing uniformity in customs policy did not imply the necessary abandonment of the idea of a General Assembly. He was convinced that some principle of unity should be established as part of the constitutional development of the Australian colonies, though he was open to conviction on the nature of the machinery which should be provided. Even before the Golden Despatch was written he had begun to look for advice on this matter. Stephen had retired from the permanent under-secretaryship in 1847 because of ill health, and his successor, Herman Merivale, was sceptical about Grey's desire to impose some form of federalism on the colonies. Grey was anxious to have Stephen's advice—and support. In order to obtain this, and to give it an air of authority, he persuaded his colleagues early in 1849 to appoint, in the guise of a revival of the eighteenth-century Privy Council Committee for Trade and Plantations, an essentially *ad hoc* body, with Stephen as the dominant member, to report on the problems of Australian government.

The committee recommended that a Bill should be introduced to give to Victoria, South Australia and Van Diemen's Land, councils modelled on that of New South Wales; the Bill should also include a uniform tariff for the four colonies, to be altered, if the colonies wanted alteration, only by a federal General Assembly consisting of a Governor-General and a 'House of Delegates', the latter elected by the four councils. This body would not be established automatically, but would be called into existence by one of the governors, who would be given a commission as Governor-General, when two or more of the colonies requested. Representation should bear a reasonable relationship to population and, while its primary function would be the maintenance of uniform duties, the Assembly would also have authority over weights and measures and various aspects of inter-colonial communication, power to establish a general Supreme Court with both appellate and original jurisdiction, and the right to accept power over matters transferred by the agreement of all the colonial legislatures. It was a well-meant and even visionary proposal, but although it was not as objectionable as Grey's 1847 scheme it seemed to the colonists to involve the same highly objectionable assumption: that Downing Street knew best. That alone was sufficient to damn it in their eyes.

Grey had allowed his enthusiasm for free trade and federalism to blind him to this fact. Without waiting for the colonial reaction to the plan he had it embodied in a Bill. In the course of debate in Parliament he was persuaded, however, that to legislate in England for a detailed colonial tariff was administratively absurd. He withdrew the clauses and schedule dealing with the tariff, transferring to the General Assembly the right to make it as well as amend it; at the same time he proposed to add to the powers of that body complete power over the alienation and occupation of Crown lands. He hoped to get the Bill accepted quickly, but there were strong objections raised in Parliament that the measure had been introduced too late in the session to allow of adequate consideration, and he was ultimately forced to stand it over until 1850.

When it was reintroduced, significant changes had been made in the federal clauses. Most importantly, the General Assembly would represent and bind only those colonies which asked for its convocation. Over these its authority in tariff matters would be complete; but colonies which did not join would be allowed to fix their own levels of duties, subject only to a prohibition on differential tariffs. The basis of representation in the federal House was altered to the advantage of the smaller colonies over New South Wales, which had fifty-eight per cent of the total population of the four colonies but would now, if all joined, have about a third of the members instead of the forty-eight per cent that the 1849 Bill would have given it. This reduction in the influence of New South Wales could be expected to make the clauses more attractive to Victorians, who might fear that federation would destroy the benefits of separation; and to South Australians, who were genuinely afraid that a General Assembly dominated by New South Wales squatters would use its powers over land to reduce the minimum price and thus depreciate what they saw as their principal asset. But since there was now no way in which New South Wales could be forced into a federation, and since its legislative councillors were hardly likely to commit it voluntarily to one in which it could be easily outvoted by its small fellow colonies, the federal scheme had lost most of its point. Grey seems to have realized this, for in the face of opposition in Parliament he first dropped the idea of federal control of lands and then withdrew the federal clauses altogether.

The Australian Colonies Government Act became law on 5 August 1850. Its basic effect was to give to Van Diemen's Land, South Australia and Victoria Legislative Councils of which two-thirds of the members were to be elected; the New South Wales Council was to retain the same proportion of elected members. Provision was made for the extension of a similar system to Western Australia when that colony should become able to pay its own way, and the right to separate the northern part of New South Wales, and to establish a legislature of the same type there, was reserved to the Crown. The government had not intended to alter the 1842 franchise levels, £200 in freehold property of occupation of a house worth £20 per year, but an amendment carried in the House of Lords halved these figures and also gave the vote to holders of squatting licences and certain leases. The various legislatures were given the right to alter their franchises and membership qualifications and, subject to the need for the Royal Assent in England, to divide themselves into upper and lower Houses. In some matters the Councils were given increased powers: they were to have control over their colonies' judicial systems, the right to make their own decisions about local government, and the right to fix their own tariff scales, provided differential duties were not charged. These were significant devolutions, but, at least in the case of New South Wales, the Act was more notable for what it did *not* grant. The 'three schedules' of the Act of 1842 were retained, with only the alterations in amount dictated by the separation of Victoria; the right to appoint all but the most junior of the colony's officers remained in the hands of the government at home; and, most importantly, the imperial government had refused to give the colonies control of their land revenue. What all this meant was that, if Stanley had side-stepped the request for responsible government, Grey had ignored it. The tone of colonial politics might now be less truculent than five years before, but vehement protest was inevitable.

The Concession of Responsible Government

This protest, though it was invariably expressed in constitutional terms, was the resultant of other irritations, over land, land revenue and transportation, and, as W.P. Morrell has pointed out, the vehemence was due to the fact that 'this much-heralded Act seemed to New South Wales almost irrelevant to the real questions of the day'. The Legislative Council, after carrying out the task imposed on it by the Act of fixing the seat distribution for its successor, passed, as its last action before being dissolved, a 'Declaration, Protest and Remonstrance' which made five fundamental demands. First, the imperial Parliament should not continue 'to tax the people of [the] colony, or to appropriate any of the moneys levied by authority of the Colonial legislature', as it did while the three schedules remained. To do so was, it was argued, contrary to the Declaratory Act of 1788 which 'solemnly disclaimed' any such power. Secondly, the land revenue, which 'derived as it [was] mainly, from the value imparted ... by the labour and capital of the people of [the] colony, [was] as much their property as the ordinary revenue', should be appropriated by the Council. Thirdly, the customs department, which was still controlled by the British Treasury even though it was to administer a tariff fixed by the local legislature, should be placed under the control of that body. Fourthly, all 'Offices of trust and emolument' except the Governorship should be under local patronage. Fifthly, 'plenary powers of legislation should be ... exercised by the Colonial Legislature' and no Bill should be reserved for disallowance unless it might 'affect the Prerogatives of the Crown or the general interests of the Empire'.

The new Legislative Council reiterated these demands. It promised, 'upon the establishment of a Constitution ... similar in its outline to that of Canada, to ... provide for the whole cost of ... Internal Government, ... the salary of the [Governor] only excepted—and to grant ... an adequate civil list, on the same terms as in Canada'. The difference between such a civil list and the schedules was, of course, that it would be a compensation for the surrender of the land revenues, not a sum additional to them. Then, when Grey rejected the original declaration, commenting, rather provocatively, that he doubted whether it 'accurately expresse[d] the feeling of the community', the Council added a threat. It replied to Grey in terms which Melbourne has described as 'more outspoken and less dignified than the original remonstrance', and announced that, though it would provide supply for the year 1853, it would not thereafter consider any estimates. Neither the old Council nor the new had used the term 'responsible government' in its protests to Grey against the Australian Colonies Government Act. Melbourne has argued, indeed, that when the phrase was used at this time it implied only the right of the legislature to influence, by financial measures, the policies of individual officers of government. Some recent writers have argued that people like Wentworth intended it to mean more than this, and it should be remarked that the Council's fifth demand, complete independence in local matters, went further than the system which had been instituted in Canada in 1847. In authorizing Lord Elgin to act there, whenever possible, on the advice of officers who could command a majority in the legislature, Grey had not abrogated the British government's right to veto *any* measure, for he realized that to distinguish between matters local and matters imperial would sometimes be very difficult.

Whatever construction the colonists might have put on the term 'responsible government' there is no doubt that they wanted a degree of autonomy which the Australian Colonies Government Act did not give them. Although the new Legislative Council was little if any more representative than the old (Wentworth and his friends having secured a seat distribution which virtually nullified the extension of the franchise) Grey was wrong in his opinion that it did not represent the 'feeling of the community'. When a select committee of the Council, appointed to consider taking advantage of the section of the Act which allowed the legislature to divide itself into two Houses, drew up a constitutional scheme based on the five demands, there was a general approval of all except that part of the scheme which dealt with the proposed Upper House. By 1852 relations between New South Wales and the Colonial Office seemed to have reached an impasse: Grey's failure to solve the problems of colonial government seemed more abject than Stanley's.

Grey left office in February 1852: in December his successor, Sir John Pakington, conceded the substance of the Legislative Council's demands. While he refused to accept the proposition that *all* colonial offices should be bestowed on colonists, and while he felt 'unable to concede the claim advanced on behalf of the Colonists to the Administration of Waste Lands as one of right', he agreed that it had become expedient to surrender control over lands and that, if the promise to provide an adequate civil list was fulfilled, financial and legislative

autonomy should be granted to the colony. The Council should, however, first draft a constitution providing for a 'new Legislature on the
bases of an Elective Assembly and a Legislative Council to be nominated
by the Crown'. Pakington also offered the same reforms, on the same
conditions, to Victoria and South Australia. In effect, the colonies were
to be given 'responsible government'.

This can be seen as a revolution in Colonial Office thinking, the
repudiation by Pakington of Grey's policy. Such was the view of one so
close to the centre of events as Frederic Rogers, then law officer at the
Colonial Office and later to be permanent under-secretary, who claimed
that 'Grey was possessed with the idea that it was practicable to give
representative institutions and then to stop without giving responsible
government', but Roger's view cannot be accepted without serious re-
servations. Grey, it is true, was 'a cantankerous doctrinaire'. Pakington
and the Duke of Newcastle (who succeeded him a few days after he
wrote the despatch which implicitly conceded responsible government)
were more pragmatic. But, as J.M. Ward has pointed out, Pakington's
despatch supported Grey 'on nearly every question of principle'. The
key difference between the two men was in their attitude to the control of
land. Grey considered that the preservation of the imperial interest in
the waste lands of the Empire was the central problem to be solved in
providing constitutions for the colonies. Pakington, probably under the
influence of Herman Merivale, seems to have felt that resistance to
growing colonial pressures might ultimately produce more mischief than
the abandonment of this interest could cause. By the time he wrote,
moreover, the full effects of the gold discoveries made early the year
before were becoming clear: the conviction that they 'must, in all human
probability, stimulate the advance of population, wealth and material
prosperity with a rapidity ... unparalleled' lay behind his decision to
abandon control over land as a matter of expediency. Once this control
was surrendered there was no longer any point in treating the Australian
colonies differently from Canada. Responsible government was a corollary of the decision on land. It came, not as a sudden reversal in colonial
policy, but as a consequence of the application of the same policy to
radically changed circumstances.

The colonial leaders had had long experience in agitation: they were
now confronted with the problems of constructive statesmanship, and
they found them to be real problems indeed. When the New South
Wales Legislative Council had first raised the cry for responsible government in 1844 it had enjoyed the almost unanimous support of the colonists, who considered the Colonial Office and its servant Gipps their
greatest enemies. But the situation had changed. The old leaders were
under challenge from new radical forces, and they had come to be as
nervous of democracy as they had then been hostile to authority. The
Canadian Rebellion Losses Bill of 1849, which compensated some of the

rebels of 1837 for loss they suffered in the suppression of the uprising, had shaken the faith of colonial conservatives in the kind of responsible government which had been sanctioned in Canada, and even when they were asking for a constitution 'similar in outline' to the Canadian they were thinking in terms of very different details. Now they sought to ensure that their new constitution would give them the local autonomy they desired without playing into the hands of the democracy they feared. The committee appointed by the New South Wales Council to draft the Constitution, the most important members of which were Macarthur, Wentworth, his friend H.G. Douglass and the colonial secretary Edward Deas Thomson, sought conservative safeguards and played down the idea of executive responsibility.

One safeguard it proposed was the establishment of an hereditary aristocracy which would eventually provide all the members of the upper house. To meet the most obvious objections to an hereditary peerage it suggested that only the holders of original patents should automatically be entitled to seats, provision being made for those who inherited titles in the future to be represented by twenty of their number elected by the whole peerage. The plan was not entirely new; something of the same kind had been considered for Upper and Lower Canada in 1791, and the South Australian John Morphett had revived the idea in 1849. It can be said for the committee that the contemporary House of Lords enjoyed a degree of prestige and public confidence which invited an attempt to use it as a model. But the prestige of the House of Lords was a product of social forces which did not exist in the colony, and the idea of what the radical Daniel Deniehy called a 'bunyip aristocracy' was too easy to deride for it to be an effective counter to democracy.

The conservatives quickly realized this, and when the committee's draft was considered by the Council the peerage was dropped in favour of an ordinary nominee chamber, to be appointed initially for five years and then replaced by one the members of which would be appointed for life. But there were other safeguards. Although it was proposed that the Lower House, the Legislative Assembly, should be elected on a franchise which would have fallen little short of manhood suffrage, there was provision for a seat distribution heavily weighted against the centre of democratic opinion in Sydney and alterable only by a two-thirds majority of members. To alter the structure of the Upper House, moreover, would require a two-thirds majority in both chambers. Despite strong opposition out of doors, these 'unusual majorities' were left in the draft constitution which was sent to the Secretary of State a few days before the end of 1853.

Draft constitutions providing for bicameral legislatures and the local autonomy in regard to land and finance which had been offered by Pakington were also submitted by the Victorian and South Australian Councils. The Victorian draft provided not for a nominated Legislative

Council but for one to be elected on a narrow property and education franchise and with a seat distribution heavily weighted in favour of rural areas: Melbourne, with about one third of the colony's population, was given only one sixth of the seats. The Legislative Assembly was to have a wide franchise, but the distribution of its seats was also to be weighted (rather less heavily) against urban voters. There was to be a high property qualification for members—£5,000 for councillors and £2,000 for members of the Assembly—but a proposal that a two-thirds majority of the Council be necessary for amendment of the Constitution was rejected. In Victoria the 1850 Act had been greeted as a charter of independence from Sydney: for this reason, and because attention was distracted by the gold-field troubles, which reached a climax at Eureka in December 1854, there was much less interest in the drafting of the new constitution than in either New South Wales or in South Australia, in which last colony as D.H. Pike has pointed out, the 1858 Act 'fell far short of what people had been led to expect'. South Australia's radical tradition dictated a wide franchise and favoured an elective Upper House or even a single-chamber legislature. However the Governor, Sir John Young, withheld from the Council a despatch from Newcastle which had withdrawn Pakington's suggestion that the British government required an Upper House of nominees: such a chamber was accordingly provided for. But no attempt was made to establish other 'safeguards' like the New South Welsh unusual majorities.

Pakington had not intended the principles of his despatch to apply to Van Diemen's Land. When he had written it he had already decided to abolish transportation to the island, and the last convict ship sailed there a fortnight later. But the high proportion of convicts in the population, as well as the economic difficulties of the colony, raised doubts about the possibility of giving to it the same form of government as the mainland colonies. However the denial to Van Diemen's Land of privileges granted to the others produced a storm of protest from people whose passions had already been aroused by an agitation against the convict system and its administration. A year after Pakington had written his despatch Newcastle was still hedging, writing of the 'peculiar circumstances of the colony' which, if they were not 'sufficient to affect the principles' of government, might 'modify the application'; and a constitution drafted by a committee of the Legislative Council, which sought to make the Governor removable by an address carried by two-thirds majorities in both houses, had no hope of acceptance in London. Later, however, a more sober Bill was proposed by a second committee, and the Secretary of State agreed to consider it on the same basis as those from the other colonies.

The Enactment of the New Constitutions

These three drafts had all arrived in London by May 1854, but the government was immersed in the problems of the Crimean War, and the parliamentary session was far advanced: they did not come before cabinet until near the end of the year. Then in February 1855 the government resigned and the Colonial Office was effectively left without a minister for several months. Sidney Herbert held the seals in the new Palmerston government for only a few days, and Lord John Russell who succeeded him spent a considerable time in Vienna discussing peace. The consequence was that the Bills were not introduced into Parliament until the middle of 1855.

By this time they had been thoroughly examined in the Colonial Office, and in particular by the law officer, Rogers. He found that all three of them contained a restriction on the right of the Crown to veto acts of the colonial legislature not directly affecting the interests of the Empire as a whole. The New South Welsh and Victorian Bills, indeed, went further: they included lists of matters which might be considered 'imperial', lists which implied a very narrow definition. He warned that the existence of the restriction could make it possible for the colonial governments to commit acts which might morally discredit Great Britain, but he seems to have thought that Pakington had already conceded to them the right to impose it and so that little could be done. Pakington had, in fact, made no such unequivocal concession. He had said that he had 'no indisposition to meet the views of the Council[s]' on the matter 'if any practicable mode [could] be devised for distinguishing Local from Imperial subjects of legislation' but had gone on to suggest that drawing a distinction would be difficult and that to restrict the power was unnecessary, for the danger that future colonial measures of purely local concern would be disallowed was 'rather theoretical than practical'. But in any case it was the existence of the lists which really worried Rogers: he pointed out that to accept those in the New South Welsh and Victorian Bills would be to leave the colonies free to close their ports to British ships, British goods and British immigrants, to discriminate against the subjects of States on friendly terms with Great Britain, or to debase the coinage. He was also uneasy about the nominee Upper House proposed by New South Wales, because it could be swamped by decision of the local executive—particularly if Downing Street surrendered the veto—and would, therefore, be unable to perform effectively the functions for which a second chamber was supposedly designed. He was less worried about the unusual majorities: their existence might seem to place a potential strain on the Constitution, but, since the future New South Wales legislature would presumably have the power to make constitutional amendments, these clauses could be eliminated by simple majority vote if the need arose. He was critical of the high property qualifications provided in the Victorian Bill, and felt that a constitution which, like this one, sought to establish a strong and independent Upper House should included a 'deadlock' clause.

The government was anxious to go as far as possible towards meeting the wishes of the colonists, but it obviously had to consider Rogers' objections. It decided not to interfere with the New South Wales Upper House clauses, despite Rogers' doubts and despite an attack on them in the House of Commons by Robert Lowe, a former New South Wales legislative councillor and a strong opponent of what he believed to be Wentworth's conservative stratagems. In the absence of any evidence beyond Lowe's assertion, Russell would not accept the proposition that most New South Welshmen were opposed to nomination; and, while he recognized the validity of Rogers' point, he was unenthusiastic about elective Upper Houses also. On the other hand, since this was the sort of upper chamber that the Victorians seemed to want, he allowed them to have it. But he dealt with the unusual majorities in the New South Wales Bill as the law officer had suggested, by ensuring that the Constitution could later be amended by normal process of legislation; and he decided not just to eliminate the attempted definition of imperial authority but to remove from the Bills all suggestion of restriction on the Crown's right to disallow Bills on any subject. The government refused to draw a hard and fast line between measures upon which the Governor would be obliged to act on the advice of responsible ministers, and matters upon which he would be required to act on instructions from London. The mem who had drafted the Bills had wanted their colonies to be fully sovereign within a limited sphere, leaving imperial interests to the British government. Russell and his colleagues were prepared to give the colonies responsible government in all matters, subject to a discretionary imperial veto. There can be little doubt that Russell's view was the wiser one. Imperial supervision could—and eventually did—quietly wither away, whereas matters specifically reserved would always be an occasion of misunderstanding and friction.

The New South Wales Constitution was adopted as a schedule to 'An Act to entitle Her Majesty to assent to a Bill, as amended, of the Legislature of New South Wales "to confer a Constitution on New South Wales and to grant a Civil List to Her Majesty"'. The body of the Act repealed all previous Acts providing for the government of the colony, conferred full control over lands and land revenue on the colonial legislature and gave this body power to pass constitutional amendment Bills; it also described the boundaries of the colony, reserving to the Crown the right to subdivide the colony later and to confer a similar constitution on the separated part, and declared the Crown's right to issue instructions to the Governor (including instructions on giving and withholding assent and on reservation of Bills for consideration in

England) as well as its right to disallow colonial Bills. A similar Act providing for Victoria went through Parliament parallel with this one, and received the royal assent on the same day, 16 July 1855. They both came into force in November.

The South Australian Bill was, however, delayed. While it was being considered in the Colonial Office a memorial from a large number of colonists protesting against the proposal for a nominated Upper House, and acquainting the government with the fact that it had been included only because the Secretary of State's views had been misrepresented by the Governor, arrived in England. The Bill was therefore referred back to the colony. A new Governor, Sir Richard MacDonnell, tried to persuade the Council to plump for a single-chamber legislature in which there would be some nominated members, some members elected on the basis of a high property qualification and the rest elected without restriction; but the election of a new Council effectively killed this plan, and a constitution was drafted to provide for an Upper House elected on a moderate property franchise and a Lower House elected by all adult males with two years' residence in the colony. As the Bill purported to place no restriction on the Crown's right to instruct the Governor or veto legislation, the British government decided that it could be given the Queen's assent without the formality of enactment by the imperial Parliament. The same treatment was accorded to a very similar Bill passed in Van Diemen's Land, or as it was henceforth to be called, Tasmania. These constitutions came into effect in October 1856. There were now to be four quasi-independent legislatures in Australia; two more were to be established before the end of the century.

The first was in Queensland. During the whole of the period 1851–55 there was agitation among the graziers in the Moreton Bay and New England districts for separation from New South Wales. This had at first been largely motivated by the desire to receive convict labour, but by the time transportation to eastern Australia was formally abolished in 1853 some popular support for the separation movement had begun to develop, at least at Moreton Bay. The British government came to the conclusion that a separate colony would ultimately have to be established there and, as has been seen, made provision for this in the New South Wales Constitution Act. An Order-in-Council defining the boundaries of the new colony of Queensland was made in 1859 and a bicameral legislature with a responsible executive came into existence the following year. Some subsequent doubts about the validity of certain parts of this constitution were removed by imperial legislation in 1861.

The other colony was Western Australia. As has been pointed out in Chapter Two, this colony was kept out of the mainstream of constitutional development by the slow rate of its economic and population growth, and after 1850 by the fact that it was accepting convicts. In 1867 the nominated Legislative Council was enlarged to twelve members, six of whom were not to be officials. The Governor, John Hampton, offered to nominate men elected by each of six districts into which he divided the colony for the purpose, and five of the six areas actually elected representatives. The next year the government announced plans to give the colony representative institutions, as no more convicts were to be sent and as the colony was now able to pay its own way. A Council consisting two-thirds of elected members and one-third of nominees was established in 1870, and enlarged successively in 1874, 1882 and 1886. Before the mid-1880s there was little demand for responsible government, but the sudden realization that the colony contained valuable gold deposits altered the situation. In 1889 the Legislative Council drew up a draft bicameral constitution and asked to be placed on the same footing as the eastern colonies. There was some opposition in the imperial Parliament to the proposal, for in 1890 this one-third of Australia still contained fewer than 50,000 people. Proposals were made for the division of the colony, reserving the area north of the twenty-sixth parallel to Crown control; but in the end responsible government was conceded without partition. In 1890 Western Australia became Australia's sixth self-governing province, and only the Northern Territory, administered by South Australia from 1863 until it was surrendered to control by the new Commonwealth in 1911, remained outside the pattern of responsible government, though in Western Australia the imperial authorities refused to surrender control over Aboriginal affairs for some years.

In the colonies given responsible government in the mid-1850s there were some problems to be solved in putting the system to work. The fact was that there were still differences of opinion about what it meant. The South Australian Governor sought to treat the first responsible ministers as if they were the officials who had advised him in the past, trying to sound them individually on matters which they were later to consider as a cabinet, and claiming the right to bring matters before the Executive Council on his own initiative. In Victoria Sir Charles Hotham held similar views, but his officers persuaded him to commission them as ministers and were able quietly to ignore his idea (surely evidence of a complete failure to understand what responsible government is all about) that he should 'not be party to the appointment of a person whose sole recommendation may be the advocacy of certain political principles'. In New South Wales there was less trouble. Sir William Denison, shrewd, experienced and adaptable, dissolved the old Legislative Council, set about forming a cabinet and holding elections at the same time, and sidestepped legal quibbles about the status of his new ministers before Parliament met. In all the colonies these problems were, however, transitional. The serious, long-term problem was to be the lack of those parties which in Great Britain were coming to serve as the cement of cabinet government. While they slowly developed, the

Governors, and their superiors in Downing Street, remained not only a strong factor in Australian government but also an indispensable condition of its continuing to function at all.

CHAPTER FOUR

The Evolution of Responsible Government

'The question of the Two Chambers has occupied a greater amount of the attention of thinkers than many questions of ten times its importance, and has been regarded as a short of touch-stone which distinguishes the partisans of limited from those of unlimited democracy.'

JOHN STUART MILL

'It is a great pity that, give as much as you will, you can't please the colonists with anything short of absolute independence, so that it is not easy to say how you are to accomplish what we are, I suppose, all looking forward to, the eventual parting company on good terms.'

FREDERIC ROGERS (1854)

When Sir William Denison opened the first New South Wales Parliament on 23 May 1856, his wife was amused to note that the colony's desire to imitate the forms of the mother country went so far as to require a 'State carriage' drawn by four horses and driven by a coachman in borrowed livery. But the members of the Legislative Assembly and Legislative Council who crowded the Council chamber that day saw nothing ludicrous in the 'pageant': to them it was merely a recognition that their country had attained the same constitutional position as the mother country. And their views were shared by their counterparts in the other colonies. Such men were aware of being citizens of polities which were definitely still colonial; but they believed that their colonies, if far from being independent, enjoyed a form of government which reflected the British Constitution. Few of them seemed to realize that the reflection was greatly distorted, that the operation of the system of 'responsible government' would not be the same in the colonies as in Great Britain. As was remarked at the end of the last chapter, the restrictions remaining on the independence of the colonies were considerable. Moreover there were to be significant differences between the Australian colonies and the mother country in the internal working of the 'Westminister system'.

The Australian experience of that system differed from the British in three ways. First, the relationship of executive and legislature was never quite the same; the party system, which was in the 1850s and 1860s becoming the 'cement of the cabinet' in Britain, developed only slowly in the Australian colonies, and when it did grow its development was along different lines; the rhythms of political change were much less regular. Secondly, reforms of a democratic nature came much more quickly in Australia, and there was a certain enthusiasm for making experiments, some doctrinaire, some more or less idiosyncratic. Thirdly, the pattern of relations between the Houses was radically different. Long before 1909, when the House of Lords began its 'sedate sort of general strike against the Constitution', the Upper Houses of the Australian colonies, particularly those which were elective, had conducted a whole series of 'strikes', most of which were anything but sedate. These are the principal facts of the history of Australian colonial government. Each of them must now be considered in its turn.

The Governor's Influence and the Slow Growth of Parties

The phrase 'responsible government' meant different things to different people: when it ceased to be a mere slogan and emerged as a principle of the colonial constitutions it stood in great need of clarification. The view generally accepted was that, save where imperial interests were involved, the Governor's executive powers, including the powers to dissolve Parliament, to give or withhold assent, and in the case of New South Wales to nominate members of the Upper House, were exercisable only on the advice of ministers responsible to the legislature; but, even apart from the fact that 'imperial interests' could be defined very widely or very narrowly, the analogy between the Governor's position and that of the Sovereign at home was by no means complete. There were some men who feared that, like George III, he might be able to build majorities by the use of placemen and dependents, particularly as the circumstances of the colonies produced some feeling in favour of the construction of ministries from men 'trained to the public business'. Such fears were fanciful, but the Governor was far from being a mere dignitary. The Constitution of each of the colonies required him to set up, and in most matters to act on the advice of, an Executive Council. There was no guarantee here, however, of collective responsibility as it was known at home. In New South Wales Denison encouraged his ministers to consider the Executive Council as a formal body and to take their decisions outside it, as a cabinet—a body which *would* be collectively responsible. But in Victoria Sir Henry Barkly was not happy with a system which treated the Executive Council as a mere means of registering decisions taken in the Governor's absence: he would have liked to establish a separate, permanent Council of senior statesmen to advise on such matters as the appointment of magistrates and to take action in an emergency. And Denison did not feel that collective responsibility should rob him of all influence; it seems that he regularly attempted to shape policy. In 1859, for example, he discussed in some detail with the premier, Charles Cowper, the Land Bill which the government was putting before Parliament. Herman Merivale quashed Barkly's bright idea of a permanent advisory Council, and later governors were in a less strong position to offer advice than the experienced administrator Denison, but for many years the three rights which Bagehot was to see as the core of the Sovereign's power, 'the right to be consulted, the right to encourage, the right to warn', were exercised rather more effectively by colonial governors than by Queen Victoria herself. The Australian meaning of collective responsibility was subtly different from the English.

The principal reason for the difference was the instability of colonial governments. In the United Kingdom between 1856 and 1900 there were twelve real changes of government; in the Australian colonies the average was about thirty. The epitome of instability was South Australia: forty-two different ministries took office in the period; twenty-one different men held the premiership, one of them, Henry Ayer, seven times; one government lasted only nine days, another eleven; in the first twenty years of responsible government there were twenty-seven changes of ministry. It has frequently been argued that the instability of governments in Australia was a consequence of a lack of great questions, that Australian politicians, once the principal political issue was resolved by the grant of responsible government, fell to quarrelling over petty personal jealousies and the spoils of office, and that parties based on principle did not emerge to stabilize the process of government until the rise of a political labour movement in the 1890s. But this view is at best an over-simplification and some modern political scientists would consider it a complete distortion. Certainly it is not a fully satisfactory explanation, for in the generation before 'the rise of labour' great issues *did* exist. In the 1850s, 1860s and early 1870s the self-governing colonies, and particularly New South Wales, Victoria and Queensland, fought out the vexed question of 'unlocking the land', supposedly locked up by the squatters in earlier decades. In the 1870s and 1880s long and bitter controversies about secular education occupied the time of the legislatures. Issues like these were enough to cause bloodshed in some countries: it is odd that they could not even produce parties in Australia.

There is no simple explanation of the instability. In part it was a consequence of the fact that the issues in colonial politics were complex and disparate. Personal ambitions, and the ideological divisions of conservative and liberal, were complicated by a tangle of questions ranging from tariff protection to sectarianism. As a contemporary observer of South Australian politics remarked,

> There is a squatting party and an anti-squatting party; a Government House party and a party opposed to Government House; a religious endowment

party and a party unfavourable to religious endowments; but as to well-defined lines of political demarcation, you might as well look for ink spots on the moon.

In part also, the instability was a consequence of political inexperience and defective education. The conditions of colonial life produced wealth without leisure: the wealthy (the graziers and city merchants) and the educated (such as they were) had little time for politics. Men educated for and aiming at a political career, men who could devote their lives to politics without sacrificing their amateur status, men of the kind who ruled England, did not exist in Australia. And payment of members did not solve the problem: it opened the parliaments to different people but not necessarily to better people. For most of the period up to federation the legislatures were dominated by lawyers, the only people with a training which bordered on the political. Their numbers in the Parliaments were always out of proportion to their numbers in society; by the 1880s they outnumbered even the graziers; and their influence was out of proportion to their membership. They, even more than the graziers and the merchants, were men who could afford to devote only a fraction of their attention to their political careers. As debaters they were often excellent, but as parliamentary managers and government administrators they were usually poor. Political instability was a matter more of lack of skill than of lack of issues.

The situation improved gradually: the cabinet system survived and itself slowly produced the parties which were necessary to its efficient working. They appeared first in New South Wales: precisely when remains a matter of some dispute among students of the subject, but Dr Peter Loveday and Professor A.W. Martin have argued cogently that the government formed by Sir Henry Parkes in February 1887 can be considered a party government and its successors were equally supported by what can be called parties in the modern sense of the term. The development was obvious by the mid-1890s: the Reid ministry, basing itself on a remarkably progressive policy of free trade and direct taxation, and made up of men who were both good administrators and clever politicians, gave the colony between 1894 and 1899 its first real taste of political stability. In Victoria the advent of the Turner government in September 1894 provided a parallel: from this time, as Professor J.A. La Nauze has shown, ' "Liberals" and "Conservatives" fairly describe the opposed groups in the Victorian Parliament'. Even in South Australia Charles Cameron Kingston was able to keep office, and to use it imaginatively, from June 1893 to December 1899. The rise of Labour encouraged, rather than caused, the development of a stable party system. The trend towards stability was to continue in the twentieth century.

Rapid Democratization of Colonial Constitutions

The result was that, while there was little formal change in constitutional theory, the 'working constitutions' of the Australian colonies changed radically in the half-century after 1856. Moreover, their systems of government underwent considerable modification in detail. In the adoption of the constitutional devices of radical democracy the Australian colonies moved much faster than did the United Kingdom. Indeed, their Constitution Acts, based as they were on Bills framed in the colonies themselves, were much more radical than a generation of English politicians who remembered Chartism, and the threat which it seemed to level at society, would themselves have liked. In South Australia, for example, universal manhood suffrage on the basis of 'one man, one vote' existed from the institution of responsible government, when the franchise in England was held by perhaps one-fifth of the adult males of the kingdom. Two other colonies soon took advantage of the power of amending their constitutions to follow the South Australian example. In Victoria there was something very close to manhood suffrage from the start, for the right to vote was enjoyed not only by those who satisfied the almost nominal property and occupation tests, but also by holders of a miner's right. In 1857 the vote was given to all adult males, partly to eliminate the possibility that the miner's-right holders (who were allowed to vote in any electoral district they chose) might swamp the votes of local residents. New South Wales legislated for manhood suffrage the following year. The smaller colonies were slower. The first 'extension' of the franchise in Tasmania in 1870 did little more than lower the qualification levels sufficiently to preserve the rights of those who already had the franchise and were in danger of losing it because of a decline in property values and incomes. After this time perhaps sixty per cent of adult males were electors. A real extension came in 1885, after a mining boom brought both prosperity and democratic pressures; the vote was given to all men in 1896. Three years earlier manhood suffrage had been established in Western Australia, and in 1905 Queensland became the last colony to abolish its franchise requirements. By this time the value of money had diminished to such an extent that they were disfranchising few apart from itinerant workers, perhaps one-sixth of the colony's male adults.

But universal manhood suffrage is not in itself democracy. In the larger colonies plural voting survived for many years. It had been established in New South Wales by the Constitution, and had been instituted in Victoria at the same time as manhood suffrage, the elector being given an extra vote in any constituency in which he held freehold land worth £50. No one, however, might record two votes in the one electorate. This limited the effect of plural voting considerably, even in a time when all elections were not held on the one day; very few people (something like five per cent of the total enrolment) were able to exercise a second vote. A rather more striking restriction on democracy, in the modern sense of the term, lay in the disenfranchisement of women; and this came under attack in the same period as plural voting. The plural vote was abolished in New South Wales in 1893, in Victoria and Tasmania at the turn of the century. By this time South Australia, where plural voting had been unknown since 1856, and Western Australia, where it was to persist in an attenuated form until 1907, had gone beyond the ambitions of Chartism to give the franchise to all adults. In Western Australia the concession, made in 1899, was perhaps intended by the old settlers of the southwest who controlled Parliament as a counterbalance to the influence of the democrats on the eastern gold-fields, where there were few women, but in South Australia, where women were given the vote in 1894, the reform is perhaps explicable in terms of the radical tradition of the colony's foundation. In the first few years of the new century female suffrage was granted in the other States. When the Commonwealth was established in 1901 its first elections were conducted on the basis of State franchises and the following year it introduced adult suffrage for all its elections. Moreover the Constitution forbad plural voting for all federal elections. The establishment of the Commonwealth thus hastened the process of democratization in the States. By 1906 women had the vote for all Lower Houses in Australia.

Perhaps the most striking of the trends towards democracy was the adoption of the secret ballot. It was introduced into Victoria with responsible government; South Australia followed at once and the other self-governing colonies within two years. So, at a time when the ballot was still being denounced as 'un-English' in Britain, it had become normal in Australia. The safeguards against the dangers of the system, impersonation and double voting, which were worked out in Victoria in 1855 were ultimately adopted throughout the world. Indeed the secret ballot became known, particularly in the United States of America, as 'the Australian ballot'.

Why, it may be asked, should the devices and assumptions of democracy have made such progress in Australia? One fortuitous cause of early democratic reform was the fact that the worst of the grievances of the gold miners matured in the period of two years between the drafting of the constitutions and the proclamation of those of New South Wales and Victoria: what had seemed to satisfy most people in late 1853 did not satisfy a majority in November 1855. As Dr R.A. Gollan has written, 'during the interval, radical opinion and feeling—in part provoked by the delay—reached an intensity that ensured that early in the life of the new parliaments democratic amendments would be carried'. A more organic cause was the structure of Australian society. Even the conservative historian of Victoria, H.G. Turner, who was inclined to blame manhood suffrage 'for injurious legislation and partisan legislators', had to admit in 1904 that 'In a country where there were no wealthy classes in the English sense, and where a high average standard of comfort engendered independence, no limitations based on mere wealth would have been tolerated'. The facts of Australian economic geography were important too. The domination of the squatting movement, which was dependent on overseas markets and therefore on seaports, over all other rural activities, gave Australia its peculiarly high concentration of people in the colonial capitals, where, as in all large towns in the nineteenth century, radical ideas flourished. It became inevitable, as Mr I.D. McNaughtan has noted, 'that control should lie with the great centres of population rather than with the "great interest" on which they chiefly depended'. This argument, however, cannot be taken too far. The members of the great squatting interest, and later of a host of lesser rural interests, might accept universal suffrage and the ballot, but they fought long and hard (and, as will be seen in Chapter Seven, with considerable success) to preserve such 'safeguards' as weighted seat distribution.

In two other matters, payment of members and the shortening of the life of parliaments, the Australian colonies long anticipated Britain's 1911 reforms. In Victoria, where the great liberal George Higinbotham advocated payment of members of the Legislative Assembly as a democratic measure and as a cure for political instability (for he felt that men with salaries to risk in the case of a dissolution would be less factious in their opposition), it was introduced for a three-year trial period in 1870. It was subsequently extended to the end of 1877 and, after precipitating the worst of the frequent crises between the Houses in that colony, made permanent in 1883. New South Wales and Queensland both provided salaries for their Assembly members in 1889, the latter after paying 'expenses' for three years. South Australia followed in 1890, Tasmania in 1891 and Western Australia in 1900. But regular salaries were not paid to legislative councillors in Victoria until 1922; in Queensland the Council was unpaid until its abolition; and in New South Wales the Upper House had to wait until 1948 for even a nominal 'allowance' payment to its members. While no one in these colonies where the principles of Chartism seemed to find at least substantial acceptance seriously advocated the sixth point of the Charter, annual parliaments (which was, of course, less a reform proposal than an attack on the British parliamentary tradition) the people quickly showed that peculiar distrust for their elected representatives which is one of the great facts of Australian political life by seeking means of making them more frequently accountable than were British MPs under the terms of the Septennial Act. South Australia included provision for triennial parliaments in its Constitution from the start; the other colonies opted for five-year terms. New South Wales shortened its term to three years in 1874 and the other colonies did likewise before the end of the century. There was, particularly in Queensland, some advocacy of 'initiative, referendum and recall', but such a radical departure from the West-minster pattern was more a Labour Party eccentricity than a seriously likely reform. In the 1920s the frequency of elections in Australia was to come under some criticism, particularly as the federal term was three years, and two States were to extend theirs to five years. South Australia did so in 1933, but reverted to three-year terms in 1939. Tasmania adopted quinquennial parliaments in 1936. In 1969 that State legislated for a return to triennial elections, but three years later an Act was passed extending the life of the existing parliament to five years and providing that future parliaments should have four-year terms.

The substantial democratization of the Lower Houses did not by any means exhaust the taste of Australian statesmen for constitutional adjustment. In at least one significant matter they anticipated the United Kingdom in desirable simplification of governmental machinery: the rule that ministers must vacate and re-contest their seats on their acceptance of office, which remained in force in Britain until 1926, was never applied in South Australia and was gradually abrogated in the other colonies—in Queensland in 1884, in New South Wales in 1906, and in Victoria in 1914. In the colonies the rule was, of course, both anachronistic (because short parliaments gave the electors frequent opportunity to express an opinion on ministries) and more inconvenient (because changes of government were frequent) than in Great Britain.

Relations between Houses

(i) *The Victorian Experience*

The various constitutions did not lay down firm and comprehensive rules on relations between the Houses: it was assumed that the colonial parliaments would follow the pattern of compromise popularly considered to be typical of the imperial Parliament. In fact such a pattern hardly existed; from 1832 to 1911 the British Constitution was in a state of highly unstable equilibrium, with the House of Lords occupying an essentially anomalous position. What happened in the colonies was that disputes between the Houses, very bitter disputes, became a recurrent theme. So when the House of Lords began its campaign of opposition to the Campbell-Bannerman government in 1906 it could almost be said to have been following the colonial pattern.

In Victoria the disputes were longer and more bitter than in any other colony. Victoria's strong, conservative Council was bound to clash with a Lower House elected by universal manhood suffrage, particularly as, being elective, the Council could claim to represent an important and coherent interest—as such a fortuitously composed body as the nineteenth century House of Lords could not. The Victorian Constitution, alone among the constitutions of the Australian colonies, contained a formal statement of the British tradition that the Upper House might not amend appropriation bills, but the Legislative Council, taking its stand on its elective nature, did not accept the implication which the House of Lords had long accepted (and continued to accept until 1909) that its power to reject such measures *in toto* was, except in an extreme case, a purely nominal one. It is only fair to point out that the disputes which occurred in Victoria were provoked by Lower House actions of doubtful wisdom and even more doubtful constitutional propriety: the Legislative Council was, in strict constitutional law, more than half right. But when the first serious crisis began in the middle of 1865 the Upper House had already built up a formidable history of obstructiveness: in the first five years of responsible government, it had rejected more than thirty bills passed by the Lower House and mutilated almost beyond recognition the most important measure it had allowed on the statute book, a Land Bill.

The crisis was precipitated by an attempt to introduce protective tariffs. The Premier, James McCulloch, was convinced that a tariff Bill would be opposed by the legislative councillors, who were large landholders and freetraders almost to a man, and he was encouraged (or perhaps persuaded) by his attorney-general, George Higinbotham, to 'tack' the tariff to the annual appropriation Bill—a very different thing. And, while they were probably right in believing that their tariff measure would be thrown out by the Council, they were, in anticipating this with a 'tack', acting provocatively. The Council reacted by voting twenty to five to 'lay aside' the appropriation Bill.

There were funds in the Treasury: the collection of the new duties had begun, in anticipation of the passing of the legislation imposing them (a perfectly normal procedure), and the regular revenue continued to come in, but the ministry was left without legal authority to disburse a penny. Government, it seemed, must come to a standstill. The ingenious Higinbotham, however, was ready with a plan. He enlisted a law called the Crown Remedies Act, which authorized the Governor to sign warrants for the payment of amounts awarded by the courts in suits against the Crown without the necessity for such payment to be included in a parliamentary appropriation. The government persuaded the London Chartered Bank, of which McCulloch was a director, to lend it the sums it needed for the conduct of public business and in due course sue for recovery: the government then 'confessed judgment' and the amounts were paid under the Crown Remedies Act. Immediate administrative problems were thus solved, but the Council naturally condemned the device as 'not only collusive but unconstitutional, if not revolutionary', and the crisis deepened.

In November the government tried to break the impasse by sending the tariff proposal up to the Council in a separate measure. But the preamble of this Bill contained a claim that the Assembly had an exclusive right to control finance, and the Bill itself included a clause retrospectively legalizing the collection of duties which had already been paid. Ostensibly for these reasons, the Upper House refused to agree to it. The ministers then went to the country on the issue, hurling at the Council as a parting provocation a sentence in the Governor's dissolution speech: 'I am glad to be able to announce that, although [the grants for the public business] have not yet obtained the form of law, they have been rendered available for the maintenance of the functions of Government and the fulfilment of its legal obligations'. In the subsequent election McCulloch won an access of strength in the Legislative Assembly.

For the time being the Council stood firm. It still refused to pass the Bill. McCulloch demonstrated his popular support by resigning and having his Assembly majority prevent the formation of an alternative Administration with a declaration that the Lower House would not give its confidence to any ministry which did not insist on the tariff Bill. Then he came back and sent the Bill up a third time. The Council again rejected it. But by this time men on both sides were realizing that the crisis had continued for long enough. McCulloch himself, faced with steadily increasing administrative disorder, and with a despatch from the Secretary of State to the Governor reprimanding him for sanctioning the use of public funds without appropriation, was anxious to end it. For their part, some members of the Council were beginning to feel that their continued opposition to a measure with obvious popular support was costing them too much. Ultimately a conference patched up an uneasy compromise which, in April 1866, put the new tariff scales into legal force.

A few days later, however, all the issues were reopened by the recall of the Governor, Sir Charles Darling. The problems which faced a governor in the early years of responsible government, when his duty to act on the advice of responsible ministers was heavily qualified by his duty as a servant of the imperial government, will be discussed more fully later in this chapter (pp. 78–82). Here it is enough to note the existence of a dilemma for a governor in such events as those just discussed. A constitutional crisis being necessarily an outgrowth of a political dispute in the colony, it would be virtually impossible for him to preserve the appearance of impartiality which his office required, unless he left all responsibility to his ministers and acted on their advice in all matters; but if the advice they gave him was illegal, he, and not they, would be held blameworthy by the Secretary of State. In fact, Darling virtually ignored the problem: his acceptance of his ministers' advice was not so much dutiful as enthusiastic. As has been seen, it earned him a reprimand from Mr Secretary Cardwell. It also led to the framing of a petition to the Queen, by a number of opposition leaders, complaining of his conduct. His reaction to this petition was a long memorandum, ending with the incautious statement that if these men were ever returned to office he would find it impossible to treat their advice 'with any other feelings than those of doubt and distrust'. For this he was recalled. Cardwell pointed out that he had put himself in 'a position of personal antagonism towards ... those ... most likely to be available in the event of any change of ministry'. He had failed to observe the duty of a governor under responsible government as described in Lord Elgin's classic statement of 1847: 'I give my ministers all constitutional support ... [but] I have never concealed from them that I intend to do nothing which may prevent me from working cordially with their opponents, if they are forced upon me'. The Secretary of State could hardly have acted otherwise than he did, but in the colony Darling's recall was inevitably interpreted as punishment for his support of a popular ministry against the wealthy and conservative interests controlling the Legislative Council, particularly as it seemed clear that he would never get another governorship.

The immediate reaction of the supporters of the McCulloch government was to attempt to compensate the ex-governor: as he was still a member of the colonial service he could not accept a gift, so a select committee of the Legislative Assembly proposed that a grant of £20,000 be made to his wife and, although he himself asked that no action be taken until he had consulted Downing Street, the Assembly petitioned the Queen asking that he be allowed to accept the money on his wife's behalf. The Secretary of State replied that acceptance would be interpreted as 'a final relinquishment by Sir C. Darling of Her Majesty's service and all the emoluments or expectations attaching to it'; but he refused Darling's request for an inquiry into his conduct which might have opened the way for a pension. In April 1867, therefore, Darling resigned from the service and announced that his wife would accept the money if it were voted. The government then included the sum in an appropriation Bill covering various additional estimates: this was passed by the Assembly and, predictably enough, rejected by the Council. So the first Victorian crisis merged into the second.

The government tendered its resignation to Darling's newly arrived successor, Sir J.H. Manners-Sutton but, as no alternative ministry could be formed, the Governor was forced to re-commission McCulloch and, after the appropriation Bill was again passed by the Assembly and rejected by the Council, to grant a dissolution of the Lower House which resulted in a sweeping electoral victory for him. Before the new Assembly met, the Duke of Buckingham, now Secretary of State, intervened with a despatch to the Governor counselling him not to sign the necessary Vice-Regal message for the grant to Darling unless it was sent up to the Council in a separate Bill. This attempt to resolve the crisis only deepened it: the ministers resigned in protest against 'the interference of the Crown in a matter so completely within the discretion of the Assembly as the form of a Bill of supply', which, they claimed, 'threaten[ed] the existence of responsible government'. A ministry formed by Charles Sladen was censured and forced to resign within a fortnight of meeting Parliament. Public business had come almost to a standstill; this time the Supreme Court prevented the use of the Crown Remedies Act; but neither side was prepared to give in. The only way to break the impasse was to remove its immediate cause, the conviction of the Victorian government that Darling was being unfairly treated. Buckingham eventually realized this: in June 1868 Darling was told that if he were to renounce the grant to his wife and ask permission to withdraw his resignation he would be retired on an imperial pension of £1,000 per year. He complied and the crisis disappeared; but although the Victorian Legislative Council magnanimously agreed when he died two years later that the colony should confer a similar pension on his widow, with provision for the education of his children, the basic issues which had caused the deadlock were unresolved.

The problem presented by the existence of an exclusive Upper House which could neither be dissolved nor swamped, and the absence of any machinery for the resolution of deadlocks (a problem the seriousness of which Frederic Rogers had perceived in 1854) remained. The Council agreed in 1869 to halve the property qualification for both membership and the franchise, but it would not hear of any modification in its powers. An attempt to amend the Constitution to provide a deadlock procedure also failed, but in this case the trouble was opposition in the Assembly to the machinery proposed—the so-called 'Norwegian scheme' of a joint sitting after two rejections of an Assembly Bill by the Council. It was resisted not only by conservatives but also by Higinbotham and some of his friends, who believed that it involved the implicit acceptance of the Council's claim to a right to reject money Bills. Further trouble between the Houses was inevitable.

When the next crisis came in 1877 the issues were more complex than those of the years 1865–68 and the dispute was even more acrimonious. It began over the question of the payment of members of Parliament. As has been remarked, payment had been authorized since 1870 by temporary legislation, which was due to expire at the end of 1877. The government led by Graham Berry brought down a Bill to continue the practice and, although it apparently expected the Council to reject the measure, it included an amount to cover the expenditure in the annual appropriation Bill. The Legislative Council objected to this as a 'tack': after unsuccessfully attempting to persuade Governor Sir George Bowen to intervene, it rejected both measures. The ministers then asked the Governor to sign warrants for the issue of money on the basis of Assembly votes alone and, while he was consulting the Secretary of State on whether he would be justified in consenting—whether this was one of those 'extreme cases' in which, Rogers had suggested in 1854, it might be necessary to allow 'the Crown and Assembly [to] legislate alone'—they further advised him to authorize the dismissal of a large number of public servants. Convinced that 'the present ministry [was] supported by a majority of about two-thirds in the Legislative Assembly and ... there [was] no reason to suppose that this proportion would be materially altered by the dissolution of an Assembly which was almost fresh from the country', Bowen reluctantly complied, insisting only that the ministers 'limit themselves to making such reductions in the public service to which ... no exception could be raised on the score of illegality'.

The government claimed that the dismissals were necessary to make supplies already voted last longer. Its opponents alleged that, since most of the men dismissed were relatively senior and well-paid officers, it was in fact carrying out what a later conservative sympathizer called 'an act of reprisal on the council, by hurting it through its friends'. Probably the opponents were right, but in any case the issue of the dismissal notices on 'Black Wednesday', 8 January 1878, is an indication of the strength of the passions aroused by what, even more clearly than the events of 1865–68, was a collision between reformers and conservatives. Both sides sent addresses to the Queen. The Legislative Assembly claimed that the Council was causing the trouble by refusing to be guided by what were believed to be the traditions of the House of Lords in the matter of finance: its view was endorsed by the Governor (and accepted as reasonable by the Secretary of State, Sir Michael Hicks Beach, who was, however, understandably reluctant to intervene and who strongly deprecated the dismissal of civil servants). The Council rejected the analogy, standing on the letter of the Victorian constitution. In March an uneasy compromise was patched up, the Council agreeing to pass the appropriation Bill and a Bill to continue payment of members provided the matters were kept separate, but, as in the earlier crises, the real issue, that of the Council's powers, was not resolved.

Berry was anxious that it should be: when Parliament was prorogued in April he announced that, 'to avoid the possibility of the recurrence of such a conflict in the future', he intended to prepare proposals for amendment of the Constitution. But any slight chance that the Council may have been prepared to accept amendment was destroyed by his deciding not to reinstate all the dismissed officers (a decision which smacked of the American 'spoils' system) and by the fact that the proposals were very radical. In July he brought down a measure proposing that money Bills might be presented for the Royal Assent if passed by the Assembly and not passed by the Council within one month, and that all other Bills should go up for assent despite Council rejection if passed in two successive sessions by the Assembly, except that the Council might demand a plebiscite, which would be decisive. The Assembly passed the measure, but the Council rejected it. The Assembly then, with magnificent disregard of the fact that in the earlier crises it had strongly condemned imperial intervention, resolved to send Berry and his principal adviser, Professor C.H. Pearson, to England to ask for imperial legislation amending the Constitution Act so as to enable the Legislative Assembly to enact, in two consecutive sessions, a measure of constitutional reform. The Secretary of State declined to intervene 'unless the Council should refuse to concur with the Assembly in some reasonable proposal for regulating the future relations of the two Houses ... and should persist in such refusal after the proposals of the Assembly ... [had] been ratified by the country'. Hicks Beach reinforced these hints to the government on the need to be sure of its popular support and to the Council on the folly of pushing resistance to extremes, with a direct lecture on the duty of both Houses to interpret their powers 'with that discretion and mutual forbearance which has been so often exemplified in the history of the Imperial Parliament'.

Whatever Berry thought of the lecture, he apparently decided to take the hint. In July 1879 he submitted another reform Bill. This proposed that henceforth the Council should have no control whatever over finance—that money should be available immediately after being voted by the Assembly—and that Bills other than money Bills should be put to plebiscite if passed twice by the Assembly and rejected by the Council. It also provided for the gradual replacement of election of members of the Upper House by nomination. Failing to get an absolute majority for the Bill in the Assembly, Berry went to the country and was defeated; but when his successor, James Service, also failed, with a much more conservative measure, a second general election brought him back to power, though with a dubious enough majority to suggest moderation. He abandoned hope of breaking the Council's power, financial or legislative, and was satisfied with a measure to narrow the gap between the respective electoral bases of the two Houses. This proposal, which the Council accepted in June 1881, increased the membership of the Upper House from thirty to forty-two, reduced the term of its members from ten years to six, and made another substantial reduction in its property qualifications and franchise. The value of freehold property required by a member was reduced from £2,500 to £1,000. The basic electoral qualification (originally the possession of £1,000 worth of landed property and since 1869 the possession of such property to the value of £500) was replaced by one which gave the vote to the owners of property with an annual rental value of £10 and also to £25 leaseholders. The effect of the change was to increase the number of voters from about 30,000 to over 100,000—half the number on the Assembly roll. Henceforth the Council was to be rather less exclusive, but no less powerful, and little, if any, less conservative.

Several unsuccessful attempts were made to weaken the position of the Victorian Upper House in the 1890s and one, after another serious crisis, in 1903. In that year there was a further reduction in the property qualification, to £500, and a nominal extension of the franchise; and the Constitution was amended to provide a deadlock clause. But the arrangement, which provided for a simultaneous dissolution of both Houses if a deadlock persisted after a dissolution of the Assembly, and which gave the Council a limited right to suggest amendments to money Bills, actually strengthened its position. In return for getting what Higinbotham would never have accorded it, a formal power to deal with finance in detail, the Council conceded nothing but a deadlock process which was quite inoperable; for, as Geoffrey Serle has remarked, it would 'take at least three years and ... require unimaginable tenacity and willingness to jeopardize immediate legislative intentions on the part of a government'. As will appear in Chapter Seven, the Council was to remain a powerful force in Victorian political life into the third quarter of the twentieth century.

Relations between Houses

(ii) *Other Colonies with Elected Councils*

The secret of the Victorian Council's strength was its elective nature. Though unable to match its performance, the other elective Upper Houses remained ready to dispute the right of their colonies' Lower Houses to legislative supremacy for considerable periods. Indeed the South Australian Legislative Council, which was based from the beginning on a wider electorate (one about half the size of the House of Assembly's electorate and one paying almost all the taxes) went further than the Victorian in some of its claims, particularly as regards finance.

Trouble began in the first few weeks of responsible government when the Council, ignoring the precedents of the House of Lords, sought to amend a money Bill. It announced that it refused to allow the House of Assembly's 'limited right of originating' such Bills, which the Constitution conferred, to be extended 'to the unlimited right of dealing with them exclusively'. After an acrimonious dispute, a conference between representatives of the Houses agreed to an informal working arrangement which accorded great influence to the Council. It was to have the right to 'suggest' amendments to any money Bill except 'that proportion of the Appropriation Bill that provides for the ordinary annual expenses of Government' and, at its discretion, to accept or reject the disputed measure if the Assembly declined to adopt its suggestions. In the case of the annual appropriations it was to have the right to demand a conference at which its views could be stated on any clause it found objectionable, and proposals for expenditure of an entirely new kind were not to be tacked to the appropriation Bill.

How much power the Council could wield was shown by its conduct in 1876–77. It first forced the government to make a reduction in the loan estimates, by refusing to pass them at all when its 'suggestion' of a reduction was not accepted. Then, when the government commenced preparations for the building of new Houses of Parliament, it protested at not being consulted and, as a reprisal, declined for a time to go ahead with legislative business and subsequently took control of that business out of the hands of the chief secretary, who was the government's representative in the chamber, and insisted on electing its own 'leader'. The crisis was only ended by the defeat of the government in the House of Assembly and the acceptance by its successor of the Council's views on the matter originally in dispute.

Quite apart from the financial influence which the South Australian Legislative Council exercised, an influence hard to reconcile with the British tradition that 'it is the privilege of the Commons House to grant aids to the Crown', that Council, like its Victorian counterpart, had its general legislative position strengthened by the absence of a deadlock procedure which a government might use to get its way when its public support was proven, as the British government could use the royal prerogative of creating peers in similar circumstances. In 1881 the South Australian government tried to persuade the Council to agree to a constitutional amendment providing that a joint sitting, at which a two-thirds majority would be required to resolve the question in the affirmative, be used to break deadlocks. It failed: the most the Upper House would accept was a provision that if a Bill were twice passed by the House of Assembly, with a general election intervening, and twice rejected by the Legislative Council, the Governor might either dissolve both Houses or issue writs for the election of one or two extra members for each of the Council's four electoral districts. Like the Victorian scheme of 1903, this procedure was so clumsy, so heavily weighted in favour of the Upper House and so inconclusive, that as a means of reducing friction between the two Houses it was useless.

That friction steadily became worse, and with the advent of Labour governments in the twentieth century it was to become critical. The Council, fortified in its conservatism by the pride of many of its members in belonging to 'old families' which believed themselves to be carrying on the traditions in which the colony was founded, and encouraged by the failure of an attempt by Kingston to weaken its position in 1898–99, was to be a stern, and remarkably successful, opponent of Labour administrations.

In Tasmania also the attitude of the legislative councillors was subtly conditioned by the colony's origins. The convict era left a deeper mark on the life of Tasmania than on that of any of the other former convict settlements: the gulf which had separated the officials and few free settlers of that time from the convicts and emancipists remained for long after 1856, in a rigid distinction and mutual suspicion between the narrow Council electorate and the mass of the people.

As in South Australia the first clash came over finance, in 1857. The Governor authorized the levying of certain new duties on the resolution of the Assembly, and the Council protested that such an action was 'without legal authority'. The obvious answer, that a similar procedure would have been adopted in Britain, it would not accept. Like the South Australian Upper House, it contended that since its members were elected there could be no analogy between the practices of the House of Lords and those it was entitled to adopt. Its position was strengthened by the complete absence from the Tasmanian Constitution of any provision to regulate relations between the Houses. A conference was held, but it left most of the issues in the air, and the Council was in practice able to assert a right to amend money Bills. In 1879 it made a wider claim: after failing to persuade the Governor to intervene against the financial practices of ministers, it adjourned for three months and virtually brought government to a stop. Successive Administrations, therefore, were forced to treat the Upper House with great care, and the Council continued to assert that its powers were co-equal with those of the Assembly. At the end of the century the determined Braddon government tried to counter its claims by asking the Secretary of State to refer the question of its powers to the Judicial Committee of the Privy Council, but Chamberlain held that the Privy Council was not competent to intervene. As will be seen (p. 77), the Committee had earlier given an opinion on issues in Queensland, but in that case it had been requested by both Houses. Braddon then tried to introduce a deadlock provision, one based on that just adopted for the Commonwealth. His proposal was rejected by the Council, which continued to assert an unrestricted right to deal, in principle and in detail, with Bills of all kinds. As in South Australia, the advent of Labour governments stiffened its attitude.

Relations between Houses

(iii) *The Colonies with Nominated Upper Houses*

In New South Wales and Queensland the pattern of dispute between the Houses was modified by the fact that, as the Legislative Councils were nominated, there always existed the possibility that they might be coerced by a threat to 'swamp' them with additional nominees, as the House of Lords had been coerced in 1832 and was again to be in 1911. For some time the Upper Houses were protected by the probability that the Colonial Office would deprecate, and even prevent, swamping except in extreme cases. As was noted at the end of the last chapter, Rogers had warned his minister in 1854 that a nominated Upper House might be reduced to a cipher by a colonial government if the Governor was intended always to accept its advice on the matter of nominations; and for nearly three decades a succession of Secretaries of State made it clear to succession of Governors that this was not Her Majesty's government's intention—particularly in view of the ephemeral nature of colonial administrations and the general willingness of at least the New South Wales Council in the early decades of responsible government to follow the precedents of the House of Lords in dealing with finance. But the Colonial Office's protection was only temporary.

The New South Wales Legislative Council came under attack early. In 1858 Charles Cowper found some of his measures blocked by its veto and asked Denison for fifteen nominees; the Governor would, however, do no more than fill the seats which happened to be vacant and add two other members. Three years later Cowper again tried to establish his supremacy over the Upper Chamber. He got a Bill through the Assembly to make the Council elective, but the Council threw it out and also emasculated the government's proposals for land reform. He then asked the new Governor, Sir John Young, to swamp, and threatened to resign if the Governor refused. Young, aware that the Premier had strong Assembly and electoral support, at least on the land question, reluctantly agreed to make twenty-one nominations, on the understanding that the nominees would hold their seats only for the few days remaining of the five-year term for which the Council had originally been appointed. But the action was circumvented by the Council itself. When the new members entered the chamber, the president, Sir William Burton, resigned rather than swear them in and was followed from the chamber by nineteen other members. Without president or chairman of committees the House stood adjourned to the next regular sitting day, which was one day after the members' terms expired. In choosing the new Council, Young selected men a majority of whom were sympathetic to Cowper's policies, but he was heavily criticized by the Secretary of State, Newcastle, for agreeing to the original swamping, and in 1865 he was to refuse ministerial advice to add more members. For a short time Cowper continued to advocate the replacement of the new Council by an elective one, before becoming convinced that such a body would be as difficult for a government to handle in New South Wales as in Victoria. Parkes made a similar proposal in 1873, after having had trouble with the Council, but it came to nothing. The Council had thus survived some serious threats, but more were to come.

By the end of the 1880s the protection afforded by the Governor and the Colonial Office was beginning to appear less reliable than it had been in the past. During a brief period as Premier in 1889 George Dibbs was able to persuade the Governor to make a large (and, his opponents alleged, partisan) batch of nominations. He repeated the performance in 1893. In neither case was the Governor criticized by his superiors. The extent of the deterioration of the Council's position since the first years of responsible government became clear in 1895. The government of

George Reid, returned to office with a comfortable majority the year before, proposed a radical change in the colony's fiscal system by basing it on direct taxation. The Council, ignoring the precedents it had hitherto respected, rejected his land-tax and income-tax Bills. Reid appealed to the electorate, promising, if his policy was supported by the voters, to reform the Council, 'to clear the fossils out' as he put it, and when his appeal was successful he had no difficulty in getting eleven new councillors appointed. Since his tax Bills had been rejected in the Upper House by forty-one votes to four, eleven members hardly added up to swamping, but they persuaded the Council to give way on the financial questions. He then produced a quite radical scheme of Council reform. It provided that members should sit for five years, not life; that appropriation Bills should receive the Royal Assent one month after having been passed by the Assembly, with or without the approval of the Council; that the Upper House should be forbidden to reject any other money Bill, but allowed to propose amendments to it, these to be finally pronounced on by the Assembly; and that general Bills passed by the Assembly and rejected by the Council in two successive sessions should go to plebiscite and be presented for assent if, with at least 100,000 people voting, they received a popular majority. But when the Council rejected this measure, Reid let it drop. He was a shrewd enough politician to be satisfied with the substance of victory: he had defeated the Council as it stood, and could do so again, as he showed in 1899, when he had it swamped after it had tried to prevent a second referendum on the federal Constitution. In 1908 its numbers were again considerably augmented in order to force legislation through. The New South Wales Legislative Council had not, perhaps, 'become a cipher', but it had become a fairly small quantity. A proposal made in 1910 to prevent future swamping by reducing the now quite large House to a fixed size proportionally related to the size of the Assembly, and to provide a deadlock arrangement involving a joint sitting (a scheme which might have helped the Upper House to retain at least its dignity) collapsed when the government, led by its sponsor, Gregory Wade, was defeated at a general election.

The Queensland Legislative Council, meanwhile, had also come under attack. The Order-in-Council of 6 June 1859, which separated the colony from New South Wales, provided (contrary to the intention of the Act on which it was based) that Queensland should have a constitution identical with the constitution of New South Wales as enacted by the imperial Parliament—not as existing at the time of separation—until altered in accordance with the imperial Act. Although a half-hearted suggestion was put forward in 1862 to make the Upper House elective, and although two years later the Council rejected a suggestion that its members be appointed for six years instead of life, not until 1867 did the Queensland Parliament make a serious examination of the colony's Constitution; and the Constitution Act passed in that year retained the 'unusual majority' clauses which had been removed from the New South Wales Constitution in the early months of its operation. The clause requiring a two-thirds majority in the Assembly for any change in its size or seat distribution was removed in 1871, but the Council held on for forty years to the provision that any alteration in its structure would require two-thirds majorities in both Houses. As Queensland governments tended to be even more unstable than New South Welsh ministries, there was less likelihood that it would be threatened with swamping. It seemed, therefore, to be in a rather stronger position than the New South Wales Council.

It was certainly less cautious about interfering in financial affairs. There were several early cases in which it insisted on making amendments in money Bills: as the issues were trifling the Assembly agreed in each case to compromise, while making a declaration reserving its privileges. There was also a certain amount of bickering between 1866 and 1877 over the Council's desire to have provision for its running expenses embodied in permanent legislation rather than the annual appropriations, but this was a matter of form rather than substance. In 1876, however, matters took a more serious turn. In October of that year the Council forced an amendment to a stamp-tax Bill in order to repeal an existing tax. Then in 1885 there was a real crisis: the Council sought to amend the Appropriation Bill to remove provision for expenses for members of the Legislative Assembly, after having previously declined to pass a specific measure authorizing them to be paid. After the Assembly insisted that the Council was bound by the precedents of the House of Lords and the Council denied that it was, the two agreed to submit the question to the Privy Council, the Upper House deciding not to insist on its amendment in this case. In April 1886 the Privy Council ruled in favour of the Assembly; but the Council declined to accept the ruling as more than an opinion and in 1915 it was to attempt to amend Bills proposed by a Labour administration to impose heavy taxes on land and speculative profits. In the meantime various proposals had been made for the reform of the Council and a serious crisis had resulted in the destruction of its absolute legislative veto.

During the 1890s there were two attacks mounted on the Upper House, one on its composition, the other on its powers. In 1893 a Bill was brought down to convert it into a body elected on a property franchise with the colony voting as a single constituency, but this idea, like similar proposals in New South Wales, found opponents at both ends of the political spectrum, and the Bill perished with the usual batch of slaughtered innocents at the end of the session. Two years later an early Labour member moved to deal with deadlocks by the drastic means of allowing the Royal Assent to be given to any measure passed by the Assembly and not passed by the Council, provided only that it was reaffirmed at the end of the session by the former House: this Bill did not get past its first Assembly reading. Few opponents of the Council were prepared to go as far as this towards effective unicameralism.

Further serious trouble flared up in 1907. Two Bills which the government led by William Kidston looked upon as vital, and which went through the Assembly with comfortable majorities, were rejected by the Council. Kidston asked for a dissolution and when it was refused he resigned. But his successor, Robert Philp, was unable to control the Assembly and the Governor was forced to dissolve: Kidston returned with an overwhelming majority. The Legislative Council, obviously warned by the experience of the New South Wales Upper House, decided that it could not stand out against a clear electoral mandate. It gave way, adopted the government's policies and also agreed to repeal the clause in the Constitution which required a two-thirds majority for Bills affecting its position. Subsequently it accepted, by a majority of seventeen to fifteen, Kidston's Parliamentary Bills Referendum Bill, which provided that if a Bill was rejected, laid aside or unacceptably amended by the Council in successive sessions, with an interval of at least three months, it could be put to referendum and if accepted by the electorate receive assent. The Council's acceptance of this measure is perhaps surprising: it was, as the Assembly's clerk C.A. Bernays said, 'unpalatable', but a plebiscite is a device a government would be unlikely to use except in an extreme case, and the alternative to acceptance may well have been swamping. The Queensland Upper House had lost its veto, but it had not had to suffer the indignity which had so seriously weakened the New South Wales Council.

The Governor's Role 1855–66

By the beginning of the twentieth century the 'working constitutions' of the Australian communities had undergone considerable development. The adoption of democratic forms and the change in the pattern of relations between the Houses of their parliaments were significant aspects of this. Equally significant was a gradual change in their relationship with the mother country. As was suggested in Chapter Three, the concept of 'responsible government'—the idea of a sovereign who reigned but did not rule, who could in theory, as Bagehot was later to point out, 'disband the army . . ., sell all . . . ships of war and naval stores . . ., make peace by the sacrifice of Cornwall and begin a war for the conquest of Brittany', but who in fact was not free to do anything without the advice of ministers accountable to Parliament—was not fully grasped by many people in mid-nineteenth-century England, including Queen Victoria herself. The British monarchy was not yet quite the royal republic it has since become. The contradictions between theory and fact, the attitudes surviving from earlier days, the idea that Britain enjoyed a 'mixed government', not only obscured for all but a few lawyers some features of the Constitution, but also affected its working. And if there were obscurities and contradictions in the idea of responsible government as it operated in England, there were many more in its application to the Australian colonies. Britain possessed unlimited sovereignty; the colonies did not. More importantly, the limited sovereignty they did possess was not, as Wentworth had wanted it to be, complete sovereignty within a limited field, but rather an authority exercisable under general supervision. The Queen, acting on the advice of her ministers, could do no wrong. The Governor, even when supported by the advice of his, could—and might be punished by recall. There was much scope for development in the British Constitution after the 1850s; there was a great deal more in the constitutions of the Australian colonies.

The grant of 'responsible government' to the colonies in 1855–56 altered their status, in strict law, only in one particular: certain subjects, most importantly land and land revenue, on which their former legislative councils had been forbidden to legislate, were transferred to their new bicameral parliaments. In all other ways their dependent status remained unchanged. Certainly it was understood that, as Sir Kenneth Bailey has pointed out, 'save in exceptional circumstances and under the Royal Instructions, a Governor would act upon the advice of ministers responsible to the local Legislature', in other words he would act as a local 'sovereign'. But the Crown (that is the British government) retained three very important legal controls. The first was the right to issue the royal instructions to which Bailey has referred. The standard instructions in the early decades of responsible government forbad the Governor to give the royal assent, except in an extreme emergency, to Bills on a long list of subjects, which included not only such obvious matters as those affecting treaty obligations, military and naval discipline, imperial trade and shipping, and the rights and property of subjects in other parts of the empire, but also such questions as restrictions on freedom of worship, the granting of divorce, grants and gratuities to the Governor himself. the establishment as legal tender of anything 'except coin of the realm or other gold or silver coin', and the imposition of differential duties. Such Bills were to be reserved for consideration by the British government. The instructions also made him personally answerable for having 'each different matter . . . provided for by a different law, without intermixing in one and the same Act such things as have no proper relations with each other', in other words, for preventing his ministers from committing irregularities in the drafting of Bills. The second control retained by the imperial government was its power to disallow colonial legislation. Every Bill to which a governor gave assent had forthwith to be transmitted to the Secretary of State, and could be voided by simple Order-in-Council at any time within two years of receipt. The third control lay in the 'doctrine of repugnancy', the principle laid down in the Australian Colonies Government Act and earlier Acts, and not altered in 1855, that no colonial law 'repugnant to the law of England' would be valid.

Consequently the Crown's representative, the Governor, was, as was remarked at the beginning of this chapter, far from being a mere dignitary. He was very much an agent of the British government, bound by his instructions to uphold what that government saw as its interests. But some of his instructions were very general, and Downing Street's view of what its interests were was subject to change; so the Governor's personality counted for a great deal, and considerable development was possible in the real meaning of 'responsible government' without serious formal change in its legal basis.

A major share of the task of making responsible government work fell on Sir William Denison, Governor of New South Wales 1855–61. He, and his colleagues and successors, sometimes got into trouble in their efforts to reconcile their two roles, of imperial agent and local 'sovereign'. But in the early years of responsible government the difficulties were minor, and their resolution helped to point the direction of future development. In 1858, for example, Denison, in his capacity as agent of the British government, ran foul of a Legislative Assembly jealous of its privileges. He asked for a grant of about £3,500 to buy horses for an artillery detachment being transferred to India to help suppress the Mutiny, and when he was refused he sent the Assembly an angry remonstrance. The House promptly condemned his protest as unconstitutional. The Governor had acted on his own initiative, without consulting his ministers, but Cowper, the Premier, who believed Denison to have been wrong, nevertheless agreed to accept responsibility for his action and offered to resign. The matter was then allowed to drop, but it had the important effect of clarifying one detail of the complex problem which the Governor's dual role presented, by establishing the principle that when he dealt with his parliament he should normally be understood to be acting on advice. Denison was to be involved in one more personal fracas with the Assembly, when in 1861 it censured him for himself affixing the seal to a land grant when the responsible minister had declined to do so, but in this case he was completing a transaction begun before the imperial government had surrendered control of lands and so was clearly acting as an imperial agent. There would have been no problem had land not at that point been a sensitive political question: there was, in fact, no constitutional issue involved. Denison was no mere figurehead; some comment has been made already on his influence on the policy of his early ministries; but he seems to have tried to keep his roles distinct.

The first Governor of Queensland was perhaps less convinced that it was desirable to do so. On taking office he announced his intention 'to maintain, with the assistance of his [Executive] Council, a vigilant control and supervision over every department of the public service'. This was reasonable enough, though the 'assistance' of his ministers is not quite the same as their constitutional 'advice', but he went on to say that he considered himself to have the 'undoubted right and duty to disallow ill-advised acts of the colonial legislature', and to claim that he was '*a fortiori* bound to refuse his sanction to the employment in the Queen's service of individuals of dubious character, and especially to the nomination of such persons to offices like those of judges and magistrates'. His views were endorsed by the Secretary of State, Newcastle. But the discretionary power to decide what is 'ill-advised' and who is 'of dubious character' is a dangerously wide one, as Newcastle saw. He told Bowen that 'in matters of purely local politics' a governor was bound, 'except in extreme cases, to follow the advice of a ministry which appear[ed] to possess the confidence of the legislature'; and he endeavoured to define an extreme case by drawing a parallel with 'such extreme and exceptional circumstances as would warrant a military or naval officer in taking some critical step against or beyond orders'. By thus placing the onus of proof on a governor who declined to accept ministerial advice, Newcastle was taking an important step towards defining the rights of the colonies *vis-à-vis* the British government.

But he was not by any means abdicating the right of imperial supervision. As has been seen, he, and his successors for many years, acted through the governors to protect the identity of the nominated upper houses. Moreover the royal instructions were taken seriously, by both Downing Street and its representatives. A furore in Queensland in 1866 showed how seriously. In that year the Macalister government tried to meet an acute financial crisis by the issue of inconvertible paper currency, but Bowen refused his assent to their proposal as irreconcilable with his instructions, and persisted in his refusal in the face of his ministers' resignation. Though the immediate issue was resolved by Parliament's agreeing to an alternative proposal by Macalister's successor, R.G.W. Herbert, for the use of Treasury Bills (which the Governor was able to sanction) there was widespread hostility in the colony to the Governor and those who gave him his instructions. These seemed to go beyond the protection of legitimate imperial interests and to derogate seriously from the principle of self-government. They seemed to indicate that the British government did not trust the colonies. Downing Street might well, of course, ask why it should. The colonies were important fields of British emigration and investment, but were small, mutually jealous and ridden with faction. Close supervision appeared to British ministers to be natural and it should be remarked that the supervision actually imposed left the colonies free in many matters where to the British mind they seemed prone to abuse their freedom. For example, the Colonial Office would not accept the advice given to it by Governor Barkly of Victoria in 1860 that it should intervene to prevent his colony and New South Wales from imposing border tariffs. As will be seen, control was gradually to be relaxed over tariff policy generally and over other important matters such as the exercise of the prerogative of mercy and the regulation of immigration, and eventually the practice on the reservation of Bills was considerably modified. But before the range of Australian self-government was extended in these evolutionary ways, the position of the colonies was to be affected by two important events, the passage of the Colonial Laws Validity Act (1865) and the 1865–67 crisis in Victoria.

The Colonial Laws Validity Act and the Victorian Crises

The Colonial Laws Validity Act was intended to confirm, and even to enlarge the powers of self-government in the colonies. It was rendered necessary by the eccentricities of a South Australian judge, Benjamin Boothby, who chose to put such a wide interpretation on the doctrine of repugnancy that he virtually brought the government of his colony to a halt. He held as 'repugnant to English law' and therefore invalid, not only such a treasured local reform as the Real Property Act of 1857 and various other acts of a kind never impugned in the other colonies, but also certain aspects of the Constitution itself—particularly the omission of the traditional rule that ministers must recontest their parliamentary seats on accepting office, the existence of an elective Upper House which could not be dissolved, and the provision that the attorney-general should sit in Parliament. The 1865 Act laid down that henceforth a colonial law should not be voidable because of departure from traditional rules of common law but only because of irreconcilability with a specific Act of the imperial Parliament applying to the colony 'by express words or necessary intendment', or with an order or regulation made under the terms of such an Act. It also provided that a colonial Act would not be rendered unenforceable simply because the Governor might have acted against instructions in assenting instead of reserving, and it spelled out the power of a colony's legislature to establish, abolish or reconstitute courts, and to amend the constitution under which it operated, provided that the amendment Act was in the 'manner and form' provided by any relevant imperial or colonial law.

The Act was intended to be as A.V. Dicey described it, 'the charter of colonial legislative independence'. It was never intended, in the phrase of Keir and Lawson, to be a 'Colonial Laws Invalidity Act'. But, as Sir Keith Hancock has said, 'although it removed doubts as to the powers of colonial legislatures within their own spheres', it 'emphasized the fact of their subordination'. Though the emphasis was, except in matters such as merchant shipping, extradition and the right to legislate with extra-territorial effect (where international law presented problems), more theoretical then practical, the 'manner and form' clause remains, as will be shown in Chapter Seven, of some significance even to the present day.

The activities of Judge Boothby had raised some questions about the meaning of colonial responsible government: the crisis which blew up in Victoria just as an answer to them was being worked out in the Colonial Laws Validity Act raised the question whether the system could survive the contradictions which lay within it. The root cause of the crisis was not the existence of those contradictions but the structure of the Legislative Council. However, once the trouble began the imperial government was inevitably drawn in, and the right of the colony to settle its own affairs, even purely internal ones, was impugned. As has been seen (pp. 67–8), Downing Street intervened openly three times in the affair. First Darling was censured for sanctioning expenditure by the use of the Crown Remedies Act; then he was recalled; finally Manners-Sutton was forbidden to sign the message for the Darling grant unless his ministers agreed to send the proposal to the Council in a separate Bill. In each case the British government claimed to be acting to prevent illeg-ality. Even this involved making a claim to a suzerainty which was hard to reconcile with the popular view that the colonies had been given 'self-government'; but worse, Cardwell was not clear of suspicion that his intervention had political rather than strictly legal motives, for as early as February 1865 he had written to tell Darling that it would be 'a matter of sincere regret to Her Majesty's Government' if the Governor's ministers went ahead with their policy of protection. If the Secretary of State was able to intervene politically, under the pretext of 'upholding the law', against an obviously popular administration, then the right of a self-governing colony to make its own laws seemed to many Victorians to be pure fiction.

Most of them were prepared to forget this reminder of their sub-ordination to Downing Street when the crisis was resolved with Darling's pension, but not all of them. At the end of 1869, George Higinbotham, who had already resigned from the government because it had been willing to leave what he saw as the great issue of principle unresolved, and who was highly suspicious of the contemporary efforts of 'a self-constituted and irresponsible body of absentee colonists' in London to 'strengthen the bonds of empire' by establishing what became the Royal Colonial Institute, led a parliamentary attack on the control exercised by the Colonial Office through the Governor. He could not accept the anomalies of the existing system. Moving in the Legislative Assembly a series of resolutions on the subject, he argued that the Governor was 'an independent Sovereign in Victoria' and that for the Secretary of State to bind him with instructions on internal matters was unconstitutional. Worse, he suggested, it was not even the Secretary of

State himself who exercised the control, but the permanent officials of the Colonial Office. He told the House that, just as 'It was said of the Athenian Republic ... that it was governed by the poodle dog of a courtesan', so also 'the million and a half of Englishmen who inhabit these colonies, and who during the last fifteen years have believed they possessed self-government, have really been governed during the whole of that time by a person named Rogers'. And he carried against the government a declaration of his view of the proper state of affairs:

> That the official communication of advice, suggestions or instructions, by the Secretary of State for the Colonies to Her Majesty's representative in Victoria, on any subject whatsoever connected with the local government, except the giving or withholding of the Royal assent or the reservation of Bills passed by the two Houses of the Victorian Parliament, is a practice not sanctioned by law, derogatory to the independence of the Queen's representative, and a violation of the constitutional rights of the people of this colony

Higinbotham's opinion that the Crown did not have the strict legal right to instruct the Governor, as it did in both royal instructions and despatches, was wrong. His exception of instructions concerning the Royal Assent was hardly logical. And his effort to draw a distinction between 'local' and 'imperial' affairs was little, if any, more wise in the late 1860s than it had been when Wentworth attempted it in the early 1850s. Not only would such a distinction involve 'closing the door which Russell had left open' and through which the colonies were to pass to wider independence without altering their constitutions; it would also have deprived the Governor of the advice which ministers occasionally gave him on imperial questions. Such advice, not binding certainly (and in the upshot not very wise), Higinbotham and his colleagues had given Darling in 1865 when an armed cruiser of the Confederate States of America had put into Port Phillip for coal and provisions and had thus confronted Darling with delicate problems of neutrality on which he had no time to consult London. But as Bailey has put it, 'Statesman rather than lawyer, Higinbotham had the future with him'. The British government would not accept his views in 1869, but they pointed the way to what was to become known in the early twentieth century as 'dominion status'. And his forceful expression of them warned the Colonial Office that it would be wise to tread more lightly in the future.

The Colonial Office was certainly more circumspect in its handling of the next Victorian crisis. When, with the crisis looming, Governor Bowen asked Lord Carnarvon what action he should take if his ministers asked him to acquiesce in 'tacking' the controversial proposal for payment of members to the Appropriation Bill, Carnarvon replied that he should follow their advice. A few months later, after the Council rejected the Bill and it became a matter of signing warrants for expenditure not sanctioned by Act, he was told that 'here again H.M.G. would expect a Governor to follow the advice of his Ministers and not (as was held in Downing Street not so long ago) to consider himself bound to resist his Ministers when they desired to proceed irregularly in financial matters any more than in other local matters'. The permanent under-secretary, R.G.W. Herbert, who wrote these words, emphasized the point by adding: 'As a broad and general rule, you may take it that it is now held here that the power of self-misgovernment conceded to the Australian colonies has hardly any conceivable limitation, so far as intra-colonial questions are concerned'. That comment led Bowen to go further, however, than the Colonial Office intended he should—to allow the 'Black Wednesday' dismissals and, worse, to consent to the government's decision not to reinstate some of the dismissed officers. The latter action drew a sharp reprimand from the new Secretary of State, Hicks Beach, who held that it was 'no ordinary occasion' of the kind discussed by Herbert but 'involved constitutional principles of great importance not only to Victoria, but (as being a precedent) to all colonies living under constitutions granted by the Crown or by the Parliament of Great Britain'. Precedents *were* a problem, one intimately connected with the question whether the imperial connection was to continue to have any real existence. The eminent constitutional lawyer, Sir William Vernon-Harcourt, went to the heart of the matter when he wrote in *The Times* in June 1879: 'As a matter of abstract right, the Mother Country has never parted with the claim to ultimate, supreme authority for the Imperial legislature. If it did so it would dissolve the Imperial tie, and convert the colonies into foreign and independent states'. But from the common-sense point of view Bowen was right when he called the permanent removal of the officers 'a less formidable evil than the practical dismissal of a Ministry possessing an overwhelming majority in the Assembly and in the constituencies, and the consequent endangering of the internal tranquillity of the colony, and of its existing happy relations with the Imperial Government'. Vernon-Harcourt's 'Imperial tie' could not, in the last instance, be maintained unless the British government were willing, and able, to use coercion—as of course it was not. The Australian colonies had begun to follow Canada along the path leading to the point where 'the Empire' became an almost meaningless expression, which, in due course, was to be replaced by one completely meaningless, 'the Commonwealth of Nations'.

No one worked more persistently to keep them on that path than George Higinbotham. His retirement from politics to join the Supreme Court bench in 1880 did not deflect him. After he became Chief Justice four years later he sacrificed the honour traditionally associated with that office of being appointed Lieutenant-Governor because he made clear that if ever required to administer the colony in the Governor's absence he would refuse to communicate with the Colonial Office on matters of domestic policy. In 1888 in the important case *Toy* v. *Musgrove*, in which the plaintiff, a Chinese whose entry to the colony had been refused in consequence of an order signed by the Governor, claimed that the order was illegal because the exclusion of aliens was a matter for the imperial government, he delivered a minority judgement holding that the exclusion was legal because the royal prerogatives exercisable in the United Kingdom by the Queen on the advice of her ministers were in Victoria exercisable by the Governor on the advice of his. When the Victorian government appealed to the Privy Council against the majority decision that the man had been improperly prevented from landing, that body balked the constitutional issue by upholding his exclusion on the simple ground that an alien had no right enforceable by action to enter a dominion of the Crown.

But Higinbotham had one important victory. His continuing heavy criticism of the royal instructions given to the Governor on appointment, and particularly the clause in them that the Governor might legally act in some cases against advice tendered by his ministers, eventually persuaded the Colonial Office to compromise on the issue. In 1886 Sir Henry Holland (later Lord Knutsford) asked the Office's old antagonist for his detailed views on the current royal instructions. Higinbotham replied the following year. Noting that 'no substantial alteration' had been made in them since 1850, he repeated his old claim that the establishment of responsible government five years later had abrogated the Crown's right to instruct the Governor except as regards imperial affairs and the royal assent to bills. He went on to argue that

> The claim of the Colonial Office to interfere in local affairs by ... control of the representative of the Crown in the exercise of his powers in that character must be once for all officially and openly withdrawn. All existing public and private instructions to the Governor should be recalled, and instructions addressed to him solely in his character as an officer of the Imperial Government should be substituted.

His unabated 'extremism' perhaps discouraged the Colonial Office for a time, but in 1892 the standard instructions were considerably modified. Higinbotham's son-in-law and biographer claimed that 'The improvement was enormous', that 'For the first time Responsible Government [was] recognized ... [and] the Governor ... instructed to accept the advice of his Ministers'. This is an exaggeration, but Higinbotham's efforts had certainly not been in vain. The new instructions, while still authorizing the Governor, should be 'see sufficient reason', to act against the advice of his Executive Council in a particular case, were so worded as to make such action seem a much more remote contingency than had the old. Moreover, the clauses in the earlier instructions which enjoined the Governor to see that his ministers did not include different matters in the same Bill and which required him to send home copies of the journals of both Houses were omitted; an important change, discussed below, was made in the clause regarding the prerogative of mercy; and the Governor was relieved of the rather ambiguous personal responsibility formerly imposed on him in matters of Aboriginal welfare. The Colonial Office's idea of responsible government was still not the same as Higinbotham's, but the two were now closer together. And, as Mr McNaughtan has noted, 'The essentials of Higinbotham's conception . . . were [to be] reached, in the end, because the system of divided responsibility proved, piece by piece, unworkable'.

Attention must now be given to three of the 'pieces', imperial supervision over tariffs, over the prerogative of mercy and over immigration policy, in which the system was clearly becoming unworkable when Higinbotham wrote.

The Decline of Imperial Control

The British government would have liked to preserve the Empire as a great free trade area, but it learnt early that this ideal was unattainable. Canada successfully insisted on full fiscal independence in 1859, and in 1866 the practice of reserving all tariff Bills passed by the Australian parliaments had to be abandoned. The Australian colonies were still not permitted to impose preferential tariffs; but in 1873 Downing Street, faced with the possibility of the worse evil of inter-colonial tariff wars, conceded them the right to give preferences to each other. Though an effort was made to maintain the prohibition of preferences on goods imported from overseas, this eventually (in 1895) was also given up as impractical. In this important matter, therefore, imperial control of policy was completely surrendered forty years after responsible government had been established.

Control over the exercise of the prerogative of mercy also caused such trouble that it eventually had to be abandoned. Clause XIII of the original standard instructions provided that in cases where the commutation of the death sentence was involved the Governor should ask for a written report on the case and require the trial judge to attend an Executive Council meeting in order to answer questions. The Governor was then to hear his ministers' advice and 'extend . . . or withhold a pardon or reprieve according to his own deliberate judgement', reporting his reasons 'at length' to London if he did not accept his ministers' advice. The instructions did not make clear whether the Governor was to have the same discretion in the remission of prison sentences, and in the early years of responsible government governors sometimes seemed to have followed their ministers' advice automatically in such cases. In 1869, however, Belmore in New South Wales asked for specific instructions. Lord Granville's reply was a little less definite than Belmore had hoped:

> The responsibility ... rests with the Governor, and he has undoubtedly a right to act upon his own independent judgement. But unless any Imperial interest or policy is involved, as might be the case in a matter of treason or slave-trading, or in matters in which foreigners might be concerned, the Governor would be bound to allow great weight to the recommendation of his Ministry.

A circular despatch from Granville's successor Kimberley in 1871, which told each governor that he was 'bound to examine personally each case' but should pay 'due regard to the advice of his Ministers', retained the element of vagueness. When Sir Hercules Robinson became Governor of New South Wales two years later, he found that his predecessor had generally decided on petitions of mercy himself and accepted personal responsibility for his decisions. Robinson did not like this situation, but when he asked for further instructions Kimberley virtually repeated his earlier statement.

Clearly the position would be awkward if a controversial case arose. Should a governor make an unpopular decision in such a case he would face public and parliamentary criticism (which would be derogatory to the dignity of his office) or his ministers would have to accept responsibility—which, particularly if they did not agree with him, would be grossly unfair to them. And Robinson did have to deal with a controversial case: the issue of a pardon to the former notorious bush-ranger Gardiner, who was recognized, arrested and convicted years after having apparently reformed. There was some reason for believing that an imperial interest *was* involved here, for it was proposed to release Gardiner on condition of his leaving the colony, and Robinson, apparently for that reason, decided that he should reject a petition for pardon. Many people, however, believed that the matter was a purely local one, and that the ministers should be held to be responsible. The Premier, Henry Parkes, seems to have felt that it would be better for the Governor to decide such doubtful cases alone: he certainly did not like the idea of tendering advice which might or might not be accepted. But in the circumstances of factional politics it was inevitable that he and his colleagues would be forced to take a stand, either against the Governor, which would mean resignation, or for him, which would involve defending the decision when it was attacked in the House. They adopted the latter course, with the result that, after a dissolution, they were defeated. The issue in this case was further complicated by the fact that Robinson chose to reply to criticism of his actions in terms which, but for the casting vote of the Speaker, would have been condemned by the Assembly as a breach of privilege. Clearly the attempt to keep the exercise of the prerogative of mercy outside the framework of responsible government was leading Downing Street and its representatives into trouble.

After a conflict on the matter in Tasmania, various cases in Canada, and another in New South Wales, it was brought up at the 1887 Colonial Conference. Some of the delegates, notably Higinbotham's devoted disciple Alfred Deakin, urged that the ordinary conventions of ministerial responsibility should be applied in mercy cases, but his Australian fellows were more interested in such questions as imperial policy in the Pacific and no united pressure was put on the Secretary of State.

The next year there was trouble in Queensland, when the government of Thomas McIlwraith advised Governor Musgrave to authorize the release of a comparatively minor offender. Since the advice was to parole the man under the terms of the Offenders Probation Act of 1866, the prerogative, strictly speaking, was not involved; but the Act, following the practice as regards the prerogative, provided that the power to parole be exercised by the Governor without making it clear whether he was to act on advice; and Musgrave refused to order the man's release. The government resigned in protest and no administration could be found to replace it. It became necessary for the Secretary of State to cable instructions to the Governor to accede to McIlwraith's advice in order to have the resignation withdrawn. Although Knutsford subsequently repeated the views of Kimberley, telling Musgrave that a governor, in the exercise of the prerogative of mercy 'may (and indeed must, if in his judgement it seems right) decide in opposition to the advice tendered to him', it was becoming clear that, if ministers persisted to the point of resignation and could not be replaced, the right and duty to use discretion was a fiction. After further trouble in New Zealand the Colonial Office decided to recognize the realities in this matter, as in the matter of tariff policy, and in the new royal instructions of 1892 the principle was laid down that henceforth mercy should be granted or refused on the advice of ministers.

Strangely enough, in the more important (because internationally sensitive) matter of immigration policy imperial control faded earlier. Probably the Colonial Office realized that hostility to Asian immigration, stemming as it did from the experiences of the gold-rush period when rapid expansion re-formed and set so many social attitudes, went deeper in Australian society and united Australian opinion more than questions of tariff policy or nice points about the prerogative of mercy. The imperial government was always unhappy about immigration laws which discriminated against Chinese, not only as gravely complicating factors in foreign policy but also as contrary to the traditions of a multi-racial empire in which another great Asian country, India, was becoming increasingly important; but even less than a decade after the establishment of responsible government it was confining itself to deploring restrictive Acts passed in Victoria, New South Wales and South

Australia. It vetoed the particularly harsh Goldfields (Amendment) Bill passed by the Queensland Parliament in 1876 and reserved by Governor Cairns as possibly repugnant to imperial obligations under the Treaty of Tientsin, but the Secretary of State agreed to accept a substantially similar Bill which was rather less offensively worded, and in 1888 his successor allowed, despite vehement Chinese protests, what were virtually exclusion Acts passed by the four mainland colonies.

In each of these cases the imperial government relaxed its control with some reluctance; but in each of them something could be said for its attitude; and in none did it persist in the face of strong and united colonial protest. Its willingness to allow the colonies the greatest freedom which it considered compatible with the maintenance of the Empire, and to liberalize gradually its view of how much freedom was compatible, is nowhere seen better than in its attitude to the reservation and disallowance of Bills, where even Higinbotham was prepared to acknowledge its rights.

From the first the Governor's power to reserve was used sparingly, and the Crown's power to disallow more sparingly still. Up to the end of the century only fifteen of the hundreds of Bills passed by the New South Wales Parliament had been reserved, and all of them had been given the royal assent in London; only five Bills passed by any Australian legislature were disallowed. Except, perhaps, as regards Bills for divorce (where English social attitudes were important and imperial uniformity obviously desirable) and Bills concerning merchant shipping (a very sensitive matter for a mercantile empire) reservation was always, as Professor Bailey has pointed out, 'little more than a means of securing consultation and delay'. By 1880 it had come to be accepted that the only Bills, apart from those to amend the Constitution and those concerning divorce and imperial shipping, which were to be reserved were Bills that made grants to the Governor, established anything except gold and silver coin as legal tender, imposed duties inconsistent with treaties, affected naval and military discipline, the royal prerogative or the rights of subjects resident elsewhere, or contained provisions to which assent had already been refused. Even in most of these cases, unless there was clear repugnancy under the terms of the Colonial Laws Validity Act, the Governor might give assent if he was satisfied that urgent necessity existed, subject to disallowance by Downing Street after his reasons had been considered.

In the next twenty years the attitude became more liberal still. After 1890 no effective control was exercised in the case of divorce and, although the imperial government was careful for a time to reserve its rights in matters concerned with shipping, the establishment of the Commonwealth in 1901 led to the virtual abandonment of control in most other cases. Though the federal Constitution contained provision for the Governor-General to give or withhold assent or to reserve 'for the

Queen's pleasure', and for the disallowance by the Crown, within one year, of any law, it was always assumed that the power to reserve (except in the case of Bills relating to Privy Council appeals, which will be discussed in Chapter Five) was exercisable on advice; and the power to disallow was never used in the generation which elapsed before, as will be seen (pp. 160–61), it was abrogated by the Statute of Westminster of 1931. As for the States, the Australian States Constitution Act of 1907 limited reservation to Bills which altered 'the Constitution of the Legislature of the State or of Either House thereof' (not including such Bills as dealt with electoral districts, franchises and the qualifications of members), which affected the salary of the Governor, or were specifically provided to be reserved in their own text or by another State law. Even in these matters reservation was obviously to be a formality. No law was ever disallowed after 1900. Some authorities argue that the right to disallow could still be exercised if the Commonwealth government tendered advice that a particular State law was contrary to the interests of Australia as a whole, but S. 109 of the federal Constitution, which voids any State law repugnant to a valid Commonwealth law, would seem to provide better protection than could Downing Street.

By the beginning of the twentieth century, therefore, the degree to which the Australian governments and legislatures were subordinated to Downing Street had been greatly lessened by the Colonial Laws Validity Act, by evolutionary change in such matters as tariffs and immigration, by the new letters patent of 1892 and by the Australian States Constitution Act. Moreover, a Privy Council decision of 1885 had removed a grave legal doubt about the status of colonial parliaments as law-making bodies. A case appealed from New South Wales raised the question whether the colonial legislatures were not mere agents of the imperial Parliament and so, in terms of the legal principle that delegated authority cannot be further delegated (*'delegatus non delegare potest'*), unable to confer power to make regulations or by-laws. The Judicial Committee ruled 'that a Colonial Legislature is a ... legislature restricted in the area of its powers, but within that area unrestricted, and not acting as an agent or delegate'. But despite all these developments the fact of ultimate imperial supremacy remained, and was to continue to affect not only the States but also the Commonwealth, the establishment of which must now be discussed.

CHAPTER FIVE

The Federation Movement

'The erection of a new government, whatever care or wisdom may
distinguish the work, cannot fail to originate questions of intricacy
and nicety; and these may, in a particular manner, be expected to
flow from the establishment of a constitution founded upon the
total or partial incorporation of a number of distinct sovereignties.
'Tis time only that can mature and perfect so compound a system.'

ALEXANDER HAMILTON

The Early Federal Proposals

That forty years should have elapsed between the establishment of
responsible government in five of the six Australian colonies and their
decision to come together in a federation may seem remarkable. These
were climactic years for the nationalist movement among European
peoples, and few peoples had more in common than those who lived in
Australia. The common language of the country had no rival; at no time
were fewer than ninety per cent of the population of British or Irish
origin; no other race save a handful of Aborigines, a handful pathetically
easy to ignore, shared with this remarkably homogeneous population an
island large enough to be called a sixth continent. And the shadowy idea
of a common identity was as old as the first spreading of settlement
beyond the hinterland of Sydney and the out-station of Norfolk Island:
not until the 1890s was the slogan 'a nation for a continent and a
continent for a nation' invented by the man who was to be the first
Prime Minister of the Commonwealth, but the name 'Australia' was
coined by Matthew Flinders in the first decade of the century and used
by Governor Macquarie in public documents in the second.

It is significant that even so imperfect a glimpse as this of a future
nation should have come to officers of the British Crown: for a generation after Macquarie's time no serious advocacy of inter-colonial
union came from other than English sources; the constitutional tendencies of the colonies themselves were centrifugal. It has been pointed out
in Chapter Three that in 1847, when Port Phillip was urgently demand-
ing separation from New South Wales and the same pressure was beginning to build up in the Moreton Bay district, Earl Grey, who sym-
pathized with the former movement and encouraged the latter, sought
to mitigate the less desirable effects of such fragmentation with a scheme
of government which can best be called quasi-federal, and that, after he
had been constrained to abandon this, he wrote a proposal for a federal
General Assembly into the Australian Colonies Government Bills of

1849 and 1850. His ideas evoked no real response in the colonies; nor did a less ambitious suggestion by Governor FitzRoy, for the appointment of an imperial officer to adjudicate difficulties between colonies without the need to refer them to Downing Street. A few men showed some interest, but the ordinary articulate colonist, who still thought of himself as an Englishman or an Irishman first and a New South Welshman or a South Australian next, could not appreciate the concept of Australian nationhood.

In fact neither FitzRoy nor Grey had glimpsed such a concept either: they saw only the possibility of establishing a regular system of inter-colonial co-operation which might solve various future problems, particularly problems of inter-colonial trade. Grey, the devoted freetrader, grasped the fact that there was need to prevent the erection of customs barriers, which might be only trivial annoyances at first but which would develop with the growth of the colonies into a formidable threat to their prosperity. When he failed to convince Parliament of the need for either a uniform tariff or a General Assembly he did not abandon all hope that the colonies would federate: he saw the power which the Australian Colonies Government Act gave the colonies to impose tariffs provided they gave no preferences, even to each other, as giving them a strong motive to agree to a federal union. But for the present he had to be content with conferring upon the Governor of New South Wales the title of Governor-General and issuing new commissions which would enable him to supersede the 'Lieutenant-Governors' of Victoria, South Australia and Van Diemen's Land if he felt that the existence of inter-colonial problems made this necessary.

This would have been little more than a gesture even if the first Governor-General had been more willing to intervene in other colonies than was Sir Charles FitzRoy, who held the office until the beginning of 1855; Grey's successors failed to follow up the matter by treating the Governor-General as such in fact as well as in name, and in his dealings with the other colonies FitzRoy was always guided by the interests of New South Wales. The title was also conferred on his immediate successor, Sir William Denison. Although the second Governor-General was not given the theoretical powers which FitzRoy had been given he was able to use his titular pre-eminence to exercise a useful leadership on matters of common concern such as steamship mail subsidies, the provision of ocean lights and the problem of tariffs on the Murray River border. But this was in the future. Grey's encouragement completely failed to bring the colonies together.

Ironically enough, however, they soon showed what might have been signs of coming together to oppose him. The evident intention of the British government to continue transportation to Van Diemen's Land, whence escapees and expirees frequently made their way to the mainland, gave rise in the early 1850s to a movement of protest which united opinion in all the colonies, though South Australian interest was slight, into the Australasian League for the Abolition of Transportation. The League was grandiloquently referred to as a 'confederation' by many of its members; there were suggestions that it could become the nucleus of a federal union of the colonies and that if such a union existed Downing Street would be forced to abandon transportation. The League was perhaps significant as providing the first airing of the assumption that a federation would carry more weight in London than the colonies separately, but, as Professor J.M. Ward has pointed out, 'the sense of union given to the opponents of transportation by their struggle against British policy was not grounded in any kind of Australian nationalism'. Indeed, the migration of ex-convicts from Van Diemen's Land to Victoria, particularly after the gold rushes began, exacerbated relations between these two colonies; and when transportation to eastern Australia ended in 1853, inter-colonial common feeling rapidly faded. Moreover the fact that the more radical supporters of the 'anti-felon confederation' spoke angrily of united resistance and repudiation of allegiance to the Crown and that one prominent member, John Dunmore Lang, established a republican 'Australia League' in 1850 and published an appeal for the establishment of a United States of Australia in 1852, tended to make respectable colonists a little wary of federal proposals. Certainly in 1853 a committee of the New South Wales Legislative Council, in criticizing a Victorian decision to reduce gold-licence fees because New South Wales had to follow (or face disorder on the gold-fields), argued that such decisions should properly be taken by a 'General Assembly' representing all the colonies; and the lack of inter-colonial co-operation which resulted in the adoption of different railway gauges by New South Wales and Victoria, as well as difficulties over mail subsidies, led to suggestions for 'federation'; but there was no hint of united action in the fight for control of executive government and Crown lands. Governor Denison, who did much to iron out differences between colonies, did not agree that a federal union was necessary; and though the select committees which drafted constitutional proposals in both New South Wales and Victoria in 1853 spoke of the desirability of federation, nothing came of their remarks. In London to see the Constitution Bill through Parliament, Wentworth tried to interest Lord John Russell in a General Assembly, but Russell quite reasonably declined to take any action unless the colonial legislatures agreed to request it.

Grey's proposals, it should be emphasized, had been for no more than a formal system of consultation and co-operation; and, with one exception, those colonists who thought dispassionately about federation in the decade after the establishment of responsible government thought in the same terms. Towards the end of 1856 the distinguished editor of the *Sydney Morning Herald*, John West, wrote a series of articles on the subject:

these concentrated on such manifest inconveniences of disunion as tariffs (especially in relation to trade on the Murray River), the need to make inter-colonial arrangements for posts and telegraphs, the difficulties of gold-field regulation and the problem caused by the fact that the various colonies were tempted to raise revenue by selling land cheaply in competition with one another, to the long-term disadvantage of all. Edward Deas Thomson, the last New South Wales Colonial Secretary before responsible government and at this time vice-president of the Executive Council, lent his influential support to West's case. Their advocacy of federation encouraged Wentworth, who was still in London, to take up the matter again. Under his inspiration an unofficial lobbying group, the General Association for the Australian Colonies, asked the Secretary of State, Henry Labouchere, for a Bill to authorize the Australian colonies to establish a General Assembly. Wentworth envisaged a body with power to legislate on a range of subjects similar to that set out by West and also on defence (for Her Majesty's government was clearly expecting the colonies to take more responsibility for this) and other matters which might later be referred to it by the colonial parliaments. Labouchere consulted the government's expert on Australian affairs, Robert Lowe, Wentworth's old antagonist and now vice-president of the Board of Trade: he criticized the scheme heavily and so Labouchere declined to act upon it, agreeing, however, to circularize the Australian governors to find whether there was support for it in the colonies.

Like West and Deas Thomson, Wentworth did not consider that the General Assembly should have executive powers, or even its own finance; he saw it as 'little more than a court of registry for its own acts', which would be put into force by the various colonies. The three men were concerned only with the inconveniences of disunion, but there was in Australia one man who saw beyond these inconveniences and seized upon them as arguments to be used in support of a view of federation which, if less radical than the republicanism of Lang, was in its motivation essentially nationalist. This was the Young Irelander, Charles Gavan Duffy. In the 1840s he had seen in a nationalism transcending the divisions between Catholic and Protestant, and between Celt and Saxon, the hope for the future of Ireland; emigrating to Victoria early in 1856 he was struck by the existence in Australia of inter-colonial rivalries which he felt should be arrested quickly lest they come to divide his new country as deeply as his native land had been. His prestige carried him into Parliament where, less than a year after his arrival, he chaired a select committee on federation which reported that, as 'neighbouring States of the second order inevitably become confederates or enemies', Victoria should take the initiative in calling immediately a conference of the self-governing colonies to consider proposals for union.

The response of the Victorian Legislative Assembly to Duffy's appeal was lukewarm. By this time there had developed in Victoria (to supplement the inter-colonial jealousies which had helped to wreck Grey's scheme) an attitude of superiority, generated by the colony's spectacular economic progress, which other Australians found particularly galling, and a confidence that prosperous Victoria could do better for itself by negotiation on individual inter-colonial difficulties as they arose than it could by agreement to federate. Nevertheless, the government agreed, without committing itself, to invite the other colonies to the conference which Duffy suggested.

In 1857, therefore, the Australian colonies had before them two separate federal initiatives, that of Wentworth, transmitted without enthusiasm by Labouchere, and that of Duffy, transmitted without enthusiasm by the government of Victoria. It was inevitable that they should meet with a cool reception. South Australia, while not declining to be represented at a conference, had virtually determined that a conference would be the end of the matter; Tasmania was prepared to agree to federal proposals, but only because, small and threatened with economic stagnation, it could not afford to remain outside if the other colonies federated; in New South Wales, despite the efforts of Deas Thomson, the matter was shelved.

By this time the arguments of convenience in favour of federation had been considerably weakened. This was particularly true of the tariff problem. The strenuous efforts of the chambers of commerce in Melbourne and Sydney had led to the adoption by the three eastern colonies of substantially similar tariff policies and by South Australia of one which eliminated the worst inconsistencies. The associated problem of trade on the Murray River, which flowed between New South Wales and Victoria and through South Australia, and since 1853 carried an increasing steamer traffic, was dealt with (albeit temporarily and after very hard bargaining) by a free border agreement signed in November 1855 and revised in May 1857. Conflicts over the Murray trade, as Ward has said,

> showed that federation might be a desirable means of resolving them, but they also provided plenty of evidence about the difficulties in the way of any movement towards federation ... And the fact that an agreement, however unsatisfactory, had been reached was quoted as evidence by those who claimed that the colonies could settle their differences by negotiation without entering into a complicated system of federal union.

Where arguments of convenience failed, more elevated appeals were unlikely to succeed. The nationalist sentiments of Duffy struck no spark: the movement which he sought to further stagnated for two decades.

The Origin of the Federal Council

But the movements of the 1850s left a legacy: the word 'federation' assumed a peculiar significance as an expression of the ultimate destiny of the Australian colonies, a destiny remote enough to be taken for granted without requiring any immediate effort from anyone: the idea was always there for use by politicians in after-dinner speeches; when the New South Wales colonial secretary, Henry Parkes, proposed in 1867 the establishment of an inter-colonial committee to handle mail contracts, he was able without being laughed at to describe the minor administrative body he was trying to establish as a 'Federal Council'. Duffy himself never gave up hope. His frequent attempts to revive interest in federal union—once coupling the idea with a proposal for obtaining for Australia an international recognition of neutrality comparable with that accorded Belgium—failed, but they contributed significantly to the development of a psychological atmosphere in which nationalism could grow. After 1862 an informal system of co-operation which manifested itself in fairly regular meetings of the Premiers of the self-governing colonies, and which was of the utmost importance in maintaining a degree of uniformity in administration, law and constitutional practice, contributed to the process. The similarity of the political histories of the colonies in the third quarter of the nineteenth century is, indeed, quite remarkable. Of the three great issues which divided opinion in the colonies during these decades, two, those concerning land settlement and education, were handled in a strikingly similar manner in all of them; in the case of the third, the question of protection, all but New South Wales followed more or less the same policies. Australian nationalism grew more slowly than Duffy had expected, but perhaps in the end it was the stronger for that. Certainly when federation did come, inter-state rivalries and jealousies, though they had by no means disappeared, had become as a result of common political experience much less irrational, much more a matter of definite and therefore potentially reconcilable clashes of interest.

For some time after the failure of Duffy's proposals the several colonies were taken up with internal political problems, particularly with the clash between conservative and radical ideas in the matters of land policy and electoral reform, but the problem of inter-colonial tariffs had not been finally settled by the compromises of the mid-1850s and, as Grey had foreseen, it was bound to become critical in the long run. The prohibition imposed by the British government on the charging of differential duties by the colonies inevitably aggravated it. For a time the aggravation was less serious than it might have been, because trade among the colonies was, in general, not in the same classes of goods as trade between Australia and the outside world and because the colonies principally affected were parties to the Murray River free border agreement. This compact, which provided for South Australia to collect duties at the river mouth and for cash adjustments to be made among the colonies, lasted (with many frictions and vicissitudes) until 1873. In the very year it collapsed, the prohibition on the granting of preferences was removed; but by this time another factor was coming into play.

The Australian colonies had begun to come under the influence of the movement which produced protective tariff policies in the United States, Russia, France, Italy and Germany. The colony most affected was Victoria. It had a relatively high population density, so when the numbers engaged in mining fell off sharply at the end of the 1850s its 'golden-age' prosperity came to an abrupt end: by 1861 the level of real wages was half the level in the boom year 1854. In the new circumstances Victorian working men, hindered by the opposition of the Legislative Council from gaining the land reform which they saw as one solution to their problems, were ready to respond to a vigorous campaign for the protection of local industries. Such a campaign was initiated in 1861 by the proprietor of the Melbourne *Age*, David Syme. By 1866 the Victorian tariff had begun to take a definite protectionist slant, and in 1877 a high level of protection was established as the permanent policy of the colony. South Australia and Tasmania followed the Victorian lead fairly closely, if without the fervour of the disciples of Syme; Queensland moved some distance along the road; only New South Wales held firm to the doctrine of free trade. Border tariffs became a much more serious cause of friction between the colonies than they had been in the 1850s.

And they were not the only border irritations. Inter-state competition for trade took on a cut-throat character as the State-owned railway systems radiating from the sea-coast capitals reached out towards the borders. In the late 1870s New South Wales lines began to push into the Riverina and tap a region which had for many years been the preserve of South Australian merchants interested in the Murray river-boat trade, and had more recently been penetrated by Melbourne merchants using the Victorian railways, which had reached the Murray by the beginning of the decade. Price wars began: differential rates (lower ton-mile charges on long hauls than on short) were used by New South Wales, which needed heavy traffic to make its long lines economical; Victoria countered with 'preferential' rates (lower charges on, for example, wool grown in the Riverina and consigned to Melbourne than on wool grown in Victoria and carried the same distance).

There was an artificiality about frictions like these between colonies with so much in common in history and culture which made their removal by federation seem only commonsense. But if they provided an incentive to unite they also placed grave practical obstacles in the way. Questions concerning a federal tariff arose: would a federation of the colonies involve a common tariff? If so, would it be protectionist or not? The latter question could only be answered if one of the two largest colonies agreed to abandon its fiscal policy. Later a Victorian premier called this problem 'the lion in the path' of a federation movement. And what of the railways, now in active competition with one another? Would a federal government forbid, in the interests of interstate free trade, the use of preferential (or even differential) rates? If it did, would the colonies, which had gone heavily into debt to build their lines, be relieved of responsibility for the payment of interest? Never capable of solution in one bold stroke, as Duffy had thought, the problems of Australian federalism were becoming more complex with every year that passed.

The forces which might produce a national sentiment strong enough to cut through the complexities were, however, intensifying at the same time, and by the late 1870s were beginning to produce a situation in which federation might be seriously discussed. The expansion of farming settlement was bringing people of at least some of the colonies into actual contiguity with those of others; business firms and trade unions were establishing inter-colonial contacts; and if the railways caused rivalry they also made intercourse easier. Definite attempts were being made to foster national patriotism, particularly by the Australian Natives' Association, which was founded in Victoria in the early 1870s and which, though always stronger there, gained a considerable membership in other colonies; the first Australian cricket team toured England in 1878. Moreover the *Pax Britannica* under which the colonies had grown up seemed to be developing cracks: some Australians were becoming aware of their isolation and disunity in an increasingly threatening international climate.

Fear and xenophobia are powerful emotions: external 'threats', though always exaggerated and often quite imaginary, provided even more potent arguments for federation than did tariffs or wasteful railway competition. Two incidents raised a doubt whether Britain, increasingly concerned with its own problems and its relationships with other great powers, could be relied upon always to protect the colonies' interests. The first serious stirring of colonial opinion came in 1876, when the French government made a request to the British Foreign Office for entry rights to Australia for political prisoners, survivors of the rising of the Paris Commune, who were about to be released from New Caledonia on condition that they did not return to France. Although there was never any real danger that London would accede to such a cheeky request, it drew attention to the proximity of a penal station from which emancipists and escapees might make their way to Australia, served as a reminder that the colonies were absolutely dependent on Britain in such matters and provoked the suggestion that, disunited as they were, they might have difficulty in bringing pressure to bear in their own interests. Then there arose the question of eastern New Guinea. During the 1870s a number of representations had been made to the British government by missionaries and humanitarians concerned with the continuation of 'black-birding' for the annexation of that part of the

island not claimed by the Netherlands (the part east of the 141st meridian); but in 1878 the Colonial Office made clear that Britain would
accept no responsibility unless the Australian colonies agreed to make a
contribution towards the cost of administration. The difficulty of arrang-
ing this shelved the matter for a time, but after 1880 growing interest in
the area by the large German trading concern Godeffroy und Sohn
began to cause alarm in Queensland, and in April 1883 the Premier of
that colony, Sir Thomas McIlwraith, precipitately ordered the annexation of the southern coastal area. His action was disallowed by the
Secretary of State for the Colonies, but the British government repeated
that it would consider at least a protectorate if the colonies united in
helping to finance it.

This led to an attempt, the direct initiative for which came from the
Victorian Premier, James Service, to establish a formal body representing the common interests of the colonies. At the end of the year he
succeeded in bringing together in Sydney a convention of delegates from
the Australasian colonies which agreed to recommend to the governments that they should meet British requirements for the protectorate
and ask for an Act of the imperial Parliament establishing a permanent
Federal Council to deal with future matters of common concern. The
protectorate was duly proclaimed, after a series of negotiations with
Germany in which, the colonies felt, Britain let that country get away
with too much (the north-eastern part of New Guinea and practically
the whole of the Bismarck Archipelago), and in 1885 the Federal
Council was set up.

The Council was given the power to pass Bills, which would receive
the royal assent from the Governor of the colony where it was meeting,
on 'the relations of Australasia with the islands of the Pacific' (a fairly
meaningless phrase given the admitted control of the imperial government over external affairs) and on the exclusion of criminals, the service
of judicial process and enforcement of judgement beyond the borders of
a colony, extradition, the custody of offenders on colonial vessels and the
regulation of fisheries. Moreover, any two colonies could refer to it the
right to pass laws, which would have force only in the colonies concerned, on a wide range of other subjects including defence, quarantine,
patents, bills of exchange, marriage and divorce, and naturalization. But
it had no executive authority, and no permanent existence as a body,
being composed of two (after 1895 five) delegates from each of the
colonies which became members. It was, therefore, essentially what
Grey had called a 'General Assembly' forty years before. It met for the
first time in Hobart in January and February 1886 and reassembled for
short sessions in 1888, 1889 and then in alternate years until its dissolution in 1899.

The foundation members of the Federal Council were Victoria,
Tasmania and Queensland, Western Australia, which did not yet have

responsible government, and the Crown colony of Fiji; South Australia joined in 1889 but withdrew in 1891; New South Wales (and New Zealand) did not join at all. On the surface, the abstention of New South Wales seems surprising. Resentment against Britain's 'mishandling' of the New Guinea affair and her alleged lack of interest in Australian fears about another Pacific development—the proposal of the French government to exile to the New Hebrides a large number of *récidivistes* (who were imagined to be the worst type of professional criminal though they were in fact the least dangerous type, men who were caught frequently)—should have aroused enough national sentiment to overcome traditional objections to federal proposals. But the New South Welsh suspicions of Victoria were deep. Rapid Victorian economic development in the wake of the gold rushes had created jealousies to which was added in the 1880s a slightly self-righteous disapproval among Sydney people towards a great speculative land boom then building up in Melbourne. An exuberant after-dinner boast made by Service when he returned to Melbourne from the Convention that he had 'woken up' New South Wales did not help. Most importantly, no influential New South Welsh political leader was sympathetic. The elder statesman Sir John Robertson was wont to call Victoria a 'cabbage garden' and to say that if Victorians wanted unity they could give up the status of a separate colony achieved in 1850. Robertson's great rival, Henry Parkes, who had submitted to an inter-colonial conference in 1881 a memorandum proposing the establishment of just such a body as now set up, had been overseas at the time of the Convention; he returned, not to embrace the Federal Council but to announce that 'maturer thoughts on the subject' had led him to regard the Council 'as a thing which must prove abortive on trial'. Whether or not Victorians who attributed his change of heart to vanity and jealousy of Service were right, he was able to prevent it from getting the trial he expected it to fail.

The Council passed a few ordinances on such matters as *bêche de mer* fishing; it made a formal protest against the supposed complaisance of the Foreign Office towards French activities in the New Hebrides; but without New South Wales it was crippled. Certainly it was, as Parkes said, 'half a loaf', but there is no need to accept his opinion that its existence was an obstacle rather than an aid to a future movement towards closer union. Its constitution was such that, if it had been joined by New South Wales, it might have gradually built up a corpus of uniform legislation upon which the superstructure of a federal government could have been easily fitted. Parkes, perhaps deliberately, underestimated the importance of functional co-operation as a step towards political integration. It became a point of honour for New South Welsh politicians, supporters and opponents of Parkes, to have nothing to do with the Federal Council: the mother colony preferred to face its problems alone, even when they included such obviously continental issues as restriction of Chinese immigration. But the Council was, for all that, one of the influences which turned minds towards the ideal of Australian unity; the very fact of its existence was a reminder of common interests; as Alfred Deakin of Victoria said, it 'became influential by the excitement it occasioned around Port Jackson', by serving as a challenge to New South Welsh politicians to win back the initiative Service had seized from them.

The Parkes Movement

There were other influences at work also. The population of the Australian colonies rose by about forty per cent during the 1880s, more by natural increase than by immigration, so that by the end of the decade about three-quarters of the people in Australia were native born; and a self-consciously nationalist literary movement was springing up around the Sydney weekly *The Bulletin*. External stimuli were intensifying. In the 1860s and 1870s talk of federalism could lead to an uneasy feeling that the bloodbath of the American Civil War might be the nemesis of the system, but by the 1880s the United States had recovered sufficiently to enter upon an impressive period of economic expansion; German precedents seemed equally propitious; and if the encouragement from Canada was less clear it could be argued that in that country there were race problems unknown in Australia. Continuing apprehension about German and French activities in the South Pacific and a growing awareness of both Russian expansion across Asia and the potential power of China were important factors. And in 1888, the centennial year, when the future greatness of a federated Australia seemed a natural theme for patriotic orations, the completion of a bridge over the Hawkesbury River closed the last gap in a railway system linking Adelaide, Melbourne, Sydney and Brisbane.

The next year the railway was to provide a setting for Parkes to take up the challenge of Victorian leadership and try to place his colony—and himself—at the head of the federal movement. His real motives in this remain as obscure as in many other actions in his long political career, but the facts upon which speculation might be based are clear enough. He had been in Parliament, with only short breaks, since responsible government; he became Premier for the fifth time in March 1889; he was the admitted master of the factional manoeuvres which had provided what cohesion there was in colonial politics for thirty years. But he was losing his way as more definite parties began to emerge: he now led a free trade party the younger members of which distrusted his leadership and looked towards a more positive policy than his, and even with their precarious support his majority was small. In June he wrote to the Premier of Victoria, Duncan Gillies, offering, if

Gillies and the other Premiers would give him some encouragement, to take 'a prominent or leading part in the cause of Australasian Federation' by convening a 'Parliamentary Convention of Australia' which might consider the framing of a federal constitution. When Gillies failed to give him the encouragement, he looked for means to extort it. He looked particularly in the wording of a report on the defence needs of the Australian colonies completed in October by an imperial officer, Major-General J.B. Bevan-Edwards—wording which, indeed, he seems to have influenced. Edwards suggested that 'a federation of the forces of the different colonies' was desirable. Parkes drew the attention of the Premiers to this phrase and made a trip to Brisbane in an attempt to interest the Premier of Queensland in the ideas which were still evoking no response in Victoria. Again his reception was cool, and so, on his way back by the Brisbane-Sydney rail service he broke his journey at the border township of Tenterfield and delivered a speech in which he argued that 'a federation of the forces' was impossible without political federation—a speech which was intended to be a dramatic appeal, over the heads of the unco-operative premiers, to Australian public opinion.

It fell rather flat: as patriotic oratory it was uninspired, and the choice of Tenterfield, which was intended to give the speech symbolic force, in fact limited the publicity it received. But Parkes had now committed himself publicly to the view that federation was urgent. Despite the fact that some of his senior colleagues in the New South Wales cabinet were annoyed at his failure to consult them before acting openly, he threw himself into a hard campaign. He bombarded the Premiers, particularly Gillies, with letters alleging both an urgency and a public enthusiasm which were purely imaginary, and the bombardment only ended when, after they had tried unsuccessfully to persuade him to discuss common defence with the Federal Council, they agreed that they and some of their colleagues should, 'as representative public men', meet him at the end of the Council's forthcoming meeting. The result was a conference in Melbourne in February 1890. This resolved to invite the Parliaments of the various colonies, including Western Australia (which was about to become self-governing) and New Zealand, to appoint delegates to a convention in Sydney the following year.

When the National Australasian Convention met on 4 March 1891 Parkes, as Premier of the host colony, was elected to the chair. After consulting with the leading figures from the other colonies, he commenced proceedings by moving a series of resolutions which sought to lay down the principles and outline the form of a federal constitution. As principles he proposed that specified powers should be transferred to a federal legislature and that residual powers should remain with the States; that trade between the States should be free; that, subject to agreement on the distribution of revenue, the federal Parliament should have exclusive power to levy customs duties; and that defence should be a federal responsibility. The constitution he envisaged would provide for a bicameral Parliament, a responsible executive and a judicature including a court of final appeal. The two houses of the legislature would be a House of Representatives with membership proportional to the population of the States and with 'sole power of originating and amending all bills appropriating revenue and imposing taxation', and a Senate representing the States equally, which should be indissoluble, one-third of its members to retire at a time. The pattern was obviously the Constitution of the United States of America: the only departure from this model was in the prescription of responsible government.

After a long debate, in which several delegates raised objections to Parkes's schema and many (foremost among them the doyen of colonial politicians, Sir George Grey of New Zealand) rode personal hobby horses, the Convention accepted it as the basis of discussion, without, however, committing members to support of its details. Then select committees were appointed, and their deliberations were consolidated into a draft constitution by a small committee, of which Sir Samuel Griffith of Queensland was the dominant member. This was then subjected to a clause-by-clause debate in which the great issues were canvassed and many minor amendments made.

In all these discussions the main issues turned upon what R.R. Garran later called 'the fundamental problem of the federal system: how to reconcile the principles of government by the will of the majority of the people and government by the will of the majority of the States'. To meet this problem—although he did not perceive its seriousness and thought that he was just humouring difficult people from smaller colonies—Parkes copied the American device of a second chamber with equal representation for the States, but this in itself was not a solution. Once the establishment and composition of this chamber were conceded the question of its powers, particularly its powers over money Bills, became crucial. In general the delegates from Queensland, South Australia, Tasmania and Western Australia wanted to give the Senate, which was to be elected by the colonial parliaments, absolute equality of power with the House of Representatives, so that it would be in a position to guarantee the sovereignty and welfare of the small colonies despite the fact that the larger would out-vote them heavily in the Lower House: these men wanted the Senate to have the right to reject or amend all measures, even taxation and appropriation Bills. The delegates from the larger colonies wanted the Lower House, the composition of which would reflect (at least roughly) the States' various contributions to federal finances, to have ultimate supremacy in money matters. The position was, however, complicated by the fact that some of the more conservative delegates from the larger colonies, men like J.P. Abbott and Patrick Jennings of New South Wales, were tempted to support the small-State view, while the radical C.C. Kingston of South

Australia strongly supported the other side. Such people saw the Senate as having some of the characteristics of an ordinary Upper House and had their attitude to it conditioned by their attitude to the history of relations between the Houses in their own colonies; Victorians, with more bitter memories of Upper House intransigence than New South Welshmen, gave the impression of being more strongly opposed to a powerful Senate.

The Convention's answer to the question of Senate powers was the adoption in the draft constitution of the arrangement which had existed in South Australia since 1857: the Senate was to have the same power as the Lower House over all Bills except those for taxation and appropriation; these it might not amend, though it might reject them or 'suggest' amendments. The difference between amending a Bill and suggesting an amendment, with the power of outright rejection in the background, is, as the Tasmanian delegate Inglis Clark admitted, at best a fine one, so this 'compromise of 1891' leaned heavily towards the States'-rights school and was a remarkably good bargain for the small colonies.

And alone it did not solve Garran's 'fundamental problem': this had another aspect, the question of the relations between executive and legislature. The American federal system, which so obviously inspired the plan for the composition of the federal legislature, depended upon the separation of powers; and many delegates believed that the responsible government to which the colonies were used could not work in a federation where, by definition, two co-equal Houses represented different interests; in a serious dispute between the Houses a responsible executive would be unable to carry on but be virtually incapable of being replaced. The West Australian Winthrop Hackett reduced the problem to an aphorism: 'Either responsible government will kill federation or federation ... will kill responsible government'. Yet the system, the idea, even the phrase, was too closely associated with the traditions of Australian constitutionalism to be lightly abandoned. In the end this very important issue was evaded. Despite the reference to responsible government in the opening resolutions, the draft constitution which the Convention produced went no further than to state that the executive government would be invested in a Governor-General acting on the advice of ministers who *might* be members of Parliament.

Here was an illustration of the real weakness of the 1891 Convention's work, the tendency to avoid serious issues. The problem of federal finances was likewise brushed aside. Obviously if the federal government was to take over customs and excise, the basic source of the revenue of all the colonies (for at this stage the difference between protectionist Victoria and free-trade New South Wales was essentially in the *incidence* of duties) it would have to hand most of the proceeds to the States. The draft constitution provided that in the period between federation and the working out of a federal tariff, while the federal authorities were collecting duties on the old colonial scales, the surplus over federal needs was to be returned under a 'bookkeeping system', in proportion to the amounts collected; but as goods imported into a particular colony would not necessarily be for consumption there, and the abolition of border customs would often prevent the collection of revenue in the colony where they were consumed, a bookkeeping system was no more than a stop-gap; and the Convention was unable to agree on a permanent basis for reimbursement of revenue, but left the matter to be decided by the federal Parliament after uniform duties had been established. This decision, and a tacit agreement not to argue over the 'fiscal issue' (the question whether the federation should adopt free trade or protection) may have been inevitable, and even visionary; but they were felt in New South Wales to have been potentially dangerous. They seemed to amount to a pretence that the 'lion in the path' was non-existent.

The rest of the draft constitution requires little comment. It provided for a Parliament composed as Parkes' resolutions suggested, with powers generally similar to those contained in the Constitution which was ultimately to come into force in 1901, and a Supreme Court which should be a court of final appeal, subject only to the Sovereign's right to grant leave to appeal to the Judicial Committee of the Privy Council in cases where imperial interests might be involved. It provided no machinery for resolving disputes between the Senate and the House of Representatives.

Before adjourning for the last time the Convention recommended that a Bill embodying the draft constitution should be passed by the various colonial legislatures and then submitted for enactment by the imperial Parliament. But the first step was to prove impossible. No one really expected New Zealand, where the width of the Tasman Sea seemed to provide 'twelve hundred reasons' for not joining an Australian federation, to ratify the Bill; Victoria, Queensland, South Australia, Western Australia and Tasmania, aware of the crippling effect the absence of the mother colony had had on the Federal Council, were unwilling to act until New South Wales did so; and in New South Wales the signs were not propitious.

Parkes was widely suspected in his own colony, and even in his own party, of pushing the federal movement in order to bolster up his shaky political position, and there were fears that under the influence of his enthusiasm the Convention had drafted its Bill too hastily, with too little attention to the vital details which Parkes, a man of large ideas, was notoriously prone to overlook. G.H. Reid, rising star in the free trade party in New South Wales and a strong critic of Parkes' leadership, had already before the Convention met emerged as an advocate of extreme caution in federal negotiations. In the six weeks which elapsed between the dissolution of the Convention and the opening of the New South Wales Parliament in May 1891, he made several speeches critical of the

Bill at public meetings; he clearly intended to oppose its ratification. Then, when Parliament met, Parkes made the mistake of adopting a course which confirmed the fears of those who suspected him of trying to rush his colony into federation.

Forewarned by Reid's public statements, the Premier gave notice, as soon as the members of the Legislative Assembly had returned to their chamber after hearing the Governor's speech, of a motion concerning the Constitution Bill, and the speaker (the Convention delegate Abbott) over-ruled a protest against the introduction of business before the address-in-reply debate. Parkes' action, and the form of his motion, were later described by the federalists Quick and Garran as 'strategic devices to answer in advance the expected attack'; to his opponents, however, they looked more like an attempt to evade it. The most important section of his motion, a provision that Parliament should have the right to propose amendments and that the Bill should finally be submitted to the judgement of the electors, was incompatible with his insistence at the Convention that the Bill should be put to the various Parliaments for 'adoption' as a whole, not for 'consideration', and therefore was rather too obviously a 'device'.

Reid's reaction was to move an amendment to the address, affirming support for federation 'on principles just to the several colonies' but attacking the Bill as it stood. Although the amendment, virtually a censure motion, was defeated, the debate, which raked mercilessly over the details of the draft constitution, seems to have shaken Parkes' confidence: he decided to drop federation from first to third place on his legislative programme, below Bills on local government and electoral reform. It had still not been brought into the House when his government fell five months later. Parkes' attempt to bring about federation had failed.

The principal reason for its failure was the apparent haste of its originator. It was haste which aroused suspicion of his motives and it was haste which led him and his colleagues to 'sink the fiscal issue'. Hindsight assures the modern student that the only solution to the tariff problem was to leave it to the federal Parliament, but the speed with which it was reached suggested to New South Welsh freetraders that it involved a betrayal of principle by a free trade premier. Reid was able to pour scorn on a proposal which was equivalent to a teetotaller's agreeing to set up house with five drunkards and to leave the question of beverages to be decided later. Haste also accounts for the lack of a complete solution to Garran's 'fundamental problem', and for the acceptance by the Convention of trade and commerce provisions which, since they could be interpreted as giving the federal authorities power to disallow railway rates designed to make the long lines of New South Wales economical, were highly suspect in that colony, where the heavily capitalized railway system accounted for the greater part of the government's large interest payments. Under attack the constitution drafted in such a hurry appeared not only unsatisfactory but also potentially dangerous. The American Civil War had occurred in the lifetimes of most Australian electors, and the frictions of the Canadian system were well known. There were many people, and not only in New South Wales (in Victoria, for instance there was George Higinbotham), who agreed with Reid that a federal constitution 'must be clear, express and unambiguous', as the Convention's Bill was not, if the federation were to avoid 'disputes, ill-feeling and perhaps violence', and that the draft constitution provided too little guarantee of popular sovereignty.

The Victorian, Tasmanian and South Australian parliaments all dealt with the Bill in part, but no government was prepared to go ahead without New South Wales, and there was little chance of the movement's being revived there for some time. Parkes was succeeded in the premiership by a strong anti-federalist, George Dibbs, and in the leadership of the free trade party, which he resigned at the same time, by that critic of his Bill, George Reid. His first lieutenant in federal affairs, Edmund Barton, who now became the acknowledged champion of the cause, joined the Dibbs government, with a promise, however, of freedom to bring on a parliamentary discussion of the Convention Bill. The promise was useless, for the Labour Party, which had just entered Parliament and which was in a position to hold a balance of power, was hostile, wanting preference to be given to domestic reforms; public opinion generally was, in the midst of a serious economic crisis, apathetic about such a grandiose scheme. Despite the best efforts of Barton and his friend Richard O'Connor, nothing serious had been accomplished before the two resigned from the ministry at the end of 1893.

The Convention of 1897–98

Before this time Barton had despaired of making any progress until public interest was aroused and had set about arousing it by organizing local federation leagues, at first mainly in districts near the Murray border. Business groups which felt that a federation of the colonies might afford some shelter from the economic blizzard seconded his efforts, and by the middle of 1893 he had been able to set up a Central Federation League in Sydney. At the same time an effort was being made in Victoria, particularly, under the influence of Alfred Deakin (who had been a member of the conference of 1890 and the Convention) by the Australian Natives' Association, to stir up public opinion. At a meeting between representatives of the A.N.A. and the border leagues at the Murray township of Corowa in July a delegate from Bendigo, John Quick, put forward a plan which has come to be regarded as the starting point of a new federal movement, one more popularly based than that associated with Parkes. The importance of the Corowa meeting can easily be exaggerated; it produced no spectacular upsurge of popular interest and was represented by some New South Welshmen as a Victorian protectionist plot; but the plan which came from it met problems the existence of which was not realized by Parkes in 1889. Quick proposed that the colonial parliaments be asked to pass identical enabling Acts providing for the election by the people of delegates to a convention which should draft a constitution, and for the submission of the draft to popular ratification. The advantages of the scheme were two: first the election of the convention could be expected to arouse popular interest lacking in the work of the previous body, which represented not people but Parliaments; secondly, as the whole process, from the election of delegates to submission of the constitution to the electors, was to be provided for in advance, the new convention's Bill could not be shelved as the old one's had been. A similar scheme emanating about the same time from the Central Federation League, which envisaged separate elected conventions in the various colonies, to be followed by intercolonial negotiations and a referendum, had similar advantages.

Both, however, the latter perhaps more particularly, had weaknesses: the Bill drawn up by a new convention, even by an elective one, might prove unacceptable at referendum and the whole grand project end in failure; and there was no certainty that the Parliaments would pass, or even get a chance to consider, the uniform enabling Bill on which everything depended. In the removal of these two difficulties the critical role was to be played by the man who had done more than any other to prevent the acceptance of the Parkes-Griffith bill, George Reid.

Reid became Premier of New South Wales in July 1894. His primary policy was the repeal of a semi-protective tariff which his predecessor had enacted and the orientation of the colony's fiscal system not towards the traditional dependence on revenue tariffs but towards direct taxation. However he showed an immediate if subsidiary interest in the federal question. Partly, perhaps, this was a matter of political tactics, of trying to assuage the hostility of prominent federalists to the 'arch-enemy' of their movement, as Parkes called him; partly it reflects the need for a minister to be more constructive than a private member; partly, too, it was a result of a growing conviction, stemming from the landslide acceptance of his policy of free trade and direct taxation, and from his reading of happenings in Victoria and overseas, that his fiscal policy was capable, as Parkes' negative view of free trade was not, of converting the other colonies from the drunkenness of protection. In any event, when he was approached, soon after taking office, by a deputation from the Central Federation League, he was able to tell its members that he had already contacted the other Premiers and invited them to consider the plans for a new start. The Premiers of the six Australian colonies met in Hobart in January 1895, and decided to put the Corowa scheme into operation. Reid agreed that the enabling Bill which they drafted should be put through the Parliament of New South Wales first, as an earnest of his colony's serious intentions, and the Premiers made an important modification of the plan: their Bill provided for an adjournment of between thirty and sixty days in the proceedings of the convention, after it had completed a first draft of the constitution, to enable the colonial parliaments to comment upon it. This was seen as making the final acceptance of the constitution more likely. There was some disapproval among conservatives in all the colonies of the implication that the method of submission to the electors would be by referendum, but when the Premiers finished their meeting the new federal movement seemed fairly launched.

There were, however, to be delays. Reid's domestic policies involved him in the dispute with the Legislative Council which was discussed in the last chapter (p. 76); the royal assent to the enabling Bill was not given until the end of the year. Within a few more weeks it had been passed by the Parliaments of Victoria, Tasmania and South Australia, but then the attitude of Queensland began to cause trouble. In that colony the question became deeply entangled with republicanism, controversies about the use of Pacific Island labourers on the canefields, the movement for the establishment of a separate colony in the north and hostility between the Upper and Lower Houses of the legislature. During 1896 strong efforts were made by the Premiers of the other colonies to persuade the Queensland government to compromise with its opponents on the method of selecting convention delegates, which became the principal point at issue, and so obtain representation at the convention even if not in the strict terms of the Hobart Bill, and at one stage Reid thought he had succeeded; but the situation had become too complex. New Zealand had shown no interest in federation since 1891, and so when the Convention finally came into existence in Adelaide in March 1897 it was composed of ten delegates each from New South Wales, Victoria, South Australia, Tasmania and Western Australia, those from the last-named having been appointed by Parliament.

The most obvious and not the least important difference between this Convention and that of 1891 was in the length of their deliberations. The first met for a little more than a month; the second held a session of four weeks in Adelaide, assembled again after a four-month adjournment for three weeks in Sydney, adjourned again and then held a two-month meeting in Melbourne, dissolving itself almost exactly a year after its first meeting, having spent just four times as many days in session as its predecessor. During the first adjournment the various Parliaments gave much time to the Convention's proposals: certainly the criticism of the 1891 Bill, that it was a product of haste, could not be made of the one which emerged from the final session of the second Convention in March 1898.

The Convention began much as its predecessor had, with a general debate upon principles. Barton, who was elected 'leader', moved a series of resolutions similar to those Parkes had moved in 1891. He proposed that a federal Parliament should assume specific powers, leaving all others to the States; that among the transferred powers should be defence and customs; that interstate trade should be free; and that colonial boundaries should not be altered without the consent of the colonies concerned. He envisaged a legislature consisting of a States' House and a popular chamber, the latter to have sole power of originating money Bills; a court of final appeal; and an executive vested in a Governor-General and his advisers, the question whether those advisers were to be responsible being left for consideration at a later stage of the Convention's proceedings. There was again a general debate, which ended in the formal adoption of the resolutions and the appointment of constitutional, finance and judiciary committees to provide the material from which Barton, Richard O'Connor and Sir John Downer drew up a draft Constitution Bill, the outlines of which were very similar to the Griffith draft of 1891. In the debates which followed, in Convention, Committee of Convention and the Parliaments, there were a number of dominant themes.

One question was dismissed fairly quickly. As has been pointed out, the failure of the 1891 Constitution Bill to prescribe responsibility of executive had caused much uneasiness; but in 1897 responsible government was written into the Bill without serious objection. The delegates had come to realize that Hackett's opinion of its incompatibility with a federal system was only valid if there was no way of resolving serious disputes between the differently-based Houses, and that the failure of their predecessors to provide a means of breaking deadlocks was one which they must remedy. Once this was accepted the traditional system of relations between the executive and legislature was accepted and debates on the nature of the deadlock clause took the place of debates on responsible government as an aspect of the 'fundamental problem' (see p. 104). It was closely related to the other aspect, the question of the composition and powers of the Senate (as the Upper House was again to be called). Equal representation of the States in the Senate was considered absolutely indispensable by the delegates from the smaller colonies, but there were serious doubts about the principle in the minds of many of the Victorians and New South Welshmen: they abhorred the corollary of equal representation, the possibility that the larger colonies could be out-voted, and the many liberals among them distrusted strong Upper Houses as such. In general the large-colony men were prepared to sink their doctrinal objections to equal representation if they could be sure that the Senate was not made completely equal with the House of Representatives. There were two ways in which their views could be met: either the Lower House could be given the dominant voice in taxation and appropriation, or a deadlock provision could be drafted to give ultimate supremacy to the popular Chamber.

The obvious starting point for discussions on the relative power of the Houses over money Bills was the 'compromise of 1891'. Some of the delegates from the large colonies, particularly New South Wales, were hostile to this: while they were willing to concede to the Senate the right to reject a money Bill considered 'grossly unjust', they were unhappy about the right to 'suggest' amendments. But the delegates from the smaller colonies were not happy about the compromise either: at the first session of the Convention they demanded for the Senate not only the *de facto* power to amend all money Bills which the right to suggest amendments provided, but also a *de jure* power to amend one type, Bills imposing taxation. The Victorians and New South Welshmen were outraged: with Baker of South Australia in the chair and the West Australian Hackett absent, there were twenty-eight small-State delegates ranged against twenty men who represented a vastly greater electorate; a real danger existed that the Convention would break down. It was saved by the decision of five delegates from the smaller colonies, Kingston and Glynn of South Australia and Lewis, Brown and Henry of Tasmania, to vote against their colleagues. The 'compromise' was bad enough from the large-State point of view: the attempt further to strengthen the Senate presented a picture of small-State intransigence which fortified the desire of the New South Welsh and Victorian delegates to get their way on the related question of deadlocks.

But even here they got only half of what they wanted. Two proposals were considered. One, for a 'consecutive double dissolution' (a dissolution of the House of Representatives followed, if after the resulting election the two Houses still did not agree, by a dissolution of the Senate) clearly favoured that chamber: it would be able to force members of the Lower House to the expense and hazard of an election while its own members risked nothing, and give way without suffering any inconvenience if the electorate were to support its opponents. The other, for a simultaneous dissolution of both Houses in the case of a deadlock, was favoured by the larger colonies and a few of the more radical delegates from the smaller and was accepted. But there remained the question of what was to be done if the Houses were still at issue afterwards, as could well be the case. The answer was a joint sitting of the two Houses, at which a three-fifths majority would be needed to carry the point at issue. It was objected that the three-fifths majority provision could weight the scales heavily in favour of the smaller colonies if an issue ever arose where State and popular rights clashed. Complicated calculations were made by both sides in the dispute, but there is little doubt that the three-fifths clause was potentially undemocratic. The New South Welsh delegates, and especially Reid, were very hostile to it, but it was the best they could get: some small-State delegates argued, indeed, for a two-thirds majority.

The Convention's answer to the fundamental problem of federalism was not one which commended itself to opinion in the larger colonies. Moreover in New South Wales there was dissatisfaction with two other sections of the draft constitution, the financial arrangements and the trade-and-commerce provisions.

New South Wales was particularly interested in questions of federal finance, both as the wealthiest colony and the only one faithful to free trade. The delegates from the mother colony were generally anxious to prevent federal expenditure from becoming too great because they could see their State's being cast in the role of financial fairy godmother to the smaller States, particularly Tasmania and Western Australia. Rather short-sightedly, they wanted a constitutional limit placed on federal expenditure, but such a limit was struck out of the draft at the last session of the Convention. They hoped to keep out of the finance clauses any detail which might seem to make high tariffs inevitable; but here, too, they were faced with determined opposition, motivated less by doctrinaire protectionist sentiment among other delegates than by the desire of the smaller colonies, whose finances were always precarious, to get as much as possible in payments from the federal customs revenue. As in 1891, there was general agreement on the use of a bookkeeping system for the payment of surplus customs revenue to the colonies in the period preceding the working out of a uniform tariff, but this time there was a desire to write into the Constitution a permanent 'reimbursement formula' rather than to leave it to the federal Parliament, and many delegates wanted this formula to include a 'guarantee' that a definite proportion of the revenue would be paid to the States. The New South Welsh freetraders, two of whom, Reid and William McMillan, were members of the Convention's finance committee, opposed any such guarantee as likely to force the federal government, anxious to get an adequate revenue itself, into a high-tariff policy. The committee proposed that the bookkeeping system should be continued for five years after the imposition of uniform tariffs, with a gradual adjustment towards per capita payments but with no 'guarantee'. The disadvantages of the bookkeeping system were generally recognized, but to adopt per capita payments immediately, without a transition period, would be unjust to New South Wales if the federation were to be even slightly protectionist, because New South Wales, having followed free trade policies in the main for many years, would be used to importing freely goods which would now be dutiable, and would, until consumption habits changed and new industries developed, contribute per capita more to the federal revenue than the national average, while being reimbursed only at the average figure. The amounts involved would perhaps be small if the federal tariff was moderate, but from the New South Wales point of view the matter became serious when the smaller colonies, led by the Tasmanian Braddon, insisted on a guarantee that three-quarters of all revenue from customs and excise should be paid to the States, a guarantee which would make a high federal tariff inevitable. The delegates from New South Wales, not only free traders like Reid and McMillan but also the federal enthusiast Barton, whose fiscal views were mildly protectionist, opposed the Braddon clause strongly. They were prepared, reluctantly, to agree to it as a temporary measure to meet the needs of small States while they were making adjustments to their budgetary policies, but the small States insisted on permanence. Here, as on the questions concerning the Senate, New South Wales had reason to be dissatisfied with the final draft of the Constitution.

So, too, in questions of trade and commerce, which narrowed themselves down to the regulation of railway rates and the control of inland rivers. New South Welshmen were uneasy about the decision of the Convention to provide for the establishment of an 'Interstate Commission' with power to disallow railway rate concessions deemed to interfere with interstate freedom of trade: there was some doubt whether the differential rates which were economically vital to the New South Wales system might not come within the Interstate Commission's powers. But the rivers were a more serious problem. There was only one navigable inland system in Australia, the Murray-Darling. To New South Wales it was a great potential source of water for the irrigation which was coming to be seen as a necessity for the future development of the colony; but South Australians, with interests in the river-boat trade (which they were unable to see was virtually moribund) wanted it preserved as a highway. The difficulty lay in the fact that because of Australia's low and erratic rainfall the two functions were likely to be mutually antagonistic. At the first session of the Convention the South Australian delegate Sir John Downer moved that the federal Parliament be given control of 'rivers running through or on the boundaries of two or more States'—a delicate way of saying the Murray system—in order to maintain water levels, as far as possible, at those necessary for navigation. His proposal was resisted by the men from New South Wales because it would mean handing over almost the entire surface water resources of their colony west of the divide: in a future drought it might mean the ruin of inland agriculture. The Melbourne session of the Convention decided that there should be no separate provision for federal control over rivers, that the power over interstate trade which the draft constitution gave the federal government would be sufficient; McMillan moved a proviso that no State should be denied the use of the waters of rivers for conservation or irrigation. A South Australian, Symon, then moved to insert the word 'reasonable' before the word 'use' in McMillan's clause, and his amendment was carried on the casting vote of the president, Sir Richard Baker, himself a South Australian. Its effect was virtually to destroy the proviso, because it meant that the Constitution would not give irrigation precedence in any conflict of interests: the best New South Wales could hope for, it seemed, was continuous litigation to define 'reasonable' in every place and circumstance.

A Nation for a Continent

The Constitution Bill which left the Convention in March 1898 was, therefore, far from satisfactory to New South Wales, which, as in 1891, was the key State. While interest in the deliberations of the Convention had done much to give a federalist slant to the growing nationalism of Australians, and thus to make for acceptance of the Bill in the referendum which must now follow, there was a strong body of opinion in the mother colony opposed to its acceptance without considerable amendment. This body was stronger in the mother colony than in any other, though in Victoria Isaac Isaacs (constitutional lawyer and future Governor-General) was hesitant, H.B. Higgins (the liberal leader who became the architect of the industrial arbitration system) opposed it as insufficiently democratic, and the influential *Age* wavered almost to the last moment. In New South Wales much depended upon Reid. He was Premier; he had taken the first steps towards calling the Convention; at its meetings he had laboured continuously to hammer out a satisfactory Bill; he was, perhaps, as one of the South Australian delegates said, the best platform speaker in the Empire. He could swing many votes for or against the Bill: his attitude became the great question. For three weeks after the dissolution of the Convention he kept his counsel; then, on 28 March 1898, he addressed a huge meeting in the Sydney Town Hall. For nearly two hours he subjected the defects of the draft constitution to detailed examination: although admitting that in providing for a Senate to be popularly elected rather than elected by the State Parliaments it was more liberal than the 1891 Bill, he pointed to the undemocratic elements in the clauses dealing with Senate representation, money Bills and deadlocks; he catigated the financial arrangements and the trade-and-commerce provisions; he argued that the Bill, rather than leaving the choice of a federal capital to the federal Parliament, should have placed it in New South Wales as compensation for financial sacrifices. But he concluded by saying that he could not 'become a deserter from the cause' of federation: he exhorted each voter to 'judge for himself' and promised to cast his own vote for the Bill. The speech, and his repetition of his criticisms at three large provincial centres in the weeks that followed, did much to crystallize vague fears about the Bill in New South Wales.

When the referendum was held in June a large majority of votes was cast in favour of the Bill in Victoria, South Australia and Tasmania. In Western Australia, where the old settlers of the south-west corner had been taught suspicion of 'eastern radicalism' by an influx of 'T'othersiders' to the gold-fields, where government finance depended to an extraordinary degree on inter-colonial tariffs which would be eliminated after federation, and where the government was not bound by the Enabling Act which bound the other colonies, no referendum was held; in New South Wales the Bill was approved by a small majority of the electors who voted, but the affirmative vote fell short of the 80,000 minimum (about thirty per cent of the electorate) which had been made necessary for acceptance by an amendment of the Enabling Act forced by the Labour Party during the second adjournment of the Convention. The implication was that New South Welshmen were unhappy about joining the federation unless the Constitution Bill was amended.

Though this was technically the end of the matter, federation had too much support, even in New South Wales, for the whole project to be allowed to die: Reid proposed the holding of a Premiers' conference to consider the Bill's amendment and re-submission to referendum. This was an obvious course, but the more enthusiastic federalists, in New South Wales and in the other colonies, blamed Reid's 'yes-no policy' rather than the defects of the draft constitution for its failure; moreover an election was due in New South Wales, and Barton, the devoted federalist, had assumed the leadership of the opposition; he was able to persuade the Premiers to refuse to meet Reid, holding out to them the prospect of being able to negotiate after the election with a supporter rather than a critic of the Bill. The election campaign was essentially a re-fighting of the issues of the referendum. Reid put up a policy of seven proposed amendments; Barton agreed to ask for the most important three of Reid's points. Reid, though his large majority was heavily cut, won clearly: the other Premiers were thus forced to meet him, and he was in a strong bargaining position.

The Premiers met in Melbourne in January 1899 and agreed on two vital amendments, to replace the three-fifths majority clause by one requiring merely an absolute majority at a joint sitting and to restrict the operation of the Braddon guarantee to a period of ten years. Reid was unable to persuade his fellows to meet his objections to the trade-and-commerce clauses, but they agreed to have the federal capital placed in New South Wales, at least a hundred miles from Sydney, as compensation. The conference also revised the requirements for future constitutional amendment. The draft provided that an amendment should require approval by an overall majority of electors and a majority in a majority of States at a popular referendum, after approval by both Houses of Parliament. It was now agreed that if one House refused to accept an amendment proposal it could still be put to referendum on being passed a second time by the other Chamber. This was seen in New

South Wales as a democratic reform, a reduction in the conservative influence of the Upper House. In an effort to attract Queensland into the federation, the conference agreed to make in its case an exception to the rule that for Senate elections each State was to be considered as a unit: this small concession seemed likely to remove one of the obstacles to acceptance of the Bill, fear by northern sectionalists that only southerners would win Queensland Senate seats. The changes made at Melbourne represented to New South Wales a very considerable improvement. In the one area where Reid was unable to get the improvements he wanted, New South Welsh fears were to prove groundless: a drafting fault prevented the Interstate Commission from carrying out the functions intended for it and led to its eventual abolition, and the river-boat traffic quickly succumbed to its own economic weakness.

The agreements made at the conference converted Reid, and the large body of voters who clearly shared his opinions, to warm support of the Bill. He agreed to put it to referendum in its new form, and, as has been seen (p. 76), when intransigent opponents entrenched in the Legislative Council tried to prevent his doing so, he had them swamped. The Bill was endorsed in New South Wales on 20 June 1899; it had already been accepted in South Australia, and in July it received enormous popular majorities in Victoria and Tasmania. The Queensland government put it to referendum successfully in October; Western Australia remained aloof, but that colony, though vast in area, was too small in population to prevent the consummation of the federal movement.

One obstacle only remained to federation of at least of two-thirds of the continent, the British government's possible disapproval of some sections of the draft constitution—in particular S.74, which provided that the High Court of Australia would be the court of final appeal in all cases except those affecting other parts of the empire. Though it was not generally known that the Colonial Office had already, working privately through Reid, had some influence on the shape of the Bill, it was realized that British mercantile and shipping interests might be unhappy about the abolition of Privy Council appeals and that, more importantly, the Secretary of State for the Colonies, Joseph Chamberlain, looked upon the Privy Council appeal as an imperial link worth preserving. The colonial Parliaments passed an address to the Queen praying for the enactment of the 'Commonwealth of Australia Constitution Bill' by the imperial Parliament. At the British government's invitation, delegates were sent to London to 'assist and explain' while the Bill was being considered, but when Chamberlain proposed an amendment to the offending clause they protested vigorously. The Secretary of State tried to compromise; the delegates replied that they had no power to negotiate on a constitution which had been accepted at a referendum; but in the end a bargain was struck. It was agreed that no appeal was to go to London on cases affecting the respective powers of Commonwealth and States ('*inter se* cases') or on cases involving disputes between States, except by leave of the High Court; the right of appeal to the Privy Council in other cases was to be preserved, but the federal Parliament might, subject to the reservation of its Bills on the matter for the Royal Assent in London, legislate in the future to restrict further the appeal from decisions of the High Court. (Appeals as of right from the High Court in all constitutional cases were abolished in 1968. Other appeals from the High Court were blocked by further legislation in the early 1970s, leaving possible only appeals direct from State courts in matters of State law.)

Two other matters were also settled by the delegates and Chamberlain. New Zealand, which had taken no effective part in the federal movement since 1891, sought to keep her options open by asking that Parliament amend the draft constitution to allow her to enter later, with the right of equal representation in the Senate, a right accorded automatically only to an original State; not surprisingly this request was refused. Western Australia also petitioned for an amendment to allow her, as a condition of joining, to impose full interstate customs duties for five years afterwards. While there was some sympathy for the view that the colony's financial problems would not be solved by the special concession for Western Australia which the draft contained, the privilege of tapering off her interstate customs over five years, an attempt to obtain by imperial fiat what had not been gained in negotiations could hardly be entertained. Western Australia was given the choice of accepting the Constitution as it stood or remaining outside the new Commonwealth.

In fact the West Australian government was clearly out of step with popular opinion. The people of the goldfields, largely eastern in origin and sentiment, and strongly hostile to the political domination of the south-west and to the mining laws, even petitioned the Crown for separation from the colony and incorporation in the Commonwealth. While there was little likelihood that the Colonial Office under Chamberlain would be sympathetic to this 'separation for federation' movement, such a vehement gesture from a group whose treatment was already being compared with that of the 'outlanders' in the Transvaal was bound to influence the Perth government, which was also well aware of the advantages offered to an original State. In Western Australia's case these included not only equal representation in the Senate but also a guarantee of a minimum Lower House representation of five, greater than that to which population would entitle the State, as well as the transitional tariff privilege. It decided to put the Bill to referendum in August 1900. A large affirmative vote ensured that when the Commonwealth of Australia came into being on the first day of the twentieth century there was indeed 'a nation for a continent and a continent for a nation.'

CHAPTER SIX

Interpreting the Federal Constitution

'I do not care in what way you frame the Constitution, the people of Australia will mould and modify it in accordance with their ideas and sentiments for the moment, although the outward form may remain the same.'

SIR RICHARD BAKER (1891)

'Whoever hath an absolute authority to interpret any written or spoken laws, it is he who is truly the lawgiver to all intents and purposes, and not the person who first wrote or spoke them.'

BISHOP BENJAMIN HOADLY

The Problem of Formal Amendment

On 1 January 1901, at an impressive ceremony in Centennial Park Sydney, the Earl of Hopetoun was installed as the first Governor-General of the Commonwealth and proceeded to swear in his ministry. Later the same day R.R. Garran, who had already been appointed by the attorney-general designate, Alfred Deakin, as permanent head of his department, drew up the first issue of the *Commonwealth Gazette*. In later years Sir Robert used to like to recall that, being 'both head and tail of the department', he wrote out the document in longhand and took it down to the printer himself. The Commonwealth was legally in existence, if only, like Garran's *Gazette*, on paper. There was a cabinet, headed by Edmund Barton; there was a Constitution; but the machinery of government had to be constructed from the ground up, out of materials partly taken over from the States and partly quite new; and the Constitution had to be made to work. Few people at the time realized how elaborate the machinery would eventually become: most based their expectations on the federalist argument of 1899 that its annual cost to the taxpayer would be no more than that of a dog licence. Few also, perhaps, realized that the Constitution would not work automatically, and that making it work would involve moulding it to future needs—that, as R.B. Haldane had observed while it was before the imperial Parliament, it provided a 'mere framework' which would have to be filled in 'with traditions and doctrines . . . , with tendencies which are not expressed'.

The founding fathers had built into the Constitution two devices by which it could be moulded. There was provision in S.51 (xxxvii) for the

State parliaments to 'refer' to the Commonwealth legislative powers which seemed at the time of drafting best left with them, but which might appear to future generations more appropriately federal; and there was an amendment procedure requiring an alteration to be accepted at a referendum by an overall majority and majorities in more than half the States. Neither device was to succeed in giving the Constitution the flexibility intended. It has since become clear that the difficulty of getting the unanimous agreement of six separate legislatures limits the use of 'reference' to the solution of temporary problems concerning particular States: the one attempt to use it seriously, in 1942–43, was to prove a fiasco. At first there seemed to be more to be expected from the 'double referendum'. In Switzerland, the source of the scheme, it had been (and continued to be) used with success; and on the first two occasions when it was used by the Commonwealth, in 1906 and 1910, the acceptance by the electors of amendment proposals seemed to suggest that it could prevent the Constitution from becoming too rigid. This was certainly the impression of W.M. Hughes, attorney-general in the Labour government which came to office in April 1910. But the first amendment had done no more than tidy up an anomaly concerning the date of Senate elections, and the second, authorizing the Commonwealth to take over State debts contracted since federation in addition to those existing in 1900, was less important than a proposal to write into the Constitution a new financial arrangement with the States, which was defeated. When the government asked in 1911 for a considerable augmentation in Commonwealth power the electors returned an emphatic 'no'. A similar proposal was rejected two years later, and another one, more modest, in 1919. It was becoming clear that the referendum gave the Australian Constitution much less flexibility than the Swiss, and the experience of the first twenty years in this matter was to be repeated over the next fifty-seven.

In this period the Constitution was to be formally amended on four occasions. In 1929 an amendment was made to render enforceable the 1927 Financial Agreement (which is discussed in Chapter Seven). After World War II the Commonwealth's power to confer social security benefits was put beyond doubt. In 1967 some references to Aborigines which had come to be seen as offensive were removed. And in 1977 three amendments were accepted: they conferred on residents of federal territories the right to vote at future referendums; provided for the compulsory retirement of federal judges at the age of seventy; and restricted the discretion of State Parliaments in the filling of casual Senate vacancies by providing that a replacement senator must be chosen from the same political party as his predecessor (see p. 166). But many more proposals were rejected in the same period. Since 1901 nearly a hundred separate proposals for amending the Constitution have been considered by the federal Parliament, and thirty-seven have actually come before the electors. The failure of all but eight, only one of which was overtly intended to add significantly to Commonwealth legislative powers, suggests a degree of rigidity in the Australian Constitution quite remarkable even by the normal standards of federal systems.

Since most of the amendment proposals have originated from the well-known policies of popularly-elected governments, the unwillingness of Australians to ratify them requires some explanation. It happens that, because there are only six States, a majority of them is in fact a two-thirds majority, and it might be thought that this can help to account for the failure of so many proposals; but in fact only two of the twenty-nine that have been rejected (both of them in 1946) failed with an overall popular majority and the States evenly divided; two others (one in 1937 and one in 1977) were rejected four States to two despite affirmative majorities overall. The rest have all failed at the popular level. It also seems unlikely that many have failed because the electors have deliberately decided that a particular power sought by the Commonwealth is one more properly exercised by the States. Two other factors are much more significant. The first is the tendency for the individual elector, in an age when government impinges more and more on ordinary life, to resent the expansion of governmental powers—federal or State—and a 'no' vote in a referendum can be an excellent catharsis for resentment, whether it has any practical impact on the growth of 'bureaucracy' or not. The second stems from the fact that a proposal to increase Commonwealth powers (and the vast majority of rejected proposals have been in this class) has behind it a political purpose. In most cases the policy likely to be enacted in the event of the proposal's acceptance has been one to which the opposition in Parliament has been hostile, and so opposition supporters have voted 'no' almost automatically. The operation of both these factors has been strengthened by the Australian's remarkable distrust of, even contempt for, his elected representatives. As Professor J.D.B. Miller has remarked,

> At a referendum a voter gets ... an opportunity to hit at ... politicians as such; he is not bound to choose between persons and policies to the same extent as at a general election, but he is able to express his cynicism by simply declining to give politicians what they want.

What is more difficult to explain is the difference in attitude between States. Tasmania, the State which gave the strongest proportional support to the federal plan in 1898 and 1899, has since voted consistently against any increase in Commonwealth powers, while Queensland, in which federal sentiment in the 1890s was at best equivocal, and Western Australia, which wavered about joining to the last moment and which asked to be allowed to secede in 1933, have voted in favour of such increase in approximately three cases out of four. Comparative size and wealth give no better clue than pre-federation voting patterns to these different records. There remains here an element of mystery.

That a scheme of government framed in the 1890s should have survived into the 1970s, weathering two world wars, the depression of the 1930s and the twentieth-century technological revolution with quite marginal formal alteration, is a tribute to the skill of the founders; it is also a reminder that reference of powers by the States and amendment by referendum are not the only ways in which that basic scheme can be effectively modified. One can ignore, as quite unrealistic, the theoretical possibility that, as part of a British Statute, it might be amended by the British Parliament; but there proved to be several other means of filling in its 'mere framework'.

Two are quite obvious. First, an ordinary Act is sufficient to deal with a number of matters, including franchise, electoral laws, privileges of Parliament and judicial appeals, where particular sections of the Constitution are prefaced by the words 'Until Parliament otherwise provides'. Secondly, the Commonwealth was not obliged to enter immediately (or at all) most of the fields it was entitled to enter. In the case of nearly all the matters listed in the thirty-odd *placita* of S.51 there were already in existence State laws which continued in force until the Commonwealth acted to supersede them. On 1 January 1901 only customs and excise passed automatically under federal control; posts and telegraphs and defence were taken over two months later; most of the other fields were effectively occupied in the next few years, though such an obvious matter as the control of lighthouses was not dealt with by federal legislation until 1911 and by federal executive action until 1915; a federal Bankruptcy Act was not passed until 1924, and the Commonwealth did not take up its 'dormant powers' over marriage and divorce until the 1960s. With each new assumption of federal authority an important change occurred in the pattern of government without any textual change in the Constitution. And the exercise of dormant powers has been complemented by the use of what can perhaps be called 'dubious powers'. A federal law (or, for that matter, a State law) is presumed to be valid until challenged and proved *ultra vires*, outside the authority of the legislature: it is inevitable that in any federal system there will be areas of dubious authority, and if no one who can show the courts that he is adversely affected by the operation of a law in one of these fields is concerned to challenge it, the law will remain in force. The Commonwealth was thus able to establish after the First World War a Repatriation Commission and a War Service Homes Commission, which could not be covered by the defence power without a great effort of imagination; in 1926, with absolutely no authority from S.51, it was able to establish the Council for Scientific and Industrial Research (which in 1949 became the CSIRO); and after the Second World War it ramified into a wide variety of social and educational activities, and even, through the Snowy Mountains Scheme, into water conservation.

Probably only a State attorney-general would be recognized as having the 'standing' necessary to challenge the federal government's right to act in most of these fields, and in many cases for a minister to make such a challenge would be politically dangerous as well as economically foolish.

The acquiescence by the States in such benign extensions of federal power suggests consideration of another important means by which the working constitution was to be altered, the growth of Commonwealth-State co-operation. This has taken several forms. There were, as will be seen (p. 174), financial agreements between the federal government and the States in 1909-10, 1927 and 1959; and the use by the Commonwealth of S.96, which provides that 'the Parliament may grant financial assistance to any State on such terms and conditions as the Parliament thinks fit', was to prove an important agent of functional change. Other forms, discussed in Chapter Eight, such as the use of the States as agents of Commonwealth policy, and the passage by the Commonwealth and a State or States of complementary legislation, were to be equally significant.

The development of the Australian Constitution was, then, to be continuous, and indeed organic; but such development had always to be related to a written document. Regulating the relationship was the task of a court of law. As in the United States of America, the history of the Constitution was to be largely, if not exclusively, a history of judicial review. Changing interpretations and emphases were to be of critical importance in moulding the Constitution to the needs of the future, and in the process of judicial review the primary role was to be that of the High Court of Australia, which came into existence in October 1903. At that time appeal was possible from its decisions to the Judicial Committee of the Privy Council, except, as was pointed out at the end of the last chapter, in cases involving the powers of the Commonwealth and States *inter se*; in which appeal was only possible by leave of the High Court itself. But the scope of the questions covered by the '*inter se* concept' was always very wide, and the Privy Council decided in 1917 that it should be interpreted to include virtually all cases involving the extent of Commonwealth powers. On only one occasion, in a 1912 case in which the decision was made by the narrowest possible margin, has leave been given on an *inter se* matter. Some important questions, particularly those concerning such specific constitutional prohibitions as the notorious S.92 (see p. 178), continued to be appealable until 1968, but with the notable exception of the S.92 cases, where the Privy Council's decisions only served to confuse further an already confused issue, the credit and the blame for the judicial development of the Australian Constitution belongs to the High Court.

As will appear in what follows, the Court has served the country well. The legalism which A.V. Dicey saw as the essence of federalism has been tempered on the High Court Bench by a certain pragmatism, a willingness to recognize, if not political considerations in the narrow sense, at least the climate of national opinion and the dominant values of society. Some of the decisions of the Court have been open to criticism on commonsense grounds, but it has not shrunk from over-ruling such decisions later. Perhaps, in some cases, it would have done better to accept Justice Holmes' *dictum* that in interpreting a Constitution a page of history is worth a volume of logic, and to use the evidence of the federal Convention debates in deciding the meaning of particular clauses, which from the first it refused to do: but this would not have solved all the problems that have arisen, and might well have given rise to others.

Adapting the Constitution: the Role of the High Court

It was inevitable that in the first decade or so after federation many questions involving the working of the federal system would arise. Some of these were issues between the Commonwealth and the States which were not capable of judicial solution. They were less questions about specific aspects of the division of power than conflicts originating in the temperamental difficulty experienced by State leaders in coming to terms with a new government which, however limited its powers might have appeared to be, had the prestige associated with being national. In 1901 many front-rank politicians chose to transfer to the federal sphere: those who did not naturally reacted by seeking to emphasise the importance of the States, and their reaction was strengthened by their consciousness, in all except Western Australia, of a long tradition of autonomy. Some of the State Premiers of these early years, and particularly J.H. Carruthers of New South Wales, went out of their way to be uncooperative, even at times to obstruct the Commonwealth's efforts to establish its own governmental machinery. Carruthers went so far as to prevent the distinguished New South Wales government statistician, T.A. Coghlan, from accepting the appointment of Commonwealth statistician, by threatening to deprive him of accumulated pension rights. One of Carruthers' successors, the Labour leader W.A. Holman, justified obstructive behaviour as an attempt to rectify the consequences of a federation for which he claimed to be unable to see any purpose. 'I have always been deeply dubious', he said in 1909, 'and at this day, after ten years, I do not see any function worth speaking of carried out by the Federal parliament that could not have been performed by a mere customs and military union among the States'. Holman became the architect of an attempt to make a regular system of Premier's conferences, convened and provided with a Secretariat by his State, a real if informal check on federal power. As late as 1916 he tried unsuccessfully to get the federal government to accept a procedure whereby the Commonwealth would only approach the States through 'the executive officer' of the Premiers' conference, Holman himself! Carruthers and Holman were extremists in these matters, but the co-operation of all the States with the Commonwealth in the years before the First World War, even in such vital co-operative fields as health and quarantine, was often very reluctant.

State resentments were aggravated by the policy of the Colonial Office with regard to communications between London and the States. In 1901 Chamberlain directed that, while State governors would still be able to communicate directly with the Office, copies of all despatches should go to the Governor-General. The States protested and he then agreed that only matters of 'general interest' need be so treated, leaving this rather vague term undefined. In most matters Downing Street found it more sensible to deal with one government than with seven, but the Premiers' very different view was demonstrated when in 1902 they declined invitations to Edward VII's coronation which were transmitted through the Governor-General.

By this time a sharp dispute on the issue had begun. In August 1901 at Port Adelaide some crew members of a Dutch merchant vessel, *Vondel*, struck work and deserted the ship; the master asked the State authorities to act against them in terms of a convention of 1856 between Britain and the Netherlands which bound the colonies, but the South Australian government, perhaps because of some public sympathy for the men, used a legal technicality to refuse co-operation. In due course a protest was made to the British government, and the Colonial Office asked the Governor-General to report on the matter. Deakin, who as acting Prime Minister was the Governor-General's responsible adviser, wrote to the Premier of South Australia for information—which the State government refused to give, offering instead to report to the Secretary of State through the Lieutenant-Governor of South Australia. The dispute dragged on for a long time, partly because the Commonwealth was anxious to assert its supremacy in any matter involving external affairs, partly because of clumsy handling in Downing Street, and partly because of State sensitivity to federal 'interference' in such a domestic issue as the behaviour of the police in a particular case. The State seems to have had the better legal argument, for what was involved was not the relationship of Australia as a whole to a foreign power but the duty of a State to enforce the terms of an *imperial* commercial treaty by which it was bound. But in the end Chamberlain insisted that in such matters Australia should be treated as one country. The case itself was trivial enough, but the final Colonial Office decision was important as one of the first stages in the long process of the growth of Commonwealth power at the expense of the States. Two more cases, in 1905 and 1906, both involving claims by Australians for compensation from foreign governments, reinforced the decision in the *Vondel* affair. In both of them a State government took upon itself to approach London for redress, without consulting the Commonwealth, but the imperial government was careful to maintain the primacy of federal responsibility and to uphold the principle that where their rights as British subjects were concerned Australians were always to be considered as Australians, not as Queenslanders or New South Welshmen.

The Colonial Office was little more sympathetic to State pretensions on other, related issues. One of these, concerning the respective rights of the Governor-General and the State Governor when permission was sought to land men from visiting foreign naval vessels, where imperial paramountcy in foreign affairs was mixed up with Commonwealth responsibility for defence and State responsibility for internal order, was debated from 1907 to 1911 before the imperial government finally imposed a settlement largely in accordance with Commonwealth views. Perhaps more importantly, a claim by the States to representation at the Imperial Conference was rejected by the Secretary of State, though he agreed that they should be consulted if any issue affecting them closely came up for discussion. In one matter only, the conferring of honours, did the States get their way. Their recommendations were to be transmitted through the Governor-General, but his advisers were not allowed to influence decision on them—even on a K.C.M.G. for Carruthers at a time when it might have appeared as a gesture of imperial sympathy for his obstreperous behaviour. By 1911 the Colonial Office had worked out procedures which, while leaving the States independent of Commonwealth control in matters obviously of exclusive State concern, defined the phrase 'general interest' very widely indeed.

While questions such as these were being fought out politically, others more amenable to judicial process were arising. Their decision was influenced greatly by the intellectual outlook of the men who made up the first bench of the High Court of Australia: Sir Samuel Griffith C.J., former Chief Justice of Queensland; Edmund Barton, who went to the Bench from the Prime Ministership; and R.E. O'Connor. All had taken important parts in the federal movement. Griffith was the virtual author of the 1891 draft constitution, which, as has been remarked, provided the basic framework of the document accepted in 1899; Barton had been the leader of the second Convention; O'Connor had served as what can best be described as Barton's chief of staff. All were men of conservative temper. More importantly, all held the view that a federal system embodies a balance between the central and the State governments which needs to be carefully maintained. They were all students of American federalism and believed that there existed what Griffith called a 'strong presumption' that the Constitution was designed to be interpreted within the framework of the United States tradition of judicial review as it stood in the 1890s: accordingly they were ready to use American precedents and doctrines.

They were to find, however, that these were not always perfectly reliable guides, and that one American principle in particular was difficult to follow with consistency. This was the doctrine of 'implied immunity of instrumentalities', the idea, originating like so much of the legal ·dogma of federalism in the United States Supreme Court's judgement in *McCulloch* v. *Maryland* (1819) and most clearly stated by the same court in 1871 in *Collector* v. *Day*, that it is deducible from the very nature of the federal system that the federal authority must not interfere with the activities of the States, or the States with federal activities, in any way. After some preliminary sparring in *Wollaston's Case* before the Victorian Supreme Court prior to the establishment of the High Court, the question whether there did exist an obligation of 'mutual non-interference' came before the Bench over a penny duty stamp. Commonwealth accounting practice required public servants to sign a receipt for their salary payments; the Tasmanian government required receipts to be stamped; a senior Commonwealth public servant in Tasmania refused to pay the State duty and the High Court ruled, in *D'Emden* v. *Pedder* (1904), that his refusal was justified by the necessary implications of federalism. It then proceeded, in *Deakin and Lyne* v. *Webb* and *Commonwealth* v. *New South Wales*, to hold that the States could neither tax federal salaries nor impose duties on documents transferring land to the Commonwealth, and, in *Municipal Council of Sydney* v. *Commonwealth*, to exempt federal buildings from local rates.

The question of income tax was a serious one for the States. The government of Victoria sought leave to appeal to the Privy Council on *Deakin and Lyne* v. *Webb*, and when this was refused, raised another case in the State Supreme Court and appealed direct from the expected adverse decision to the Privy Council, by-passing the High Court. In 1907 the Privy Council handed down a decision opposite to that of the High Court in the earlier cases, but later the same year the High Court declined to accept the argument that it was bound for the future by this decision (*Webb* v. *Outtrim*) because the matter was one over which the Constitution gave it final authority. To clear up this untidy state of affairs the federal government, at Griffith's suggestion, provided in an amendment to the Judiciary Act that if any *inter se* matter was in future raised before a State court the case should immediately be removed to the High Court: it thus closed up the loophole which had been used to get *Webb* v. *Outtrim* to London. Although it also legislated to allow the States to collect reasonable (that is, non-discriminatory) taxes from federal officers, the Commonwealth was now fully protected against interference by the States.

The States·were also, it seemed, protected. In 1906 in the *Railway Servants' Case* the High Court held that an award of the Commonwealth Arbitration Court could not bind State railway commissioners. But there were problems. Were the States bound by federal import regulations? If they were not, would not the control of foreign trade by the Commonwealth for which the Constitution provided be nullified? If they were, would they be liable to pay duty on goods they imported, notwithstanding S.114 which forbids the Commonwealth to 'impose any tax on property of any kind belonging to a State'? These questions, the bases of the *Steel Rails* and *Wire Netting* cases, were to prove very difficult to answer.

In the middle of 1903, before the establishment of the High Court, the New South Wales Supreme Court entered a verdict for the State in an action in which a refund was sought of duties charged it on the import of steel rails for its railways. The Commonwealth, however, refused to regard the action as a test case and continued to insist that State governments should obtain ordinary customs clearances, which meant, where goods were dutiable, paying the tariff. The Premiers protested repeatedly that the Commonwealth should either accept the New South Wales court's decision, or appeal. Finally, the egregious Carruthers took the law into his own hands: in August 1907 he sent a body of carters with a police escort to remove from a wharf at Darling Harbour some 1500 rolls of wire netting, which had been imported on government account for the use of rabbit-harassed farmers, but for which no clearance had been obtained. Most had been taken before the Collector of Customs, acting on instructions from Melbourne, marched in a body of clerks to prevent the removal of the rest by sitting on it. The next day another shipment of steel rails arrived, and the Customs Department refused to allow it to be unloaded from the ship until duty was paid. The 'Battle of Darling Harbour' at least brought matters to a head. The Commonwealth took action over the 'seizure' of the wire and the State over the detention of the rails. The decision in both cases, handed down in May 1908, was for the federal government. Implied immunity did not, apparently, give the States such strong protection as it gave the Commonwealth.

Mr Justice O'Connor provided an explanation for the Bench's flexibility (or inconsistency) in the fact that the Australian federal system gave the Commonwealth powers which it must be allowed to exercise freely: 'Wherever it is necessary for an effective exercise of Commonwealth power that a State power should be restricted, it must be taken that the Constitution intended that it should be reserved to the State in that restricted form'. This was a reasonable enough justification for relaxing the implied immunity doctrine, which, as Professor Sawer has pointed out, 'had the flexibility of all judge-made rules'. But there was the complicating factor of S.114. To get past this the Bench resorted to an ingenious if unconvincing piece of casuistry: a customs duty is not a tax on property but a tax on the act of importing, and therefore not covered by the section. In fact, the justification for the decisions had little to do with their motivation, which was purely pragmatic and depended to a considerable extent on the Court's unwillingness to allow implied immunity to give State-government trading activities advantages not enjoyed by private trading concerns. In Sawer's words,

> The Court was now aghast at the way in which a trading State government could nullify exclusive federal control of import policy, if State governments were held free to disregard Commonwealth customs laws. The decision was pure, if in the circumstances necessary, 'judicial legislation'.

Implied immunity was, then, serving to maintain that 'balance' which Griffith, Barton and O'Connor sought, but it was an untidy and unstable balance, and one with which Justices Isaacs and Higgins, who joined them on the Bench in 1906, were far from happy. Higgins in particular had been a critic of this American doctrine while still in Parliament. Even less did he like another in which his senior brethren placed great faith (greater indeed than did the United States Supreme Court) the doctrine of implied prohibitions. Shortly after handing down the *Wire Netting* and *Steel Rails* judgements the majority of the Court used this principle as the basis of a decision with much more immediate effect, for it seriously hindered the execution of a policy with overwhelming popular support.

This was the 'new protection'. Adumbrated in Victoria in the 1890s and adopted by both the Deakinite liberals and the Labour Party in the early years of federation, this policy aimed to ensure that industries enjoying tariff protection should pass on its benefits to their employees. One of the consequences of the new protection was the Excise Tariff Act of 1906. This, *inter alia*, imposed on locally-produced agricultural machinery an excise equal to the tariff on imported machines which would be waived for manufacturers who provided fair and reasonable conditions of employment for their workers. The Commonwealth Arbitration Court ruled that the conditions provided by two harvester firms were not fair and reasonable and the government took action to collect the excise. The first case, *King* v. *Barger*, was decided in June 1908. The High Court ruled, by a three-two majority (Higgins and Isaacs dissenting), that the 'excise-plus-exemption' method of carrying out the new protection was invalid. The majority held that the Commonwealth Parliament was implicitly prohibited by the nature of the federal compact from using its right to impose taxes in order to regulate conditions of employment, which did not come under any specific head of Commonwealth power. In another case, *Union Label*, the same year the doctrine was used to strike down a section of the Trade Marks Act which provided for the registration of labels indicating that goods were made by trade unionists.

Although the supporters of the new protection were disappointed by the invalidation of the Excise Tariff Act, the adoption by the senior justices of the implied prohibitions doctrine is easier to understand than their use of implied immunity. Mr Justice Else-Mitchell later argued that, if the Higgins-Isaacs view had prevailed in *King v. Barger*, 'it would have been difficult to set any limits to Commonwealth legislative power' for the Commonwealth would have been able 'to impose a prohibitive tax on any acts or transactions whatever which the Parliament wished to discourage'. And most of the social objectives sought by the Excise Tariff Act could be achieved by other methods, such as the payment of conditional bounties. A nationalist might agree with Higgins's view that, 'Unless . . . it becomes clear beyond reasonable doubt that the legislation in question transgresses the limits laid down by the organic law of the Constitution, it must be allowed to stand as the true expression of the national will'. But Griffith, Barton and O'Connor were federalists rather than nationalists, and it can be said for the implied prohibitions doctrine that it did not present the same difficulties in consistent application as implied immunity. And if it lent itself to the narrow view of Commonwealth power which they favoured (and which they were to take in other cases where the doctrine itself had no application) the Court was able to use a third American doctrine to justify its actions when World War I presented it with the need to take a wider view.

This was the doctrine of implied powers, the *dictum* of Chief Justice Marshall: 'Let the end be legitimate, let it be within the scope of the Constitution, and all means which are plainly adapted to that end, which are not prohibited, but consistent with the letter and spirit of the Constitution, are constitutional'. In 1916 an order was made under the War Precautions Acts fixing the price of bread. One Farey, convicted of selling bread above the fixed price, challenged the validity of the order and the Act on which it was based. The Bench, altered in composition by the death of O'Connor and the appointment of Justices Powers, Rich and Gavan Duffy, found by a majority of five to two (Rich and Gavan Duffy dissenting) that both were valid exercises of the defence power. The Chief Justice and Barton did not necessarily agree with Isaacs that any measure which might 'conceivably . . . even incidentally, aid the effectuation of the power of defence' should be sustained, but they concurred in the view that the duty to make laws for 'The naval and military defence of the Commonwealth' implied a power to pass and enforce laws reasonably connected with the purpose of winning the war. The judgement in *Farey* v. *Burvett* was to be of enormous importance in the remaining years of the war, and during World War II; and in combination with the specific constitutional provision for a valid federal law to prevail over a State law inconsistent with it, the doctrine of implied powers was, as will be seen in Chapter Eight, to provide some grounds for believing that the Commonwealth could use its responsibility for external affairs to regulate a number of matters apparently within the control of the States.

Such an expansive interpretation of federal powers was not typical of the High Court in the first two decades of the Commonwealth's existence. Indeed, in some matters its interpretation of them was very narrow even by the standards which its acceptance of implied prohibitions imposed on it. This was particularly so in regard to S.51 (xx), which authorized the federal Parliament 'to make laws for the peace, order and good government of the Commonwealth with respect to ... Foreign corporations, and trading or financial corporations formed within the limits of the Commonwealth'. In 1906 Isaacs, then attorney-general in the second Deakin government, sought to use this *placitum* as the basis for an anti-monopoly law, the Australian Industries Preservation Act, but in 1908, on the Bench, he was alone in dissenting from the ruling in *Huddart Parker* v. *Moorehead* which struck the Act down. The majority decision, that S.51 (xx) was solely a power with regard to corporations and not a power over monopoly practices (which might conceivably be adopted by unincorporated commercial operators) and so could not be used to extend the Commonwealth's quite distinct power over interstate trade to cover *intra*-State business as well, was, as H.S. Nicholas later remarked, 'one of the surprises of litigation'. Until 1971 this piece of logic-chopping was to serve as a very serious restriction on governmental power in Australia—for there was little practical possibility of the States being able to occupy a field thus closed to the Commonwealth. The Court also took a very narrow view of the *placitum* which dealt with 'Conciliation and arbitration for the prevention and settlement of industrial disputes extending beyond the limits of any one State': In 1910 it declared void a section of the Conciliation and Arbitration Act which purported to give the Arbitration Court power to make a 'common rule' for wages and working conditions to apply throughout an industry, and so restricted that body to dealing with disputes in the narrowest sense. However, despite strong objections from Barton and Griffith, there was some retreat from this position in 1913, and by 1925 the making of a common rule had become, in practice if not in theory, possible.

By the time of World War I it had become clear that the attitude of the justices of the High Court was to play a vital role in the operation of the Australian federal system, and that since 1906 there had been what amounted to a schism on the Bench. The difference between Griffith, Barton and O'Connor on the one hand, and Higgins and Isaacs on the other had, as Sawer has remarked, 'a political significance which to some extent corresponded with the temperament of the Justices'. The majority view led, in such cases as *King* v. *Barger*, *Union Label* and *Huddart Parker* v. *Moorehead*, to the invalidation of 'radical' measures, 'but left State socialism exposed to the federal customs power' in the *Wire Netting* and *Steel Rails* cases. 'The minority view would not only have upheld radical measures, but would have extended the powers of a central government more likely, as electoral laws then stood, to come under the sway of left-wing majorities.' The addition to the Bench in 1913 of three men who had not taken part in the federal movement, and were therefore less subject to doctrinaire views of federalism, prevented the schism from becoming a scandal. And as it turned out the tenor of the judgements of at least Powers and Rich favoured the expansion rather than the contraction of Commonwealth power: in the long run the 'balance' which the senior justices had sought to maintain was to be tilted in a nationalist, if not a radical, direction.

The Establishment of Commonwealth Primacy

That balance had begun to tilt even in the period during which the Griffith view was dominant on the Bench, as a consequence of the Constitution's financial clauses. These left the States in a much weaker position *vis à vis* the Commonwealth than many people had realized they would. The Commonwealth's monopoly of what had been before federation the principal source of colonial revenue, customs and excise, was absolute, but S.87 (the 'Braddon clause') guaranteed the States a particular share of this for only ten years. Thereafter the guarantee would continue for no longer than the federal Parliament might decide. It was generally believed, however, that the Commonwealth would not need even the one-fourth share to which it was temporarily restricted, and the Constitution made provision for the distribution of any surplus. There were short-term, 'bookkeeping' arrangements in Ss.89 and 93, and S.94 provided that 'After five years from the imposition of uniform duties of customs, the Parliament may provide, on such basis as it deems fair, for the monthly payment to the several States of all surplus revenue of the Commonwealth'; the States therefore expected much more than the amount guaranteed in the first ten years, and thought that even at the end of this period S.94 would continue to ensure them a reasonable share. They were wrong. In 1908 the Deakin government, anxious to build up reserves to guarantee the payment of old-age pensions, which were to begin the next year, put through a Surplus Revenue Act which provided for the institution of trust accounts into which any federal funds not otherwise appropriated might be paid. This allowed the Commonwealth to retain all its income except for the share of the customs proceeds temporarily guaranteed to the States by the Braddon clause. A challenge to the validity of the Act failed, and S.94 became a dead letter.

Coming when it did, just as the Braddon guarantee was about to expire, this was a severe shock to the States: here was an ill omen for the success of negotiations which had begun as early as 1903 for a financial agreement which might replace that guarantee. In 1905 the Premiers had apparently thought that they could persuade the federal government to agree to its indefinite extension, or to some substantially similar arrangement, possibly including transfer to the Commonwealth of State debts. The Commonwealth for its part, faced with the necessity of paying for its steadily growing activities, and finding its own fiscal style cramped by the guarantee to return a fixed proportion of its main revenue source, was prepared to offer much less. Constitutionally it had the whip hand, but the realities of politics dictated a compromise. Deakin had only recently ousted a short-lived Labour administration by bringing about a fusion of the old protectionist and free-trade groups, and he was anxious lest too harsh a line with the Premiers should split the 'Fusion' party's precarious unity. No agreement was made on the difficult question of State debts (though Deakin was prepared to ask for an enlargement of the Commonwealth's power to take them over in the future). But the Prime Minister agreed to propose a constitutional amendment replacing the Braddon clause with one binding the Commonwealth to pay the States twenty-five shillings per head of population per annum. The agreement was not ratified by the electors, but when the Labour Party came to power after the April 1910 election the new Fisher government sponsored an ordinary Act to make it the basis of payments to the States for ten years and thereafter until Parliament might decide. In the upshot it remained in operation until 1927. The Commonwealth also agreed to meet the particular problems of Western Australia, problems which that sparsely settled, primary-producing State blamed on a fiscal policy designed to protect the secondary industries of the east, by making use of S.96 of the Constitution which authorizes the federal Parliament to 'grant financial assistance to any State on such terms and conditions as the Parliament thinks fit'. In 1912 Tasmania began receiving similar assistance.

From the States' point of view the new arrangement had the advantage that they could depend for at least ten years on a revenue from the Commonwealth which would rise with population. But most of the advantages were on the side of the Commonwealth. The guarantee it gave was for a strictly limited time; it no longer had to consider the reimbursement question when deciding on means of raising revenue, as it had been forced to do while the States' guarantee was tied to customs income; the amount of twenty-five shillings per head was less than it had been paying under the Braddon clause immediately before the agreement—but of course its responsibilities were growing. The 1910 settlement made the States dependent upon the Commonwealth for a substantial part of their revenue with no guarantee that that part would not be suddenly cut off in 1920.

Moreover the Commonwealth now began using its concurrent as well as its exclusive taxing powers: it moved into fields of direct taxation which in the first decade of its existence it had left to the States. In 1910 the Fisher government, for reasons of social policy rather than revenue, imposed a federal land tax. After the outbreak of the war a federal tax was placed on deceased estates, and in 1915 the Commonwealth began levying income tax. After a couple of tentative moves during 1909 and 1910, the Commonwealth entered the loan market seriously for the first time in 1914: the exigencies of the war made its incursion much more significant in the years which followed. Inevitably the national government's competition for revenue, from taxation and from loans, weakened further the financial position of the States. In 1902 Deakin had written anonymously:

> As the power of the purse in Great Britain established by degrees the authority of the Commons, so it will in Australia ultimately establish the authority of the Commonwealth. The rights of self-government of the States have been fondly supposed to be safeguarded by the Constitution. It has left them legally free, but financially bound to the chariot wheels of the Commonwealth.

By 1910 many more people were beginning to see what he meant than saw his point when the words first appeared in the *Morning Post*.

In the years between federation and the Great War, then, while the High Court worked to maintain the ideal of balance which existed in the mind of Griffith, the financial forces which in the long run were to alter the balance radically had begun to operate. Tension had begun to develop between the legally restricted responsibilities of the federal government, as set out in a specific list of transferred powers, and the need for increased activity suggested by the Commonwealth's growing importance in the overall governance of the country. A natural resultant of this was the series of attempts to amend the constitution which has already been mentioned.

The first attempt followed quickly on the accession to power of the first Labour government with a clear majority. Although the New South Wales leader Holman was an almost fanatical States-rights man, the vast majority of Labour supporters saw the Commonwealth, with its electoral laws based on 'one man one vote, one vote one value' and its popularly elected Upper House, as a much better vehicle for the party's social policy than the States. Labour was particularly anxious to reverse the decision of *Huddart Parker* v. *Moorehead* and to extend the powers of the Arbitration Court. In 1911 the government put to referendum proposals to give the Commonwealth full power over trade and commerce, corporations and industrial disputes. They were defeated decisively: the overall majority against was large, and only one State, Western Australia, returned an affirmative vote. The failure was in part due to the requirement that the electors should vote either for or against the proposals *en bloc*, but more, in Professor Sawer's opinion, to the fact that the government in its enthusiasm cast its net too wide: the proposed corporations clause, for example, was so worded that if accepted it would have authorized the enactment of a whole code 'of contracts, wrongs, crime etc., applying to artificial legal persons different from that applying to natural persons'. At the same time an amendment to empower the Commonwealth to nationalize monopolies was also rejected. In 1913 the government put virtually the same amendments forward, in a rather more carefully worded form and in a way which enabled the electors to vote on them separately: they were again negatived, though by a smaller overall majority, with the States evenly divided.

In 1919 W.M. Hughes, who had been the prime mover in both these attempts at amendment but had since left the party as a result of the conscription controversy and now led a Nationalist government, persuaded colleagues who had no sympathy for Labour policy that to deal with post-war problems powers rather similar to those sought on the other two occasions should be acquired for a period of three years, pending a full overhaul of the Constitution by a convention. He could not persuade the electors, but his margin of failure was very small—one State, and, on the major issues, less than one per cent of the total votes.

That Hughes was able to get the Nationalists to agree to hold the referendum, and that he should go so much closer to carrying it than the Labour government had gone in 1911 and 1913 were in large measure consequences of the war. The tremendous expansion of Commonwealth activity which a liberal interpretation of the defence power had made possible, while legally only temporary, was to have a permanent effect: public attitudes to government are as much a matter of common consent, and even of habit, as of strict law. Moreover the events which gave rise to the Anzac legend disposed electors to think nationally as most of them had never thought before. Australia's 'becoming a nation' as a result of the Gallipoli campaign is a figure of speech which has now passed beyond patriotic oratory into bathos; but the sense of being Australian rather than New South Welsh or Victorian (or British) which the war produced was a real factor in political life. In 1919 the new importance of the Commonwealth was symbolized by the action of the federal government in convening a Premiers' conference to discuss post-war reconstruction. Hitherto such conferences had always been organized by the States themselves. Though a few more were convened by New South Wales in the next decade, it had become normal for the Commonwealth to take the initiative before the financial agreement of 1927, which is discussed in Chapter Eight, regularized the practice. The new national habit of thought was not without its influence even on the High Court Bench. There was, moreover, another influence at work; in October 1919 Griffith retired, and less than three months later Barton died; their successors, Sir Adrian Knox and H.E. Starke, were in no sense radical nationalists, but neither were they concerned to fight a rearguard action against Isaacs and Higgins in defence of the ideal balance for which the senior justices had always contended. In 1920 that balance finally collapsed.

It had already become quite unstable. In 1919 the potential difficulties of the doctrine of implied immunity were emphasized in the *Municipalities Case*. It was held (Griffith and Barton dissenting) that local government authorities, though they operated under State law, did not have the immunity from the operation of the Commonwealth Arbitration Court which was enjoyed by such instrumentalities as State Railway Commissions. The Court, which in the *Wire Netting Case* had suggested, and in another case in 1912 had sought to draw more clearly, a line between 'trading' and 'governmental' functions of State instrumentalities in the application of the doctrine, protecting the latter but not the former from federal interference, thus moved further away from the absolute protection of the States which a strict interpretation of implied immunity necessitated. This seriously weakened the already tenuous distinction with which the doctrine had been propped up since 1908. Now, with Griffith and Barton no longer available even to fight a rearguard action, circumstances arose which enabled Isaacs and Higgins, with the aid of Rich and their two new brethren, to kick the support away altogether.

In an access of socialist zeal the government of Western Australia undertook after the war the establishment of a complex of State enterprises ranging from a farm-implement factory to a string of butcher shops. In the *Engineers' Case* (1920) it claimed for its new activities the protection from Commonwealth Arbitration Court control of implied immunity; it thus effectively reduced the doctrine to an absurdity. As R.R. Garran recalled in his autobiography, the United States Supreme Court had dealt with similar cases in the past by blandly ruling that a particular State activity was or was not a proper concern of government and applying or not applying the doctrine accordingly, but the High Court of Australia, as now constituted, 'did not feel equal to the task of bringing Herbert Spencer up to date' by distinguishing 'between government post offices or railways on the one hand, and government butcher shops or liquor saloons or implement works on the other'. Instead it took the bold but sensible step of over-ruling the *Railway Servants* decision. Isaacs, who wrote the majority ruling, insisted that there is no need for a doctrine like implied immunity which would impose on a court the duty of preventing the abuse by one government, acting against another, of the powers which belonged to it by law. 'The extravagant use of the granted powers in the actual working of the Constitution', he argued, 'is a matter to be guarded against by the constituencies and not by the courts'. The High Court simply had to construe Acts in terms of the 'natural meaning' of the Constitution's words, remembering the dictum of the Privy Council in a leading Indian case decided in 1878:

If what has been done is legislation, within the general scope of the affirmative words which give the power, and if it violates no express condition or restriction by which that power is limited ... it is not for any court of justice to enquire further, or to enlarge constructively those conditions and restrictions.

In thus wielding Occam's Razor among the multiplied hypotheses of the American tradition of constitutional interpretation, Isaacs and his brethren did not cut implied prohibitions off as short as implied immunity. *King* v. *Barger* was not, like *Railway Servants*, clearly over-ruled in the *Engineers' Case* judgement. But certainly the doctrine was heavily lopped and left exposed to further pruning in the future, and the overthrow of implied immunity alone amounted to a revolution in Commonwealth power *vis-à-vis* the States. It might appear that the new policy of the Bench would cut both ways, that if the States lost the protection they had enjoyed the Commonwealth would also lose something. The High Court actually said: 'The principle we apply to the Commonwealth we apply also to the States, leaving their respective acts of legislation full operation within their respective areas and subject matters'. But, as the full powers suggested by 'natural meaning' were to be given to the Commonwealth without restriction by assumptions about the nature of federalism, and the Constitution operates by the grant of specific powers to the Commonwealth, the actual effect of the *Engineers' Case* was to circumscribe the 'areas and subject matters' left to the States; for these can only be determined after the limits of Commonwealth authority have been reached. The new attitude of the High Court was a recognition that the Constitution had to be considered as an organism capable of growth and adaptation to changing forces in society, rather than a carefully regulated machine for the balancing of these forces. The Court was now aligning itself with the tendencies inherent in the finance clauses and with the trends encouraged by the Commonwealth's leadership in war, and opening the way to a very great extension of federal influence in Australian life.

Indeed one decision almost contemporary with the *Engineers' Case* judgement, leant extraordinarily far in the direction of federal supremacy. This concerned that 'little bit of layman's language' which survived from its origin as one of Sir Henry Parkes's least successful attempts to turn his woolly oratory into meaningful English to become S.92: 'trade, commerce and intercourse among the States ... shall be absolutely free'. The High Court's attempts to interpret this sentiment when wartime marketing regulation first made it a serious issue had been far from happy: in the *Wheat Case* of 1915 the court had ruled that the compulsory acquisition of goods by a State government could not be prevented by arguing that it interfered with a producer's right to sell interstate, but two 1916 cases in which the issue was regulation without acquisition, *Foggitt Jones* v. *Queensland* and *Duncan* v. *New South Wales*, had been decided in virtually contradictory terms. Now, in *McArthur's Case*, the Bench sought to cut through the tangle it had thus created by deciding, in effect, that any regulation by a State at a border was forbidden, but that S.92 did not bind the Commonwealth in any way beyond preventing it from levying border tariffs. This is not the place to discuss the problems raised by the section in any detail—they were to become serious in the 1930s and acutely embarrassing to both Commonwealth and States in the 1950s. Here it is enough to note that this is one matter in which a willingness by the Bench to consider the evidence of the Convention debates would have saved much trouble, and that to exempt the Commonwealth in part from a prohibition couched in general terms was to exalt federal authority as against State authority to a degree which could not later be justified. The effect of *McArthur's Case* was, therefore, temporary.

The effect of The *Engineers Case*, however, was permanent; and it was supplemented by several other judgements in 1920, in particular by a decision that the Commonwealth could validly exempt the interest on its loans from State income tax and another that it could validly legislate to prevent State elections or plebiscites from being held on the same day as federal elections. It is a commonplace of American history that 'the Constitution which Americans revere is not the Constitution as it was written in 1787', that in the early years of the United States there were political changes which altered it more in effect than it has ever since been altered by formal amendment. A similar process in Australia reached fruition in 1920. The habits of thought engendered by World War I, the leadership which the Commonwealth exercised during the war years and which Hughes at least wished it to exercise in the peace, the development of a system of financial relationships loaded against the States, and a revolution in the thinking of the High Court, culminated in that year in the destruction of the Constitution as it was understood by the man who had more claim than any other to be considered its author, Sir Samuel Griffith. Henceforth there was to be no real 'balance' between federal and State power; it had been replaced by the primacy of the Commonwealth, a primacy which was to develop in the next half-century into dominance.

Democracy and Sovereignty

'It is inexpedient to suppose and to make provision for extreme cases, because in truth such cases, when they occur, will usually be found to make an adequate provision for themselves'.

SIR GEORGE MURRAY

'The power of the Parliament of the United Kingdom to legislate for the colonies is fast receding into the ghostly company of legal fictions'.

F.W. MAITLAND (1901)

The establishment of the Commonwealth was a watershed in Australian political life, but it was not a revolution. The history of the Commonwealth and its constituent States in the twentieth century was in many ways a continuation of political developments of the kind discussed in Chapter Four. The constitutional machinery which had gradually evolved towards democracy continued to change slowly; the rivalries between Upper and Lower Houses were far from settled; most importantly the Australian communities still had, in 1901, a long way to go before they could consider themselves in any meaningful sense 'sovereign'. It is necessary, therefore, to take up these questions and to trace their history in the twentieth century.

In some matters the continuity is obvious and easily explained. For example, the trend towards the stability of ministries which began to appear in the 1880s and 1890s continued after federation under the impetus of the decline in importance of State politics which is discussed in more detail in the next chapter. As the States found themselves forced to concentrate more and more on administration and became steadily less important in the overall governance of the country, politicians became less willing to put their salaries to hazard by overturning governments. The Labor Party's methods of discipline, copied to some extent by other parties, and the ability of a disciplined government to manipulate electoral distribution, have played a part in the process, but the decline of the States was critical. Since World War II the States have lost virtually the last shreds of their financial independence, and their governments have become very hard to dislodge. The point is that they are no longer fully responsible in the old sense. One party continued in power in Tasmania from 1934 to 1969; in New South Wales the same party was in office from 1941 to 1965; in South Australia one man, Thomas Playford, was Premier for over a quarter of a century, from 1938 to 1965.

In other matters the persistence of ideas which originated in the middle nineteenth century is little short of remarkable. As was noted in Chapter Four, the pastoral and other rural interests, in accepting such democratic devices as manhood suffrage and the ballot, did not surrender their claim to a powerful voice in politics: they fought hard, and successfully, to preserve it by the maintenance of a heavily weighted seat distribution. Ironically enough, they were most successful in the Province which otherwise seemed the most radical, South Australia. In 1856 about thirteen per cent of the colony's population lived in Adelaide, which elected ten of the thirty-six members of the House of Assembly, that is about twenty-seven per cent; but by 1884 the forty per cent of the people living in the capital were represented by only fourteen of the fifty-four Assembly members—still about twenty-seven per cent. By the early twentieth century the idea that there should be two country seats for every city seat had come to be accepted almost as a fundamental principle, and it continued to be accepted as such until the end of the 1960s, even by the Labor Party, though the percentage of the people living in the city had risen to about sixty. The idea of one vote, one value was not seriously considered in New South Wales before federation, but it was adopted, at least in theory, in 1902. In Queensland and Western Australia tremendous differences in population densities over the colonies made a literal interpretation of it unacceptable, even to people who considered themselves absolute democrats: in Queensland, for example, there was seldom any serious objection to giving a vote from the sparsely-settled western districts more than twice the 'value' of a metropolitan vote. In Tasmania rivalries between the northern and southern centres of population raised more controversies than an overall weighting of country representation against both which did not disappear until near the end of the nineteenth century; but in Victoria, where weighting persisted until 1953, when Victorian seats were tied to the reasonably proportional federal distribution, there was often more criticism. To call the pattern of seat distribution in the Australian colonies 'undemocratic' would be a rhetorical exaggeration, but there is no doubt that it has tempered the effects of democratization. So, perhaps to a greater extent, has the composition of the elective Upper Houses: they have shown themselves much less amenable to reform than the various assemblies. Efforts to reform them will be discussed presently, but first some mention should be made of one matter in which change was very largely a phenomenon of the twentieth century.

Parliamentary Election Systems

All the Australian communities inherited the British simple-majority or 'first-past-the-post' method of calculating electoral results, but their electorates were always complicated in organization. In the nineteenth century they exhibited a bewildering tangle of single-member, double-member and multiple-member constituencies, and combinations of the three, to untangle which would be pointless. The simple-majority system has the obvious disadvantage that the candidate with the greatest number of votes may not be the preferred choice of a majority of voters. In the 1890s and the early years of the twentieth century most of the colonies began to experiment with improvements. Between 1910 and 1918 New South Wales tried double ballots: where a candidate failed to obtain an absolute majority his name and that of his nearest rival were submitted to the electors a second time. The system worked reasonably well, in that it seemed to discourage splinter-voting, for the second ballot had to be used in only a small number of electorates, but when it did become necessary the candidates experienced considerable difficulty in keeping issues alive and voting fell off heavily. Exhaustive preferential voting seemed a better idea: its first use in Australia was in Victoria in 1911. Queensland had introduced a variant on the preferential system in 1892. This involved *permitting* electors to show an order of preference but not *requiring* them to do so: if no candidate received an absolute majority all candidates except the two with the highest number of votes would be eliminated together (instead of candidates being eliminated one at a time from the bottom of the poll as in the exhaustive system) and those of their votes on which preferences were shown would be used to determine the final result. Western Australia also tried this 'contingent' preferential system, but only from 1907 to 1911: Queensland persisted with it for fifty years.

To some people a more obvious improvement on the traditional method of counting votes seemed to be one or other of the systems of 'proportional representation', which, presupposing the existence of a reasonably clear distinction between parties, aim to produce a house divided among them in mathematical proportion to the strength of their electoral support. The first use of such a method for an Australian legislature was in Tasmania in 1896, in the towns of Hobart and Launceston where it was thought likely to provide representation for minority interests. The system used was a modification by the attorney-general, Andrew Inglis Clark, of the formula devised many years before by the English barrister Thomas Hare. In 1899 and 1901 attempts made to extend it to the whole country failed in the face of strong opposition, and in the latter year it was abandoned even in the towns. But in 1907 the scheme was reintroduced for all seats, in a form different in detail from that first used (though it has continued to be known as the 'Hare-Clark system'). It came in for some criticism because, since the State was not treated as a single constituency but as five separate districts, a small majority of seats could be won by a party which failed to win an overall majority of votes; but only once (in 1928) has this happened. A more serious problem is that all proportional systems tend, if there are only two real parties, to return closely divided and even deadlocked houses: as this problem is obviously greater in a small legislature, the survival of the 'Hare-Clark system' in Tasmania, where the House of Assembly had only thirty members until 1958, is perhaps surprising.

Strangely enough, the difficulty did not arise until after World War II. When it did an effort was made to resolve it which involved the most fundamental of all Australian departures from the strict Westminster pattern of responsible government, the remission to the electorate of direct choice of the executive. An Act was passed in 1953 to provide that electors be given not only a ballot paper with the names of the candidates but also a second paper on which to mark the name of the party each elector would prefer to see govern in the event of a tied vote. The following year this Act was repealed without having been used and replaced by one which provided that if each of the two parties won fifteen of the thirty seats an electoral commission should be appointed and decide, by examining primary voting figures, which party had the greater electoral support. This party would then be entitled to govern. The other would be entitled to nominate a Speaker and thus give the government a working majority of one; if it declined to do so the government might nominate the Speaker and draw an extra member from among its unsuccessful candidates in his electorate. A parliament in which this device had to be used to break a deadlock would expire after three years instead of the normal five. It was a clumsy compromise, and in giving overt recognition to the existence of the two major parties, it made election difficult for both independents and smaller political groups. It worked in the 1955 Parliament, but the enlargement of the House of Assembly to thirty-five members in 1958 provided a solution to the problem more in accordance with the traditions of ministerial responsibility.

In 1948 the 'Hare-Clark system' was adopted by the Commonwealth for Senate elections. Both simple voting up to 1918 and preferential voting during the next thirty years had tended to give one party or other a disproportionately large Senate majority and to leave its rival, with perhaps only a slightly smaller popular vote, almost unrepresented in the Upper House. Proportional representation was an obvious answer. But it has frequently led to the opposite difficulty, a very evenly divided Senate, and as a result honourable senators have been known to arrive at Parliament House in ambulances and to answer division bells in Bath chairs. In a second Chamber, however, and one of sixty members, equal division is not such a serious problem as in a very small Lower House; and in the first two decades after its introduction proportional representation did something to provide seats for at least one minority group which could not win Lower House places.

The system eventually adopted for most Houses in Australia was preferential voting. In theory designed to give exact expression to the electors' preference, it has probably not, in fact, influenced electoral results very greatly, though, as Professor S.R. Davis has noted, 'In moments of severe party fragmentation . . . it can be lethal . . . [and] In normal times it may sustain the odd independent' or make relations between parties in a coalition easier by enabling both to contest a partic-ular seat without serious danger to their overall position. In some cases its consequences have been a little peculiar: for example the Labor Party won majorities at four successive general elections in Western Australia between 1933 and 1943 without once gaining half the primary votes cast. The clearest fact about preferential voting in Australia is that many Australians have come to identify it with democracy: a suggestion made by the Labor Party leader A.A. Calwell during the 1963 federal election campaign that the Commonwealth revert to the 'first-past-the-post' sys-tem met with a remarkably hostile reception. Preferential voting seemed to have become a distinctive feature of Australian constitutional prac-tice. More recently, however, it has again come under some criticism from Labor leaders.

There is another feature even more distinctive—indeed to some minds downright peculiar. This is compulsory voting, perhaps the *re-ductio ad absurdum* of democracy. It was first introduced in Queensland, in 1915. New South Wales introduced compulsory registration of voters in 1921 and began imposing fines for failure to vote in 1930. By this time Victoria and Tasmania had introduced compulsion in Lower House elections, the former in 1926, the latter in 1928. Western Australia did not do so until 1939 and South Australia until 1944. The Commonwealth introduced compulsory registration in 1911, made vot-ing at constitutional referendums obligatory in 1915, and legislated for compulsory voting at elections in 1924. The policy of compulsion has been heavily criticized for producing 'donkey-voting', the quite hap-hazard completion of ballot papers, and also for encouraging people with little knowledge and less interest to copy 'how-to-vote' cards un-critically; it has also been strongly defended on the ground that it pro-tects the real interests of the ordinary citizen against tightly-organized minorities; but whether it has had much influence on election results is perhaps doubtful. The suggestion has often been made that it works slightly to the advantage of the Labor Party, at least in such 'swinging' electorates as those in suburban Sydney and Melbourne. Certainly the Labor Party thanked compulsory voting for its electoral victory in Queensland in 1915 and for this reason procured its use in federal referendums; and its use in municipal elections in New South Wales in the 1950s and 1960s seems to indicate that it can help Labor. One of the first actions of the Liberal-Country Party government which came to office in 1965 was to abolish compulsion in local government elections, and when Labor returned to power in 1976 it was restored. But the highly conservative H.G. Turner was an advocate of compulsion in the first decade of the century. He believed that most of those who did not vote regularly were members of 'the comparatively independent classes, with whom the knowledge that they are in a minority somewhat paralyses effort'. And the historian of Western Australia, Professor F.K. Crowley, came to the conclusion that in that State it 'apparently did not operate to the advantage of any party in the long run, merely serving to increase the cost of holding elections'. Before the introduction of compulsory voting sixty to seventy per cent of electors voted on average, and polls of about fifty-five per cent were frequent. The highest recorded seems to have been 82.34 per cent in New South Wales in 1927. Since compulsion was introduced the figure has fluctuated around ninety-five per cent, though the penalty for failure to vote has never been great and has become quite nominal.

Apart from the eventual adoption by all legislatures of compulsory voting, the most striking feature of Australian electoral laws is the frequency with which they have been changed. All States have changed their systems of voting at least once. Victoria and South Australia were satisfied with that. Western Australia has changed twice, adopting exhaustive preferential voting in 1911 after its experiment with the Queensland system. Tasmania's changes have already been discussed. The Commonwealth adopted preferential voting in 1918 and, despite some criticism in recent years, has used it since for the House of Representatives; but, as has been seen, it has changed the Senate system twice. The legislatures with the most remarkable records are those of New South Wales and Queensland. New South Wales has used no fewer than four different systems, having made all its changes within fifteen years: after long experience with simple voting and its experiment with double ballots it conducted a flirtation with Hare and Clark between 1920 and 1925 before adopting the preferential method. Queensland has changed three times. It persisted with the system of 'contingent votes' until 1942. Then it went back to simple voting. Since the non-Labor opposition was split into two groups and the 'first-past-the-post' system therefore helped to keep the united Labor Party in office, the change was regarded by that party's opponents as a cynical misuse of electoral machinery; and in 1963, after a Labor split brought them to power, they introduced preferential voting. This system has become the one used by all States except Tasmania, as well as by the Commonwealth for elections to the House of Representatives.

The Decline of State Upper Houses

The establishment of the Commonwealth, by taking some of the more exciting political issues out of the State parliaments, contributed in the long run towards cooling the hostility between their Upper and Lower Houses. But the process was gradual. In Victoria, where the nineteenth-century disputes had been most bitter, the Council remained a force to be reckoned with, its powers hardly affected by the clumsy machinery for the resolution of deadlocks introduced in 1903. In 1937 a Country Party ministry led by A.A. Dunstan succeeded in modifying that machinery to provide for an Assembly dissolution followed, if necessary and after a nine-month delay, by a dissolution of the Council and then, if deadlock persisted, by a joint sitting at which an absolute majority would decide the issue. At the same time the property qualification was again lowered; but the Council was compensated for these, quite marginal, concessions by a formal prohibition of 'tacking'. The Council remained able to reject a supply Bill in 1947 in order to force an Assembly election; indeed in 1952, two years after an alliance of the Country and Labor parties and the votes of some opposition members had abolished property qualifications and instituted adult suffrage, it was able to repeat the performance. But in the long run the identity of the franchises of the Houses was bound to smooth the pattern of relations between them sufficiently to bring about, after almost a century, what Geoffrey Serle has described as 'the surrender by the ... Legislative Council of a position of authority comparable to that of any second chamber in the world'—though the survival intact of the Council's legislative equality with the Lower House and the fact that its seat distribution is heavily weighted in favour of the country districts combine to make that surrender rather less than absolute.

In South Australia also the Council was reluctant to accept a subordinate role. It would not hear of any proposal which it considered 'socialistic', and twice during the years 1910 and 1911 it rejected 'Council Veto Bills' which the Labour government led by J.S. Verran had put through the House of Assembly. These provided that any measure passed twice by the Lower House in successive sessions and then, after a general election, passed a third time with an absolute majority, should be eligible to receive the royal assent without passing the Council. In November 1911, six weeks after the failure of the second Council Veto Bill, the government, with the same desperate lack of consistency as the Berry government had shown in Victoria in 1878, but, considering the recent victory of the Asquith government in Britain over the House of Lords, with a nice sense of timing, asked the Secretary of State, Lewis Harcourt, 'that the Constitution be so amended by an Imperial Act as to enable the matured will of the people of South Australia to become law'. The request was not made public until the beginning of 1912, when the Council rejected the Appropriation Bill because the government, abrogating the 'gentlemen's agreement' which had existed since 1857, 'tacked' to it proposals to establish a State brick works and timber mill. A few days earlier Verran had telegraphed

Harcourt to ask for immediate action. Harcourt, however, was even less likely to consider imperial intervention desirable than had Hicks Beach been a quarter of a century before: it would not be contemplated, he said, 'until every constitutional remedy had been exhausted', and even then only 'in response to a request of the overwhelming majority of the people and if necessary to enable government . . . to be carried on'.

The Verran ministry attempted to exhaust the constitutional remedies and to demonstrate the support of an overwhelming majority of the people with a dissolution, but it lost the election. The ministers who took its place proceeded to legislate to incorporate in the Constitution the 'gentlemen's agreement' on money Bills. So, although the Council had submitted to reductions in the terms of its members—from twelve years to nine in 1881 and to six in 1901—it retained its powers. Moreover, though its franchise was widened somewhat in 1907, given to householders in 1913 and subsequently extended to cover returned servicemen, it held out until 1974 against attempts to give votes in its elections to all adults.

In Tasmania, as in South Australia, the Upper House saw the advent of Labor governments as a challenge which it had a peculiar mission to meet. It viewed their policies with grave suspicion, and in 1924 it provoked a serious crisis by amending the Appropriation Bill after it had been passed by the House of Assembly. A conference between managers having failed to reconcile the views of the two Houses, the Premier, J.A. Lyons, asked the Chief Justice, who was Acting-Governor, to give assent to the Bill as passed by the Lower House. The Acting-Governor had, in anticipation, cabled Leopold Amery at the Colonial Office for instructions. Amery, anxious not to embroil the British government in the affair, told him that if, after consultation with his law officers, he complied, the ministers would be solely responsible and 'No question [could] arise as to the constitutionality of [his] action'. He therefore assented, to the great scandal of the conservative expert on imperial constitutional law, A.B. Keith, who had still not recovered from the shock of recent events in Queensland (see below, p. 150), and when the Council tried to amend further money Bills a new Governor, Sir James O'Grady, followed the precedent. The government won popular endorsement for its policies at a general election. It seemed that the Council had stretched its authority beyond the breaking point.

But in constitutional law the situation was at best untidy. When tempers cooled, the parties to the dispute agreed to the passage of an Indemnity Act and to the appointment of a joint committee to consider future regulation of relations between the Houses. A compromise plan which gave the Council the right to reject all money Bills, and to amend such measures as loan Bills and Bills dealing with the sensitive question of death duties, but not ordinary taxation and annual Appropriation Bills, was worked out and enacted. The Council came out of the affair surprisingly well; it surrendered only the right to amend measures which the growing financial dependence of Tasmania on the Commonwealth were making steadily less significant, and it got in return a statutory confirmation of its other powers; the government had failed to follow up its advantage. Lyons' successor, A.G. Ogilvie, had reason to regret the fact when in 1934 the Council, afraid of 'socialistic' policies and perhaps spurred by verbal provocations, struck an item providing for an extension of public health services out of the Appropriation Bill on the ground that it had been 'tacked' thereto. The government countered with an attempt to amend the Constitution along the lines of the British Parliament Act of 1911, which had deprived the House of Lords of all power over money Bills, but the attempt was little more than a gesture and when it failed the ministers were forced to use a conference to compromise the financial difference. The Council remained strong enough to be able to force a Lower House election in 1948 by rejecting an appropriation measure. By this time a gradual extension of the franchise to include all householders, spouses of householders and ex-servicemen had given it an electorate almost seventy per cent of the size of the Assembly's; its franchise was extended to all adults in 1969; henceforth it was not likely to represent a conservative brake on the Lower House but its actual power was only marginally less than it had been in 1857.

In Western Australia, where the Legislative Council became elective in 1893, there occurred the same sort of disputes between the Houses as in the other three colonies with elective Upper Houses, but they tended to be conducted in a rather more muted tone. As Crowley has put it, they 'have never paralysed administration' if they have at times 'acutely inflamed political tempers'. The nominated Upper House which had existed between 1890 and 1893 had had powers equal to those of the Assembly, except that it had not been able to initiate a money Bill. When the new Council was elected, an informal agreement was made to give it the right to reject money Bills or to suggest amendments to them. This was formalized, with safeguards against 'tacking', in 1921, the Council successfully resisting an attempt to write into the arrangement a clause forbidding it to 'repeat, press or insist upon' any suggestion for amendment. The Council was always a conservative body, but it tended also to be a circumspect one: the Labor government which ruled the State through most of the 1930s and 1940s never had an Upper House majority, but was able to put most of its policy into force, if its more ambitiously radical schemes were sacrificed in the process. Like the Tasmanian Council, the West Australian was able to keep its theoretical powers virtually intact and to retain a measure of real influence in legislation after its franchise, which through most of its life had permitted perhaps one-third of Assembly electors to vote at its elections, was extended to all adults in 1964.

The nominated Upper Houses of New South Wales and Queensland had been since the 1880s in a weaker position than the elected Councils of Victoria, South Australia, Tasmania and Western Australia, and by 1910 the whole idea of nominated Councils was coming under attack. The new Labour parties, indeed, were hostile to Upper Houses as such: the New South Wales party had had the abolition of the Council as part of its platform since 1893, and in 1908 had added to this 'plank' the words 'and the substitution therefor of the initiative and referendum'. While policies as doctrinaire as this were not necessarily to be taken literally, there was a general expectation when the party came to power on the defeat of the Wade government in 1910 that it would attempt to do something. For three years, however, the majority behind the first Labour Premier, J.S.T. McGowan, was too slender to enable him to take any action beyond having eleven new members appointed; and an increased majority in the 1913 election produced nothing from his successor W.A. Holman until the 1916 annual conference of the party virtually forced the government to agree to propose a referendum on abolition; then the split in the party over conscription, which led to Holman's expulsion and the formation of a Nationalist government at the end of the year, shelved the issue.

The next Labor Premier, J.T. Lang, was more determined than his predecessors. In 1925, faced with a very hostile Council, he asked Governor de Chair for twenty-five nominations. The Governor demurred, offered fifteen, and asked the Secretary of State for instructions. Amery's reply was that 'established constitutional principles require that the question should be settled between the Governor and Ministers'; de Chair therefore made the twenty-five appointments, on what he believed to be the understanding that they would not be used to put through an abolition Bill. Lang, however, attempted to use them for just that purpose: he failed because some Labor councillors defected, giving as reason the fact that his Bill did not provide for initiative, referendum and recall. Lang was prepared to try again by asking for more appointments, but his government was defeated at the polls in 1927.

Lang's opponents were anxious to protect the Council, which was now perhaps more valuable to them as a symbol of resistance to his noisily threatening radicalism than as a House of legislature. In 1929 the Bavin Nationalist government got an Act passed to provide that the Legislative Council might not be abolished without a referendum, and that a referendum would also be necessary before a future Parliament might repeal the Act itself. Whether or not the legislature could thus bind its successors was a nice legal point which Lang proposed to test when he returned to power the next year. He brought down Bills to repeal the Act and abolish the Council; the Upper House, confident of its legal security, let the Bills pass; an injunction was then sought to restrain ministers from presenting them for the royal assent, and in successive cases before the New South Wales Supreme Court, the High Court of Australia and the Privy Council its view was upheld.

The Council was saved, but it was obviously ripe for reform. It had been swamped by the Nationalists in 1917, and by Lang in 1925; after his failure to abolish it he added another twenty-five members to get some of his contentious financial policies onto the statute book, and after he fell in 1932 it was 'counter-swamped' by his successor with twenty-one nominations. A precedent had been established which reduced its power of legislative veto to a power to protest and invite coercion: it had now indeed been 'reduced to a cipher'. In 1933, therefore, the new government moved to reconstitute the Upper House along lines suggested by the reconstitution of the Senate of the Irish Free State four years before. It proposed, and the electors at a referendum accepted, an indissoluble body of sixty members one-third of whom would retire every three years, the vacancies being filled by the votes of members of both Houses. The new Council was to have no power over the annual Appropriation Bill beyond that of delaying its passage for one month, but it was given (in consequence of hostility by the new government to some of Lang's financial measures, particularly the Mortgage Tax Bill of 1932) the power to reject or amend other classes of money Bill. Since 1933 it has been impossible for a government to coerce the Council, but machinery exists for the resolution of deadlocks. If the Upper House rejects (or lays aside or amends in an unacceptable manner) a Bill passed by the Assembly, and repeats its action when, after an interval of three months, the Bill has been confirmed by the Lower House, the government can convene a conference between managers and then, if necessary, a joint sitting at which the Bill is discussed but not voted upon. Should the deadlock persist, the issue can then be resolved by a popular referendum. The machinery is cumbersome, but since the upheavals of the Depression years State politics have been quiet enough to make disputes between the Houses rare.

The usefulness of a Council which did little more than reflect the balance of forces in the Lower House some years earlier was, to say the least, not obvious. The Labor government returned in 1941 made half-hearted gestures at further reform in 1943 and at abolition three years later, but nothing more serious until 1958. Then it was forced to act by the party's State conference, though it had had since 1952 a Council majority—which, as some Labor MLCs pointed out at the conference, it could hope to retain for a decade even if it lost control of the Assembly. In 1959 an Abolition Bill was brought in, but a group of Labor 'rebels' joined the opposition in the Council to try to defeat it by refusing to participate in a conference between the Houses and then challenging in the courts the government's action in putting it to referendum. The challenge failed, but the proposal for abolition was decisively rejected by the electors in 1961. With no greater issue at stake than a traditional

Labor Party doctrine, voters, particularly compulsory voters, could hardly be expected to be fired with enthusiasm for the abolition of a House which was giving no one any trouble and could be represented as one of those 'safeguards against hasty legislation' for which even the most fervent democrat often has a sneaking regard. Apparently realizing this, the Labor government returned in 1976 proposed to convert the present Council into one directly elected, with the State voting as a single constituency. By compromising on details of its plan it won the support of the Council, where its opponents were in a majority. In its new form the Upper House seems likely to survive in New South Wales, as elective Councils have in Victoria, South Australia, Western Australia and Tasmania.

Only the Queensland Upper Chamber has paid with its life for its resistance to the will of a government, and it, one may perhaps say, was assassinated rather than executed. As in New South Wales, the advent of Labor administrations brought the Legislative Council under attack. There was some preliminary sparring in 1912 and 1915 before a Labor government, installed with a comfortable Assembly majority in the latter year, put an Abolition Bill through the Lower House. This was rejected by the Council, passed again by the Assembly and, after the failure of a legal challenge to the validity of the Parliamentary Bills Referendum Act of 1908 (which had not, as technically it should have, been reserved for the royal assent in England), put to the electors. They voted heavily against it. After the election of 1918 a similar Bill was passed by the Lower House and rejected by the Council, which was now bitterly hostile to the government because of a proposal for land reform which many of the councillors considered confiscatory. When the Council rejected the Land Bill the ministers reacted by asking the Acting-Governor to swamp. As deadlock provisions existed, the request was of dubious constitutional propriety; and as the Acting-Governor (William Lennon) was a recently retired Labor minister, his agreement to nominate a large 'suicide squad', which in 1921 voted to abolish the chamber, outraged conservatives and worried lawyers. Berriedale Keith henceforth considered 'Queensland' to be almost a synonym for 'political immorality'. But, as the new Governor, Sir Matthew Nathan, reported to the Secretary of State, there was no evidence of 'any very strong or widespread feeling in the country against assent being given to the Bill', which was, as the law required, reserved for assent in England. This was accordingly given and the Queensland Upper House formally ceased to exist in 1922.

The events surrounding the abolition of the Queensland Council and the failure of Lang to abolish that of New South Wales had an interesting constitutional implication. While the State legislatures generally have power to alter their States' constitutions, subject in most cases to the need for absolute majorities in both Houses and in all cases to reservation (now a mere formality), there existed now two cases in which an alteration could be made only with the consent of the electorate: the abolition of the New South Wales Upper House and the reinstitution of a second chamber in Queensland. This 'entrenchment' of particular clauses, upheld, as has been noted (pp. 148–9), by the Privy Council (which based its decision on the clause in the Colonial Laws Validity Act providing that an Act to amend a colonial constitution must be passed in the 'manner and form' required by imperial or colonial law) provides a precedent which a government could use to entrench other clauses. In fact, nothing has been done in any State along these lines except the passage by the New South Wales Parliament in 1950 of an Act to forbid the extension of the life of a parliament beyond three years without the approval of the electors at a referendum, and the passage in South Australia in 1969 of an Act making a referendum necessary to abolish either of the State's two Houses; though there have been suggestions that guarantees of 'fundamental rights' should be entrenched. Like the British Constitution, the Constitutions of the Australian States remain flexible.

In their principles they have changed little since their enactment by the imperial Parliament, but in their practical application they have undergone the same kind of subtle modification as the British Constitution itself. The tremendous expansion in the functions of government which began in the United Kingdom in the second quarter of the nineteenth century gradually led to the acquisition by civil servants of what were very close to executive and legislative powers. The process was well under way when the first responsible governments came into existence in Australia, and its development in the colonies was encouraged by some of the problems which the colonial legislatures had to solve in their early years. In particular, it was encouraged by the need which the men who drafted the closer-settlement legislation of the 1860s and 1870s discovered to give a minister very wide powers of discretion and regulation—which in practice were often exercised by his departmental officers—in order, as George Higinbotham said, 'to meet and defeat the various contrivances of fraud'. Similarly the problems of economics and geography, and in particular the necessity for the governments to build and control railways, made Australia the land of the public corporation. The 'semi-government authority' has continued to exercise wide influence, and to impinge on the life of the ordinary citizen quite as much as the State government does directly, particularly since the transfer of various important functions from the States to the Commonwealth. Moreover the development of strong, or more-or-less strong parties at the end of the nineteenth century had the effect of altering in Australia the practical meaning of collective responsibility rather more quickly, and rather more radically, than in the United Kingdom. The existence of party caucuses, and more importantly the

Labor Party's system of having cabinet chosen by caucus (a system for which some non-Labor people have considerable sympathy), has made possible an appeal over the head of the Premier to the parliamentary party, or even to the extra-parliamentary machine, by a minister who finds himself in a minority in cabinet. In the long run the development of the caucus system has had a more profound, if less easily defined, effect on the methods and problems of government in Australia, federal and State, than any change in constitutional details or in the position of the Upper Houses.

The Imperial Connection: Vice-Regal Powers

It has now been shown that, without extensive formal alteration of their constitutions, the Australian States underwent a series of quite profound changes in the operation of their systems of government during the first three-quarters of the twentieth century. In the same period even more significant changes took place in the relationship which they, and the Commonwealth, enjoyed with the imperial government. As was pointed out at the end of Chapter Four, the degree to which Australian governments and legislatures were subordinated to Downing Street had been greatly lessened by the early 1900s, but the fact of ultimate imperial supremacy remained. Both the Commonwealth and the States were frequently reminded of their inferior status. In the years before World War I, for example, efforts by the Commonwealth government, particularly under the Prime-Ministership of Deakin, to communicate directly with the British government rather than through the Governor-General and the Colonial Office were repeatedly rebuffed. Neither the States nor the Commonwealth were permitted to legislate with extra-territorial effect until after 1930: not until the Statute of Westminster was passed in 1931 was the Commonwealth granted the right, an indispensable attribute of sovereignty, to legislate fully for its citizens wherever they might be; not until 1933 did a Privy Council decision give the States power to apply *any* legislation extra-territorially, and even then it remained necessary to show the connection between the law bring applied and the State's territorial rights. Moreover the Crown refused, despite the fact that the Constitution gave the Commonwealth power over 'Trade and commerce with other countries' and despite vehement protests, to acknowledge the right of the federal Parliament to legislate in terms inconsistent with imperial shipping Acts. As late as 1925 the Commonwealth found certain provisions of its Navigation Act of 1913 voided by the High Court because of repugnancy to the British Merchant Shipping Act of 1910. Even when allowance is made for Berriedale Keith's tendency to distrust the dominions and self-governing colonies and to emphasize in exaggerated terms Britain's right to control them, it must be acknowledged that he was not going beyond the facts when he wrote in 1927 that

> any Imperial Act which by its express terms or necessary intendment applies to the Dominions binds all their people, their governments and their Courts, and the British Nationality and Status of Aliens Act, 1922 is a recent example of the frank use of such superiority over all Dominion legislation.

The difference in status between Britain and the Australian polities was underlined by the fact that Australian ministries were forced to accord more influence to the men who represented the Crown for them than British ministries accorded the Sovereign. As was noted in Chapter Four, the development of a political dispute to the point where it raised constitutional issues could place a governor in a position where he might have to choose between advisers who could control the Lower House of the legislature and his duties as guardian of the Constitution. For this reason he was more likely to have to take sides than was the Monarch, more likely to have strong motives for seeking to influence policy. Fortified by his instructions, impelled by a feeling (often well justified) that his ministers lacked skill and foresight, endowed by his extra-colonial origins and limited tenure with the status of an outside arbiter, he was better able than the Sovereign to exercise 'the right to be consulted, the right to encourage, the right to warn'. Moreover, few of the Australian governors, particularly before federation, were like Belloc's Lord Lundy who, having failed at everything else, was sent out 'to govern New South Wales': most of them were very able men who were capable of exerting a personal influence on people like Parkes or Berry which Queen Victoria could never exert on a Russell or a Gladstone. What they were able to do behind the scenes was considerable, at least until nationalism and a Labour movement developed at the end of the century.

In front of the scenes they were occasionally able to exercise a power which no Monarch exercised in the United Kingdom after the balance of the Constitution was radically altered by the 1832 Reform Act, the power to refuse a dissolution of Parliament. In 1873 the Duffy ministry in Victoria was refused a dissolution by Lord Canterbury and thus forced to resign. Several times in the next decade similar events occurred in other colonies: in each case the Governor was able to find new advisers. The confused state of 'parties' in the colonial legislatures encouraged the various governors to examine critically—more critically than would the Monarch—advice to dissolve tendered by men who had just suffered a parliamentary defeat; and after payment of members became general they could count on the approval of legislators who were not anxious to put their parliamentary salaries at risk. Even in 1899, by which time more formal parties were developing, three ministries, those of Reid in New South Wales, Kingston in South Australia and Turner in

Victoria, were forced from office by being refused dissolutions. In the first eight years of the Commonwealth, dissolutions of the House of Representatives were refused three times. The action of the Crown's representative in these cases did not necessarily prove the existence of a prerogative right in Australia which did not exist in the United Kingdom. In each of them the Governor or Governor-General had available an alternative ministry to take responsibility for his refusal to dissolve, and it is arguable that, at least in the nineteenth century, the Sovereign would have been entitled to reject advice in the United Kingdom under similar circumstances. But, as Lord Salisbury once had to remind Queen Victoria, the Monarchy had much to lose in reverence and mystique from the criticism which would inevitably follow a crisis brought about by refusing the advice of a ministry actually in office, even if that ministry could be replaced. With less to lose in these in-tangible ways an Australian governor was more likely to use his discretion.

The Commonwealth Constitution, indeed, seemed to imply that the Governor-General was intended to exercise discretion in two matters other than the dissolution of the Lower House. One of these was closely related: the question of dissolving both Houses in the event of a dead-lock. The other concerned S.128, which authorizes, but does not oblige, the Governor-General to submit to referendum a proposal for constitutional amendment passed twice in successive sessions by one House but rejected by the other. It could be argued that the Governor-General would have to exercise this power in accordance with his own judgement, not on his ministers' advice: otherwise opposition by minis-ters to a proposal emanating from the Senate could nullify the provision as far as the Senate was concerned. But when the two questions arose at the same time in 1914 Sir Ronald Munro-Ferguson seems to have de-cided to follow advice, though he also consulted the Chief Justice. A Liberal government Bill to forbid the granting of preference to trade unionists in government employment was twice defeated by a Labor-dominated Senate, which at the same time tried to force a second ref-erendum on the constitutional amendment proposals that had been narrowly defeated the previous year (see p. 134). The question of the referendum did not come to a clear-cut issue, but the Governor-General granted the government the double dissolution it sought, and there is no reason to think that he would not finally have accepted the Prime Minister's advice on the other matter. Munro-Ferguson and the Chief Justice were obviously influenced by events in Britain in 1910 when the King, despite emotional protests, followed his ministers' advice in coer-cing the House of Lords. After this time advice was invariably to be followed by the Governor-General on prorogation and dissolution, as on legislation and administration, until in 1975 a quite extraordinary set of circumstances (see below, pp. 164–8) was to arise.

There remained some doubt, particularly as time produced differences in technically legal position between the Commonwealth and the States, whether the governors of the latter were bound by the precedents to which Munro-Ferguson and his successors submitted. Clearly they could not be allowed to claim the kind of authority which Sir William Macartney claimed in Tasmania in 1914, when he sought to obtain from the Labour leader John Earle, as a condition of commissioning him as Premier, a pledge that he would formally advise a dissolution. That action was repudiated by the Secretary of State. But they have continued to look critically at requests for dissolution from Premiers who have lost the confidence of their Lower Houses. Another Tasmanian governor refused a dissolution in 1923 when a single defection transferred the government's control of the House of Assembly to the opposition. Twice in the 1950s dissolutions were granted in the same State in similar cases. In the first of these, however, the Governor first saw the Leader of the Opposition and 'satisfied himself that no alternative Government was possible', while in the second, though the Governor refused to accept an offer from the opposition to form an Administration, he told the Premier: 'It should not be assumed that my decision implies the acceptance of your submission that it is only "in extreme circumstances" that I am entitled to reject your advice to dissolve the House of Assembly'. And as late as 1952 a Victorian Premier was refused a dissolution by a governor convinced that an alternative ministry was available. But in most cases before that time and in all cases since, State Governors have followed their Premiers' advice: no Australian governor has any more right than the British Monarch to refuse a dissolution if a viable alternative administration is not obviously available. A governor must have ministers who can control the Lower House to accept responsibility for his actions, just as the Sovereign must. He may, in an emergency, take extraordinary action, as the New South Wales Governor did in 1932 in the case discussed later in this chapter (pp. 162–4), but he would be exercising the 'reserve powers' of the Crown just as, in a similar emergency, they might conceivably be exercised in the United Kingdom and as, indeed, they were exercised by the Governor-General of the Commonwealth forty-three years later.

Australians were slow to realize that the principle that a governor normally acts on ministerial advice has a fundamental implication— that they must solve their own problems and cannot complain if he does not solve those problems for them. In the past, for example in Tasmania in 1877 and Victoria in 1908, governors have been criticized by legislatures for granting their ministers a dissolution. The idea persisted for a long time that the representative of the Crown was available to punish a ministry which had seriously offended its opponents and that he was liable to censure if he did not act against them. The acquiescence of the Governors-General in the efforts of W.M. Hughes to cling to office in

1917, after the failure of the second conscription plebiscite, and again in 1923, was represented by Hughes's Labor opponents at the time (and has been represented since) as biassed political intervention by imperial officers in support of a man whose policies were favoured by the imperial government. And during the 1932 crisis in New South Wales, before the question of the legality or otherwise of the Premier's actions arose, there were people—this time in the non-Labor parties—who subjected the Governor to bitter personal abuse because he would not dissolve the Legislative Assembly against his ministers' advice. But in each of these cases the British precedent of 1910 was being followed. In the cases, subsequently to be discussed, in which a State governor and a Governor-General have dismissed ministries, questions concerning the constitutional legality of ministerial actions have allowed doubts about the relevance of this precedent to arise.

A corollary of the informal influence and formal discretion which were once the governor's was the unwillingness of the Crown to allow the colonial government any voice in his appointment. Up to 1888 the colonies were not consulted at all. In that year the Queensland government asked for advance information on who might be appointed, was refused by Knutsford, and protested strongly, with the support of New South Wales and South Australia. After this time the imperial government, though for long insisting on the right to decide, usually consulted colonial opinion. After federation there was some desire evinced to have Australians appointed to State governorships: the Labor Party wanted the office abolished and its duties performed by the Chief Justice. Although an Australian was appointed Governor of South Australia in 1924 and, despite the personal reluctance of the King, Sir Isaac Isaacs became Governor-General in January 1931, illogical hostility to the idea from true-blue conservatives in Australia, and from successive Secretaries of State, led imported Governors and Governors-General to remain the rule until after World War II. Western Australia remained without a governor, and was administered by the Lieutenant-Governor, for more than a decade after 1933 because the imperial government refused to accept a local nomination.

The Imperial Connection: Formal Independence Established

The survival well into the twentieth century of attitudes which allowed governors apparently more informal influence than the Sovereign was able to exercise in the United Kingdom should not be over-emphasized. Even in 1914 Australian governments, though they still lacked real sovereign status, enjoyed a very high degree of practical independence, and in the Empire at large there were developments which were further to increase that degree, in the case of the Federal government particularly. Ironically enough, these developments were a long-term consequence of attempts by imperial loyalists, in Britain and in the colonies, to prevent the disintegration of the Empire which seemed to be following from the growth of self-government.

In the late 1860s, as the recovery of the United States from the effects of its civil war and the progress towards unification in both Germany and Italy presaged a fundamental alteration in the political and economic balance of the world, there emerged a desire to make the Empire the great world power that Britain alone could not hope to remain. The establishment of the Royal Colonial Institute in 1869 was an obvious manifestation of this desire, one which, as has already been noted, Higinbotham saw as potentially pernicious in its effects on responsible government. While he was undoubtedly exaggerating the effect the Institute was likely to have, there were people who definitely aimed to bind the empire together more firmly than the self-governing colonies could be expected to allow. Some of these came forward with more or less hare-brained schemes for the election of colonial representatives to the House of Commons; others espoused 'imperial federation'. These latter established the Imperial Federation League in 1884. There was never any serious likelihood that this body would succeed in turning the Empire into a federal super-State, but before it collapsed in the early 1890s it had some success in making statesmen aware of the possibility that developments in the self-governing colonies implied imperial disintegration. It was largely responsible for the decision to hold, as part of Queen Victoria's golden jubilee celebrations in 1887, a 'Colonial Conference' at which British ministers discussed the problems of the Empire with representatives of the self-governing colonies. Although the speeches at this gathering ranged widely over economic, constitutional and strategic problems, it was a rather amorphous affair, and was important primarily as a precedent. Inevitably there was another meeting ten years later at the second jubilee, and a third, at which the Commonwealth rather than the Australian States was represented, on the occasion of Edward VII's coronation in 1902—after the Boer War had emphasized the collective loyalty of an apparently disorganized Empire. Both these conferences were given more direction by the presence of Joseph Chamberlain. At the second of them Britain agreed to seek the views of the colonies before signing commercial treaties, and it was decided to put the conference system on a regular basis: henceforth an 'Imperial Conference' was to be held every four years.

While the 1887 conference had been designed as a demonstration of unity, the development of a conference system which enabled colonial prime ministers to meet directly with senior British ministers necessarily implied a recognition by Britain that the participating colonies were now closer to independence than they had previously been. Their new position was emphasized by the fact that they were referred to in the report of the 1902 conference as 'self-governing dominions'. The semantic gaucherie of this description reflected the difficulty of defining the 'dominion status' which was acknowledged to be enjoyed by Canada, Australia, New Zealand and Newfoundland—and was to be accorded to South Africa in 1910 and to the Irish Free State in 1922. The English political mind, which like the English language tends at times to make a virtue of its vagueness, was at first not concerned with the problem of definition; but eventually this had to be tackled.

It was raised, at least theoretically, by the outbreak of World War I. The declaration of war shone a bright light on one basic difference between dominion status and true sovereignty: whatever the constitutional theory of the Empire might be, the fact remained that in international law Australians—and Canadians, South Africans and New Zealanders—were British subjects, and therefore as much at war on 4 August 1914 as British subjects domiciled in Yorkshire. At first it hardly seemed to matter: Australians almost unanimously supported Andrew Fisher's pledge to support Britain 'to the last man and the last shilling', and one of the first shots fired after the British declaration of war was across the bows of a German freighter attempting to break for sea from Port Phillip. The new Royal Australian Navy was officered by Englishmen, and when Australian troops laid the basis of their country's proudest legend at Gallipoli in 1915 they were commanded by a British general. Meanwhile patriotism inspired a revival of talk about imperial federation, and the British government, more pragmatically, sought to stimulate the war effort by holding 'Imperial War Conferences' in 1917 and 1918 and by inviting dominion prime ministers to sit in the so-called 'War Cabinet'. But the final effect of the war was to stimulate national self-consciousness in the dominions and to produce a desire to have their status defined.

That desire was stronger in Canada and South Africa than in Australia. The Canadian Prime Minister, Robert Borden, persuaded the 1917 Imperial War Conference to agree that post-war settlements should be based on 'recognition of the dominions as autonomous nations of an Imperial Commonwealth', and when the question of the representation of the dominions at the Paris Peace Conference came up he interpreted this rather pompous phrase as meaning that they were entitled to separate seats. Hughes also wanted separate representation, and the right to put a separate point of view, but he did not go as far as Borden, who replied to objections from other powers that dominion representation would increase British influence by claiming that the dominions were *de facto* independent States with the same Monarch—like Britain and Hanover between 1714 and 1837. And when he got separate representation and separate membership of the League of Nations he was satisfied. At the 1921 Imperial Conference he opposed moves, on this occasion mainly from Smuts of South Africa, for a clearer definition of dominion autonomy: 'We have all the rights of self-government enjoyed by independent States .... Let us leave well alone'.

Hughes was, of course, wrong. The dominions lacked at least one right enjoyed by independent States, the right to legislate extra-territorially. Moreover, their emergence into the international community after 1918 raised several important questions. Some of these concerned the application of the League Covenant to the Empire: could the League intervene to investigate disputes between member countries of the Empire? were Empire agreements 'treaties' within the meaning of Article XVIII of the Covenant and therefore void unless registered with the League secretariat? how could Empire countries apply 'sanctions' against each other? Some were more general: did the dominions have a prescriptive right to be consulted about foreign policy? if so, did this imply a share of financial responsibility for imperial defence? In some cases, like the Washington Naval Agreements, the Empire as a whole was clearly bound by a British decision: did this apply in all cases? and could dominions be considered bound by an agreement made by another dominion—such as a fisheries treaty between Canada and the United States? In the early 1920s some more-or-less desultory efforts were made to lay down principles which would apply to these questions, but in 1925 there arose issues which persuaded even the most fervent imperial patriots that such efforts were not enough. The Governor-General of Canada, Lord Byng, ignoring the precedents of the Parliament Bill crisis, refused a dissolution to the Prime Minister, forced his resignation, and then granted a dissolution to his successor. The same year in Australia there was the case, already referred to, in which the High Court voided provisions of the Navigation Act because of their repugnancy, under the terms of he Colonial Laws Validity Act, to British legislation; and the following year a Canadian law purporting to restrict the right of appeal to the Privy Council was similarly invalidated. The exercise by the Crown in Canada of a power apparently not exercisable by the Crown in the United Kingdom and two 'revivals' of the Colonial Laws Validity Act were impossible to square with the idea that the dominions were 'autonomous nations': some definition of the meaning of 'dominion status' was becoming urgently necessary. At the Imperial Conference of 1926 all the dominion representatives urged the need to face the issue, Hertzog of South Africa going so far as to ask for 'full nationhood, recognized internationally'.

The issue was faced, if not quite squarely. It was settled that henceforth the Governor-General of a dominion was to be considered as the personal representative of the King, not a representative of the British government: hence he was to observe the same conventions as the King in relation to his ministers. The British government made clear that it was willing to abrogate all rights of reservation and disallowance of Bills. And a committee under the chairmanship of Lord Balfour drew up a definition of dominion status. It defined the self-governing members of the Empire, the dominions and the United Kingdom, as 'autonomous communities within the British Empire, equal in status, in no way subordinate to one another in any aspect of their domestic or external affairs, though united by a common allegiance to the Crown and freely associated as members of the British Commonwealth of Nations'. This description left something to be desired. While Australians were not likely to ask, as South Africans and Irishmen did, whether the phrase 'freely associated' implied freedom to dissociate, they were, like Canadians and New Zealanders, aware that the Balfour Report *was* only a report (one in terms vague enough to lead a future Chief Justice of the High Court to call it 'a disorderly collection of abstract nouns') and that it could not over-ride rules of law. Alone, it did not constitute a grant to the dominions of extra-territorial legislative power; it did not abrogate the right of the Privy Council to give, in certain cases, leave to appeal against decisions of dominion courts; it did not clarify the position as regards foreign affairs; most importantly, it did not alter the provisions of the Colonial Laws Validity Act. To bring the law into line with the report it was necessary to hold an expert conference on the operation of dominion legislation which, reporting to the 1930 Imperial Conference, provided the basis for a legislative definition of the position of the dominions, passed by the imperial Parliament in 1931 and called, rather quaintly, the Statute of Westminster.

This enactment removed the last formal restrictions on the sovereignty of the Commonwealth of Australia. Apart from defining the dominions by the simple means of listing them, it provided that the Colonial Laws Validity Act should cease to apply to their laws and that the Acts relating to merchant shipping and courts of admiralty should be subject to repeal by dominion legislatures; it declared that henceforth no dominion law should be voidable through repugnancy to the laws of England; it gave the dominions full power to make laws with extra-territorial effect; and it laid down that no subsequent Act of the imperial Parliament should apply to a dominion unless at the request and with the consent of the dominion concerned. In order to prevent the federal government from using 'request and consent' to bypass opposition by the Senate, it was specifically provided that in Australia's case such request and consent should be that of the Parliament and government; and other clauses prevented the Statute from being interpreted in such a way as to give the Commonwealth power to amend the Constitution otherwise than by the means provided in the Constitution, or power to make laws on matters of exclusive State jurisdiction. As far as the Commonwealth was concerned, nothing but ratification of the Statute by the federal Parliament was needed to do away with the last vestiges of subordination to Britain.

Oddly enough, that ratification was delayed for a decade. The reasons are far from clear. Perhaps they lie partly in the economic situation of the 1930s, which gave statesmen problems more obviously urgent, and partly in the survival of the idea, expressed by Hughes in 1921, that it was somehow more in the British governmental tradition to let well alone. It has sometimes been suggested that strong influence against ratification was exerted by England-oriented conservative politicians, but it should be noted that between 1936 and 1938 the Commonwealth attorney-general, R.G. Menzies, than whom no man was truer blue, made three attempts to have Parliament pass a ratification Bill. One was finally passed in October 1942 after doubts had been cast on the validity of various wartime emergency regulations, particularly those applying to foreign shipping. Thus was put, as Menzies, now in opposition, said, 'the final touch to the technical powers of Australia'.

Long before this, those powers had been all but complete: the establishment after 1910 of the general principle that neither a Governor nor a Governor-General enjoyed discretion not enjoyed by the King in the United Kingdom was really more significant than the passage, or the ratification, of the Statute of Westminster. As has been noted, however, this fact was not always clearly understood: there were people who thought that the Governor was available as a tribunal of appeal against his ministers. He was not. But he did (and in strict law still does) have emergency reserve powers, as does the British Monarch. After 1910 Governors of New South Wales twice, and a Governor-General once, felt obliged to exercise such powers.

The Use of Reserve Powers: New South Wales 1916 and 1932

In 1916 the Labor Party split over the decision of its Commonwealth leader, the Prime Minister, W.M. Hughes, to support conscription. Among the minority of the party who followed Hughes was the New South Wales Premier, W.A. Holman. He and a few of his colleagues were expelled from the party, but he was able to retain his majority by coalescing with the opposition against most of his former supporters. The official Labor Party felt that it had the support of most of the electors, and looked forward to the general election which was due. Holman, however, proposed a year's extension in the life of the Parliament. The Governor, Sir Gerald Strickland, expressed doubts as to whether he would be justified in assenting to such an attempt to deprive the Labor Party of its chance to appeal to the country: he was promptly recalled by the Secretary of State. Ostensibly he was recalled for the same reason as Macartney had been rebuked in 1914—for claiming a discretionary right to reject advice (see p. 155). The cases, however, were not the same: Macartney had done something which, it was generally agreed, the Monarch would not be entitled to do in the

United Kingdom, but what Strickland had considered doing was something which the Monarch might well consider doing in a parallel case. As A.B. Keith, no friend of Australian Labor politicians, wrote in 1927, 'If a ministry should seek to cling to office by prolonging the duration of [a] Parliament in which it had a majority, or to govern without Parliament, the reserve powers of the Crown would be available to expel them from office'. Strickland did nothing more than contemplate exercising a legitimate reserve power. It is difficult not to agree with Keith that 'The only plausible reason for his recall is that his attitude ... was embarrassing to the Imperial Government', which was much in favour of Hughes' attempts to provide more troops for the Western Front.

By thus putting expediency before constitutional principle the British government seriously clouded the issue of the definition of the reserve powers, and thereby complicated the second case of their exercise in New South Wales.

In 1930, during the worst period of the Great Depression, a Labor government led by J.T. Lang was returned to office with a large majority and a financial policy which, if hardly radical in terms of later economic thinking, was both unorthodox and, for financial interests inside and outside the State, quite alarming. Lang proceeded to raise the political temperature by making his second attempt to abolish the Upper House. While his legislation on this matter was under challenge in the courts he went ahead with his financial programme. He tried to force a lowering of the interest rate on the State debt; when he failed he defaulted on interest payments. But the Financial Agreement of 1927 which is dealt with in Chapter Eight had given the Commonwealth overall responsibility for the management of the debt of the States. Accordingly the federal government paid the amounts owing by New South Wales and then sought to reimburse itself by putting through Parliament four Financial Agreement Enforcement Acts authorizing the seizure of the State's revenues. By this time Lang's actions—or rather, perhaps, his words, for his denunciations of bond-holders and moneyed men in general were remarkably inflammatory—and the hysterical reaction of some of his opponents (including a lunatic fringe of quasi-fascists) had produced a real atmosphere of crisis. As has been pointed out, the Governor, Sir Philip Game, was subjected to pressure to take action which would have been quite unconstitutional while the government remained within the law, as up to this time it had, however much its opponents might accuse it of acting immorally. But the Commonwealth government had forced Lang against the wall of legality: he had either to surrender or make a breach in it. He tried various means of evading the provisions of the Acts sequestering his revenues, which were held valid by the High Court under Ss.105A and 109 of the Constitution. The Commonwealth seized the State's balances at the banks. He then ordered his officers, in contravention of both the State Audit Act and proclamations made under the federal Financial Agreement Enforcement Acts, to accept payments only in cash and not to pay moneys received into banks. The definitive order to this effect was issued on 10 May 1932. Two days later Game wrote formally to Lang in words which implied a request for his resignation:

> The position as I see it is that Ministers are committing a breach of the law ... Your case as I understand it is, that Ministers are determined on their action in order to carry on the essential services of the State. Into the aspect of justification it is not, as I conceive it, my province to enquire. My position is that if my Ministers are unable to carry on essential services without breaking the law my plain duty is to endeavour to obtain Ministers who feel able to do so.

Lang replied curtly that the government would not resign. The next day he was dismissed. Game commissioned the leader of the opposition and dissolved Parliament on his advice. In the election which followed the Labor Party was defeated

On 11 May Lang had rushed through Parliament a Bill to put a ten per cent tax, payable within fourteen days, on all mortgages. For this reason, and because the fate of Governor Strickland who had supported the Labor Party in a constitutional crisis sixteen years before was well remembered, Lang's supporters believed that the Governor had acted, probably under instructions from London, in order to protect British bond-holders. The party's best lawyer, H.V. Evatt, wrote a book on the constitutional implications of the affair in which he drew a cynical inference from the fact that Game was able to remove a Premier while Strickland had been recalled for threatening to remove one: 'In each of the two cases, which are so difficult to reconcile with each other, it was the Official Labor Party ... which was seriously disadvantaged by the exercise of, and the prevention of the exercise of, a reserve power'. Evatt was right in saying that the cases were difficult to reconcile. Indeed they were impossible. And there is something to be said for his opinion that 'The moral ... is the need for definition ... of the Crown's reserve powers'. But one should add that Strickland and Game seem to have understood what those reserve powers were: they were, and are, no more than a right to intervene when no other method is provided by constitutional convention or by the courts to prevent a ministry from abusing its power. In a federal system in which federal law takes precedence it is better for a governor to be able to enforce that law against a recalcitrant State government by dismissal and dissolution than for the federal authority to enforce it by arms; in any case it is an emergency means of forcing ministers to defer to their real masters, the electors. No governor is likely to use it except in an extreme case, for he has to be confident that he can find a Premier who, after an election, will be in a position to accept responsibility for his conduct.

The action of the representative of the Crown in dismissing the government of a State, within eighteen months of the passage of the Statute of Westminster and long before a Governor-General felt impelled to take similar action, could have been seen as a consequence of the fact that, in law, the Statute applied to the Commonwealth and the other dominions and not to the States. In theory they remained, and remain, bound by such enactments as the Colonial Laws Validity Act and the Australian States Constitutions Act. But too much can be made of this theory. As K.C. Wheare has noted,

> It is difficult to accept arguments put forward to demonstrate that the States of Australia . . . are . . . to be placed upon a status of constitutional inequality in relation to the United Kingdom. A Dominion is not a Government or a Parliament, it is a territorial community. It has been declared that these territorial communities are equal in status with the territorial community of the United Kingdom. The people of Australia . . . that is to say, are in no way subordinate in constitutional status to the people of the United Kingdom, and the proposition is unaffected by the fact that the people of Australia . . . are for some purposes governed from Canberra . . . and for other purposes from the State capitals.

In theory the British Parliament could, without the consent of the government of a State, pass a law to apply to that State. But in theory it could repeal the Statute of Westminster. In theory Queen Victoria could have sold the Navy.

In practice the position is as Menzies stated it in 1942. He spoke of putting 'the final touch to the technical powers' not of 'the Commonwealth' but of 'Australia'. Much has been written, and more could be written, on the question of where sovereignty resides in Australia. But the question can easily become a sterile one, particularly in a world in which most countries depend for the ultimate protection of their sovereignty on the assistance, or the forbearance, of one or two 'super-powers'. The essential facts are that intervention by Britain in the affairs of either the Commonwealth or the States has long since become utterly inconceivable, though there remain, and perhaps will long remain, people who do not know it, and that in the critical question of reserve powers subsequent events were to show the position of the Commonwealth and the States to be not markedly different.

The Use of Reserve Powers: the Crisis of 1975

The second of these facts, however, was far from obvious. In the years which followed the dismissal of Lang the steadily continuing growth in Commonwealth powers which is the subject of the next chapter accustomed men to think of the national government as something existing on a quite different plane from the governments of the States, however much lip service might have been paid to the alleged sovereignty of the latter. World War II and a long period of profound, in the view of some people, perhaps, deadening political stability which followed reinforced the tendency. By the 1970s the reserve powers had been all but forgotten. The sudden reminder of their existence which came in 1975 was, therefore, a shock to the country as a whole, and an almost traumatic blow to the more dedicated supporters of the government against which they were exercised.

The post-war political history of Australia was quite extraordinary. The Labor government which had ruled throughout most of the war failed to satisfy the electors in the early years of peace and was roundly defeated at the end of 1949. From then until he retired in 1966 the remarkable, indeed almost charismatic R.G. Menzies was able to direct the affairs of the nation pretty much as he wished, though he was forced into a double dissolution by a hostile Senate in 1951 and had a rather close shave at the election of 1961. But after his retirement (or rather after the accidental death a little over a year later of the man whom he had carefully groomed as his successor, H.E. Holt) the grip of his coalition on affairs rapidly decayed, and in 1972 Labor came back to power.

Nearly a quarter of a century in opposition had left a mark on the Labor Party. The new ministers were inexperienced, and, finding themselves in a position which enabled them to do the things they had never been able to do, they tried to do all those things at once. The result was inevitably that they stirred up much more hostility in their opponents than would have been the case had the political pendulum swung more regularly since 1945. Within eighteen months of coming to office the new Prime Minister, E.G. Whitlam, found it necessary to obtain a double dissolution. When his government was returned with a somewhat reduced majority in the Lower House but without control of the Senate, he called a joint sitting in order to push through important measures.

The passage of these Bills was a very considerable political victory, but it was won at a price. The uncompromising determination which it showed to put his party's far-reaching policies into force as quickly as possible frightened many of the 'swinging voters' who had put his government into office and had been persuaded that they should give it a 'fair go' at the election which followed the double dissolution. More seriously, his ministers made grave mistakes. The worst concerned exploratory negotiations for a large overseas loan. These negotiations were begun without the knowledge of the Loan Council and so were arguably a breach of S.105A of the Constitution (see below, p. 174). They were carried on through unusual channels and with considerable secrecy, and so when news of them leaked out there were allegations of constitutional impropriety and, from some quarters, vague hints of corruption. The treasurer was forced to resign.

Meanwhile the country was drifting into serious economic difficulties, and tempers were fraying. Elements opposed to the Whitlam government allowed their political passions to lead them into actions as dubious as some of those into which Labor ministers had been led by their enthusiasm for rapid change. The most dubious concerned the filling of casual vacancies in the Senate. The Constitution provided that when a vacancy occurred it should be filled, until the next Senate election, by the Parliament of the State from which the former senator had come. It had become the invariable practice for the vacancy to be filled with a member of the party which had previously held the seat. But when Whitlam's attorney-general, Lionel Murphy, resigned his position to accept an appointment to the High Court Bench the New South Wales Parliament appointed an independent. There may have been some little justice in the Premier's claim that the convention, intended to cover vacancies caused by death, should not automatically apply in Murphy's case; but six months later a Labor senator from Queensland died and the Premier of that State (against the wishes of his coalition partners) forced the rejection of the man nominated by the Labor Party and the election of another.

By the spring of 1975, therefore, a resentful government, its political standing seriously eroded by the loans affair and by what was seen as a dismal failure to deal with serious inflation and rising unemployment, was faced by an opposition obviously prepared to go to extraordinary lengths to dislodge it. The crisis which had been looming for some time was touched off by further revelations concerning the overseas loan negotiations which culminated in the resignation of another senior minister. The opposition, alleging that popular confidence in the government had now been completely destroyed, acted to force a dissolution with a Senate refusal to pass necessary supply Bills until the government agreed to an election.

The question whether the opposition was justified in its actions, whether, that is, it was appropriate in a modern democratic polity that the Senate should be able to force the dissolution of a House only eighteen months old, or whether, as Whitlam claimed, governments should always be 'made and unmade in the House of Representatives—in the people's House', is not one which can be adequately discussed here: answers to it are bound to be conditioned by political sympathies. Opposition supporters argued that Australia's federal Constitution did give the Senate the right to do what it was now doing, despite the breach of convention in the matter of casual vacancies, and despite the fact, which Whitlam understandably emphasized, that no Senate had ever done it before. Government supporters argued that this was too legalistic and backward-looking a view, that the democratic principles which were the underlying assumption of Australian political life were threatened by the Senate's behaviour. What is clear is that the opposition had forced a first-class political crisis. But there was not, as yet, a constitutional crisis.

What produced this was the decision of the government not to advise a dissolution but rather, as the Prime Minister put it, to 'tough the affair out', and the opposition's equally adamant refusal to retreat from its position. Again the question of justification must be left aside. Something can be said for the Labor argument that the Senate's unprecedented action involved straining the Constitution in order to force an election at a time unfavourable to the government; and something can be said for the opposition coalition's view that in the circumstances then existing the electorate was entitled to be consulted. Both were in fact pursuing political ends, as political parties normally do.

The leader of the opposition, J.M. Fraser, announced his parties' decision to refuse supply on 15 October and the Senate passed the necessary amendment that afternoon; later in the day the Prime Minister announced his decision to stand firm. In the fortnight which followed the two leaders jockeyed for public support, and in the process manoeuvred themselves into positions from which it would be very difficult to retreat. On 21 October the Governor-General, Sir John Kerr, began attempts to produce a compromise, but it was already too late. By the end of the month it was clear that the opposition would continue to use its Senate majority to defer supply Bills no matter how frequently they were introduced, and the government, still refusing to advise a dissolution and faced with the need to find money for its public service and contractors, began to look for ways round the impasse. Its decision to do so sealed its fate. A request to the banks to provide the necessary funds on credit was rejected by them after consulting counsel: it appears that the Governor-General had already formed the opinion that raising money in this way would be a breach of the law and that he would therefore not be justified in signing the necessary documents. Early in the afternoon of 11 November he came to the conclusion that only by an exercise of the reserve powers of the Crown could the crisis be resolved: he withdrew Whitlam's comission as Prime Minister and commissioned Fraser to form a 'caretaker government', having previously ascertained that Fraser could secure the passage of the blocked supply bills and would then advise a double dissolution.

The affair produced great political bitterness. In the hours which elapsed between the dismissal of Whitlam and the dissolution of Parliament, while the supply bills were being approved by the Senate, the Labor majority in the Lower House pushed through a no-confidence motion against the caretaker government and claimed that this obliged the Governor-General to dismiss it in turn—missing the point that the alternative course, a dissolution on the advice of the Prime Minister thus censured, had since 1910 been accepted as the proper one. The action of the Speaker in protesting to London against the Governor-General's decision to take it was simply another case of an Australian's forgetting, in a moment of high political anger, that Downing Street had long since surrendered its right and duty to control vice-regal actions.

The Governor-General was subjected to unprecedented abuse. The Labor Party felt cheated and deceived. It resented the fact that he had acted immediately after consulting the Chief Justice, Sir Garfield Barwick, a former Liberal minister. It resented even more that it had not received the sort of warning Lang had received from Game the day before he was dismissed. This aspect of the affair has since led the eminent constitutional lawyer Geoffrey Sawer to accuse the Governor-General of a lack of frankness. Perhaps Kerr felt that, given a warning, Whitlam may have moved to have him recalled, thus leaving the crisis unresolved. On the other hand it can be argued that the Governor-General's action was precipitate and that by 'lancing the abscess', as one political commentator put it, he had not cured the disease affecting the body politic but simply allowed the poison to spread throughout its system. Yet again, the question is politically subjective. The objective outcome was an election which produced a landslide victory for the 'caretaker government'. As in New South Wales in 1932, the electors endorsed the exercise of the reserve powers.

That the exercise of these powers has been rare is undoubtedly fortunate, for by their very nature they cannot be used in a modern democratic society without producing the sort of political passion which can threaten that society's stability. A constitutional amendment which would, by weakening the Senate, ensure that the situation which led to their use in November 1975 could not again arise could well be in the country's interests. Even the Fraser government was prepared in 1977 to put to a referendum a proposal to reduce the possibility of clashes by having half the Senate go to the country at the time of each House of Representatives election, and another to formalize the old convention on casual vacancies. The former was narrowly rejected; the latter was passed.

It is possible to criticize the reserve powers themselves as an anachronism, but their formal elimination would require constitutional amendments unlikely to receive electoral endorsement. In the long run they may wither away, but they are part of the Westminster system as it exists at present in this country. They are neither a consequence of federalism nor an indication that Australian governments, federal or State, are in some sense still subordinate to Britain.

CHAPTER EIGHT

The Decline of the States

'Federalism is a stage in Australian political development which must now be regarded as over, and ... in most, but not quite all, functions of government we have an effective unification within a nominal federalism.... To deplore the departures from what the Founding Fathers designed is perfectly legitimate; to see dangers of centralization and overgovernment in trends away from ... federalism may be completely justified. But it is not sensible to believe that it is practical politics to secure in this country a reversion towards federalism and less of the near unitary state we have reached. The clock will not go backwards'.

S.J. BUTLIN (1954)

The High Court and the States, 1920–1939

The process of filling in the 'mere framework' of the Australian federal Constitution with the traditions and doctrines and unexpressed tendencies of which Haldane had spoken in 1900 was—and is—a continuous one, but, as was pointed out at the end of Chapter Six, by 1920 the pattern of future development had been more or less set. Not only had the *Engineers' Case* revolution determined the secondary role of the States in the Australian federal system; there had by now been built up a considerable number of local precedents and it was therefore possible to apply ordinary judicial techniques more easily; American theories and the personal presuppositions of the justices, even the surviving 'Founding Fathers', Higgins and Isaacs, became less important. During the next two decades federal powers continued to expand, though the process was complicated by the tangled history of S.92 and the arbitration power, and the High Court played a leading part in the process. The Bench naturally insisted that it pursued no policy and was concerned only with 'discovering the law', but its members were well aware that the total separation of policy and law is a myth. Indeed Isaacs, who was perhaps a little more honest with himself in this matter than some of his brethren, went close to stating a theory of judicial legislation when he said in a 1925 judgement: 'As a living and co-ordinate branch of the Government [the High Court] cannot stand still and refuse in interpreting the law to recognize the advancing frontiers of public thought and public activity'. During the 1920s and 1930s the Court's decisions in a number of areas helped to advance those frontiers further in the direction of Commonwealth dominance.

There was, for example, a tendency to give the Commonwealth the benefit of the doubt in the interpretation of such specific constitutional prohibitions as S.99, which provides that 'The Commonwealth shall not, by any law or regulation of trade, commerce or revenue, give preference to one State or any part thereof over another State or any part thereof'. In 1935–36, when a primary producer sought to destroy an export marketing board on the ground that the Act establishing it provided for representatives to be appointed from only four States and in unequal numbers, and when a seaman tried to bring down regulations made under a Transport Workers Act for the licensing of sailors in certain specified ports in four States, the actions failed. In these judgements (*Crowe* v. *Commonwealth* and *Elliott* v. *Commonwealth*) the Court required tangible commercial advantage to be demonstrated clearly before this clause could be invoked: its scope was therefore greatly restricted.

In contrast, prohibitions applying to the States were rigidly enforced: in particular the Court's interpretation of S.90, which forbids the States to impose duties of customs and excise, became in this period a serious embarrassment to them. Its definition of 'excise' when the meaning of S.90 first came before it in 1904 was the narrow and commonsense one of 'a tax on production in proportion to the amount or value produced'. This allowed the States to impose licence fees on brewers and hotel-keepers which looked like traditional excise duties but were in fact an ingenious variant—taxes based on the previous year's turnover, or sales. But in two cases in 1926 and 1927 the Court rather widened the definition. In the first, *Commonwealth* v. *South Australia*, in which the Commonwealth successfully challenged a State tax on petrol, the issue was complicated by the fact that interstate trade was involved; but the second, *John Fairfax and Sons Ltd.* v. *New South Wales*, in which a State tax on locally produced newspapers was struck down, carried the unmistakable implication that the States might not impose sales taxes of any kind. A revenue source of very great importance to the State governments in America was thereby forbidden to them. Forty years later, in the *Hamersley Case* of 1969, the Court with steam-roller logic deprived the States of another source on which they thought they could rely when it declared a stamp duty on receipts given in connection with sales to be an excise. A decision in another case (*Dickenson's Arcade*) in 1974 may seem to have relaxed the situation somewhat by allowing fees to be exacted from the retailers of tobacco and cigarettes on a similar basis to hotel licence fees, but the decision in this case was very grudging, so grudging indeed that some legal authorities wonder whether the conditions imposed in the *Dickenson's Arcade* decision might not in the long run restrict the States' ability to use hotel licence fees as a lucrative source of revenue.

The decisions of the inter-war years had consequences on policy as well as on finance. An attempt by the New South Wales government to raise money for subsidies to wheat farmers who were in difficulties by imposing a thinly disguised tax on flour sales was invalidated in 1937. The next year, when a levy on the *acreage* of chicory grown in Victoria which was intended to finance a marketing scheme was similarly treated, the meaning of the word 'excise' was stretched to almost absurd limits. Henceforth no State could compel primary producers to pay the expenses of the 'orderly marketing' of their product unless it was prepared to give authority to a Board to acquire the whole crop and re-sell it, deducting a charge for expenses. The Court's rigid view of S.90 thus forced the States into rural socialism.

The same restrictive attitude towards the States was seen in the Bench's treatment of S.109. As has been seen, most of the Commonwealth's legislative powers were made concurrent with similar State powers, and under S.109 States laws remained valid unless 'inconsistent with a law of the Commonwealth'. At first the High Court interpreted the idea of inconsistency narrowly, voiding a State law only if it was impossible for a person to obey that enactment without committing a breach of federal law, but in three cases in 1926, the most significant of which was *Cowburn's Case*, the definition was widened. Thereafter, although exceptions were made in some cases, a State law was liable to be struck down when the Court believed that there existed a valid federal law intended to provide a comprehensive code, a law which 'covered the field'. This interpretation of S.109 was of particular importance in extending the powers of the Commonwealth Arbitration Court, of which more is said below.

The tendency between the wars, then, was to give federal authority greater scope and State authority less. And by the end of the period there were signs that the tendency was being strengthened by the operation of the external affairs power. The first hint that the federal government could, by making an international agreement, acquire for the federal Parliament power to execute the provisions of that agreement even if it extended into fields constitutionally reserved to the States came in the judgement of *Roche* v. *Kronheimer* in 1921; but the leading case was *R.* v. *Burgess, ex parte Henry* (1936). This arose from the signature by the Commonwealth of the Paris Convention on Air Navigation of 1919 and an attempt to apply regulations purportedly in accordance with the convention to intra-State as well as interstate and overseas flights on Commonwealth authority alone. The court held that the regulations were *ultra vires* (outside the Commonwealth's jurisdiction) as far as intra-State services were concerned. The Commonwealth had, therefore, to ask the States which had not already done so to legislate to provide uniform rules. But the decision was based on the fact that all but one of the justices considered the particular regulations in question to go beyond the terms of the convention: they were unanimous that the external affairs power gave the Commonwealth the right to apply the convention to intra-State flights provided it did so strictly.

The *obiter dicta* (statements made by the judges in giving reasons for their decision which did not strictly form part of the judgement) considered the implications of this. Justices Starke and Dixon were anxious that the decision should not be pushed too far: they suggested that the external affairs power could only give the Commonwealth authority over matters not otherwise covered by federal powers if the treaty or convention involved was 'in an accepted area of international agreement'. Chief Justice Latham approved their caution, but wondered whether such areas were not multiplying so rapidly as to make the phrase meaningless. The other justices, Evatt and McTiernan, could see no limit to the operation of the principles of the case. They asked: 'What is comprehended by the expression "external affairs"?' and answered:

> It is an expression of wide import ... frequently used to denote the whole series of relationships which exist between States ... It would seem clear, therefore, that the legislative power of the Commonwealth over 'external affairs' certainly includes the power to execute within the Commonwealth the treaties and conventions entered into with foreign powers.

They argued, indeed, that the power extended to the implementation not only of treaty obligations but also of the recommendations of international bodies of which Australia was a member. Both were former Labor members of the New South Wales Parliament, and it was obvious that uppermost in their minds was the ILO Forty-Hour Week Convention, which was unlikely to be accepted by State legislatures with conservative Upper Houses. But Evatt in particular saw well beyond this. Later, after he had left the Bench and was minister for external affairs and attorney-general in a Labor federal government, he was, as will be seen, convinced that he had in the external affairs *placitum* a potent means of modifying the social framework of Australia. His views were, perhaps, extreme. As K.C. Wheare has said, the precise limits of the power, in Australia as in the United States, have still not been defined. But already by 1939 it had become one of the factors in the decline of the States.

Efforts to amend the Constitution formally in the years between the wars met with little more success than had those sponsored by Hughes. In 1926 an attempt was made to give the Commonwealth something close to plenary powers over both corporations and industrial disputes but, despite all-party agreement in Parliament on the proposals, it failed. At the same time a request for the power to protect 'the interests of the public in the case of actual or probable interruption of any essential service' which was bitterly opposed by the Labor opposition was also rejected. The defeat of the corporations and industrial disputes proposals was due partly to the factious opposition of J.T. Lang's Labor government in New South Wales and partly to the conviction of conservatives that they would be safer if these matters were left under the influence of State Upper Houses; but the existence of some evidence that substantially the same people voted against all the proposals is an interesting comment on the operation of the amendment process in Australia. In 1937 attempts to strengthen Commonwealth powers over interstate trade, which had been seriously weakened by recent S.92 cases, and to give it plenary powers over aviation were also rejected. The informal changes already discussed were, however, considerable, and there was one formal alteration approved in the period, one which was to have very great consequences. This was the 'Financial Agreement' amendment.

The Growth of Federal Financial Power, 1920–1939

As was shown in Chapter Six, the Surplus Revenue Act of 1908, the financial arrangements made on the expiry of the Braddon clause in 1910 and the Commonwealth's invasion of the field of direct taxation had begun by 1920 to make clear what Deakin had meant when he spoke of the States as 'financially bound to the chariot wheels of the Commonwealth'. The States entertained no real hope that the bonds could be cut, but they were anxious to prevent them from being drawn tighter at the end of the ten years for which the 1910 arrangement had been made. The Commonwealth, for its part, while it continued the twenty-five shilling per capita payments on a year-to-year basis after 1920, tried unsuccessfully to get agreement on their progressive elimination. Finally, in 1926, it proposed to discontinue the payments and in compensation to vacate the field of personal income taxation. Its idea was that federal and State finances should be 'separated as far as possible, on the principle that, normally, indirect taxation is the proper field for the Commonwealth'. It offered, however, to give temporary help with transitional problems and to continue special assistance to Tasmania and Western Australia. When the States rejected the offer the Commonwealth virtually forced them to accept an alternative plan which tied the revenue question to the question of loan funds.

One of the pre-1900 arguments for federation had been that a united Australia would be able to raise loans on better terms than six competing colonies, but after the establishment of the Commonwealth the competition continued, and in the long run was aggravated by the needs of the federal government. In 1908, when the Commonwealth first began to consider entering the loan market, the treasurer, Sir William Lyne, suggested that a 'Council of Finance' be set up to co-ordinate federal and State borrowings. No agreement could be reached at the time, but in 1924, when the problem had become quite serious, all the States except New South Wales joined the Commonwealth in a more-or-less informal 'Loan Council' designed to find agreement on such issues as the total amount which could be raised at economic rates and the proportion of the total which each government should get. Three years later the Commonwealth used a threat to end per capita payments without compensation to force New South Wales as well as the other States to agree to the establishment of the Council on a formal basis. The Financial Agreement of 1927 provided for the Commonwealth to take over the management and amortization of all State debts. The States would make regular payments to interest and sinking funds, and the Commonwealth would contribute an amount roughly equivalent to the existing per capita payments, which were abolished. The Loan Council, which in effect was a Premiers' Conference attended by the Prime Minister, would have exclusive control over all future raisings except loans for defence purposes. It was provided that on decisions about total borrowings each State would have one vote and the Commonwealth two, with, if necessary, a casting vote: the sharing of the amount raised was to be a matter for negotiation. It was agreed that a constitutional amendment should be sought to provide a firm basis for the agreement, for subsequent similar agreements, and for their enforcement. Ratification was given by the electors in 1928, and the next year S.105A became part of the Constitution.

The Financial Agreement had benefits for both the Commonwealth and the States. Although the States resented having been coerced into it, it seemed to lay the foundations for an improvement in their relations with the federal government. It provided the opportunity for a regular Premiers' Conference under federal leadership, which was to develop into an important machine of 'co-operative federalism' and to play a significant role during the Great Depression. It was the more successful as a means of resolving the economic complexities of the federal system because of an informal understanding which went with it: the Commonwealth included defence loans in the total estimates, and the States included the needs of local government and of 'semi-government instrumentalities', though not obliged to do so. But there was one feature of the agreement which was extraordinary in theory and was to have serious and quite unexpected practical consequences. Not only was the institution of the Loan Council incompatible with theories of federalism which see the essence of the system in the complete independence of each government in its own sphere; it was also incompatible with the strict theory of responsible government. It transferred to a supra-governmental institution an important part of that financial control which the Parliament of the Westminster type is supposed to exercise over the executive.

The practical effects became clear in the events of 1932 which were discussed in the last chapter: when the New South Wales government attempted to default on interest payments which it was obliged to make under the agreement, the High Court in the *Garnishee Case* upheld the right of the Commonwealth to seize the State's revenues. In theory S.105A made the Financial Agreement enforceable against any party, but it was for the Commonwealth to do the enforcing. It suddenly became clear that in the process of enforcement the 'sovereign rights' of the States could be ignored, the control of a State's revenues could be taken out of the hands not merely of its government but even if its Parliament—that in some circumstances, perhaps, the State involved might be prevented from having the government it chose. What would have happened if J.T. Lang had won the election which followed his dismissal remains unknowable, but it is impossible to believe that he could have succeeded in his defiance of the Commonwealth.

It is important to realize that the powers of self-government which the *Garnishee Case* showed the States to have lost did not go directly or immediately to the Commonwealth, but to the Loan Council. In theory that body had no right of direction of State policies, but the Depression, which was the ultimate cause of the crisis in New South Wales, gave it such a right in practice by forcing nearly all the States to rely on it to balance their budgets. In the financial situation of the early 1930s a State could not even get a bank overdraft unless the Council approved. It became, in the words of one legal commentator, 'a kind of super-government, directing the States and the Commonwealth when they should prepare and present their budgets, what lines those budgets should follow, and even (it is scarcely too much to say) where and how economies should be made'. This was a consequence not of the Financial Agreement in itself but of the agreement in combination with the attitude of the independent Commonwealth Bank Board which saw the Council as a means whereby it could force reluctant politicians, federal as well as State, to swallow the economic medicine which the Board prescribed. When recovery came, the powers the States had lost to the Council did not return to them: war soon followed recovery and after the war the situation had changed. Although established for the narrowly specific purpose of co-ordinating governmental borrowing, the Loan Council had come by the end of the Commonwealth's first half-century to exercise authority over the whole spectrum of Australian financial affairs, at least as far as the States were concerned. New economic ideas and new federal policies had turned the Commonwealth Bank into a reserve bank under the clear direction of the federal Treasury. From the establishment of the Loan Council the Prime Minister had needed the support of only two of the six Premiers to force his economic policies on them all. Now he hardly needed even two because, as Sir Douglas Copland has remarked, since World War II 'the Commonwealth Government, with its new powers over the loan market derived from its effective control of the Commonwealth Bank, has been in the position of being able in effect to veto any decision of the Loan

Council with which it disagrees'. In the inter-war period, which is at present under discussion, this nail had not quite been driven home, but it was already firmly imbedded in the lid of the States' coffin.

The destiny of the States was written between the lines of the Constitution. The distinguished economist and central banker L.F. Giblin pointed out in 1949 that 'When the decision was made for a uniform customs tariff and interstate free trade, the independence of the States was doomed'. He was right: federal monopoly of customs revenue led to the per capita payments of 1910–27, which led to the Financial Agreement, which led, in turn, to the situation just described. Giblin added: 'This verdict was confirmed by section 96, which gave the Commonwealth power to make grants to individual States without limit, and subject to any conditions'. The first hints of how S.96 could become an instrument of federal control were given in 1923, when the Commonwealth legislated to offer the States a grant for the construction of main roads: a State which accepted the grant had to provide matching finance from its own funds and agree to locate the roads under Commonwealth direction. Three years later a Federal Aid Roads Act provided more money, to be expended under particularly stringent supervision. After the High Court had made short work of a Victorian contention that the Act was in substance an Act relating to roads and so beyond Commonwealth powers, the way was open for the Commonwealth to exercise influence in any field of State responsibility where the need for finance was great. An Act of 1927 provided money for the States to assist farmers in the purchase of rabbit-proof fencing, and during the 1930s the main roads grants continued to be important. After World War II the 'matching dollar' was to be as potent a corrosive of State powers as federal control of borrowing.

Between the wars the influence of federal grants was naturally strongest in the smaller States. South Australia began in 1929 to receive special financial assistance of the kind which Western Australia had been receiving since 1910 and Tasmania since 1912. Up to 1933 the grants were more or less *ad hoc* and unconditional, but in 1933 they were put on a more business-like basis, largely as a result of the 'secession' movement in Western Australia. The complaints of that State about the alleged disadvantages imposed on it by interstate free trade and external protection, which sent up the price of fencing wire, galvanized iron and farm machinery, were not ended by the institution of special grants. With the collapse of overseas wool and wheat markets in the Depression they grew louder, while the protection extended to Queensland sugar producers was represented in exaggerated terms as the cause of a steep rise in the cost of living. Suggestions that the State would be better off if it seceded, which had been of little significance in the early 1920s, began to attract more attention in the depths of the Depression. In 1933 a plebiscite held by the State government returned a majority of almost two to one in favour of petitioning Westminster for permission to withdraw from the Commonwealth. The vote is not necessarily to be taken seriously. A case was solemnly prepared and sent to London with a counter-case prepared by the Commonwealth, and equally solemnly a committee of the two Houses of the imperial Parliament considered both. But at the same time as the plebiscite was held the Labor Party, which opposed secession, was elected to government. The joint committee in London reported, predictably, that constitutional practice forbad the imperial Parliament to amend the constitution of a dominion without the consent of its Parliament. The vote was really a gesture of protest. As that it was taken and as that it had its effect—if not, in the long run, quite the effect which the supporters of 'secession' hoped.

Before the movement was killed at Westminster the federal government had acted to alleviate the grievances which lay behind it by establishing the Commonwealth Grants Commission, a quasi-judicial body with power to investigate the financial problems of the three 'claimant States' and to recommend what special grants they needed. As has been pointed out, the main basis for claims to special assistance had been the contention that the smaller States were adversely affected by federal tariff policy and were therefore entitled to 'compensation'. But from the time of its first report in 1934 the Commission, having found it impossible to assess the grants that were needed to 'compensate' the three States, adopted as the criterion their 'fiscal need'. In other words the Commission sought to assess the amount of federal aid which would be necessary to enable the claimant States to provide for their citizens services comparable with those provided by the larger States. This involved close examination of State budgets and policies: the Commission was able to punish, by cutting down grants, what it considered extravagance. It was, and is, able to do a great deal for the material needs of the claimant States, but although special grants have always been a marginal supplement to their budgets rather than a central form of revenue, its activities have provided yet another restriction on them. A Premier who has to justify to a Commonwealth officer the need for some particular expenditure must have his tongue very tightly in his cheek when he describes his State as 'sovereign'.

In the operation of the Australian financial system, then, as in the developments which the High Court sanctioned in matters like excise duties, external affairs and inconsistency of laws, the inter-war period was one of steady growth in Commonwealth power at the expense of the States. In two other matters which were important in this period, the operation of S.92 and the problems of the arbitration power, the States also lost ground, though the advances of the Commonwealth government were less clear.

Complicating Factors: Interstate Trade and Industrial Arbitration

In the case of S.92 the development was very confused. The 'little bit of layman's language' is capable of a wide range of interpretations. Probably the majority of the Convention delegates of the 1890s, and of those electors who thought about it at the time of the referendums, took it to be a guarantee of that 'interstate free trade' which had been one of the advertised advantages of federation, a guarantee that border tariffs (or their disguised equivalent) would be abolished permanently. It is possible that some of the 'conservative men of property', as L.F. Crisp has described the bulk of the delegates, put a wider interpretation on it, seeing the phrase also as some sort of protection against government regulation of a 'socialist' nature; but no one could have foreseen the confusion of shifting interpretations which made it in the 1920s and 1930s the bane of governments and the gold-mine of constitutional silks. The decision of *McArthur's Case* (see pp. 137–8) that the clause forbad all regulation by a State of trade which crossed a border, but did not bind the Commonwealth at all (except insofar as inter-state tariffs would be invalid even if federally imposed) had little to recommend it in theory; but if the Commonwealth had accepted the invitation thus extended to it by the Court to develop the kind of legislative code on interstate trade which the United States government had developed, the judgement might have provided a basis for a practical arrangement. This was not done: matters which were becoming of great importance, particularly the rationalization of uneconomic primary industries and the regulation of long-distance transport, were left to the States, and the way was left open for the *McArthur's Case* principle to stultify the States' efforts in these fields.

It was with a particularly difficult primary industry, dried fruit production, that the trouble began. The South Australian government, anxious to share the limited, high-price Australian market among its growers, passed an Act requiring all growers to provide a quota of their production for export. In 1927 a large producer named James, whose efficient methods enabled him to sell in Australia much more than the Act permitted him, challenged it on the ground that by preventing him from fulfilling interstate contracts it contravened S.92. Although the new Act was not in any direct way intended to interfere with trade between States, but affected such trade only incidentally and marginally, the Court, applying *McArthur's Case*, found unanimously for James. The Commonwealth then, rather reluctantly, introduced an interstate quota scheme, and in *James* v. *Commonwealth* (1928) its right to do so was upheld, though the actual regulations made were destroyed on technical grounds. The Court was here again using its *McArthur's Case* rule, but in two almost contemporary cases the rule was not applied so strictly. Particularly significant was *ex parte Nelson* in which the Bench divided equally on a contention that a New South Wales regulation forbidding the import of cattle from parts of Queensland where there was an epidemic of stock disease was invalid. In accordance with the normal practice, the Chief Justice's opinion that the regulation should be upheld prevailed. The odd situation thus existed that an incidental hindrance to absolute freedom caused by the operation of State law was demolished, while a direct prohibition imposed by another State law was allowed to stand.

The matter was then further complicated by Mr James and the Privy Council. In the interval between *James* v. *South Australia* and the decision of the Commonwealth to involve itself, the State government had tried to deal with its troublesome dried-fruit grower along lines suggested by the 1915 *Wheat Case* (see p. 137) by compulsorily acquiring his crop. James challenged the action, lost in the High Court and appealed successfully to the Privy Council. The Privy Council's decision in the case *James* v. *Cowan* (1932) effectively over-ruled the *Wheat Case*, thus restricting State powers in these matters even more than the High Court had restricted them, but it left unresolved the important question of whether the *McArthur's Case* principle should stand.

By this time the problem of regulating interstate road transport had become pressing. The first important case was *Willard* v. *Rawson* (1933) in which four justices held valid a Victorian Act requiring an interstate haulier to take out Victorian registration although he already held New South Wales papers, on the ground that it could not be shown to discriminate against interstate operators as all vehicles used in Victoria were required to pay fees on the same scale. There was one significant dissentient, Owen Dixon, who had joined the Bench in 1929. This was his first clear demonstration of a view which he was later to make dominant, that S.92 forbad both Commonwealth and States to interfere in any way with business activities which were carried on interstate— that it was, as far as such activities were concerned, a guarantee of the freedom of private enterprise. He would have invalidated the Act because it was intended, really if not ostensibly, to protect State-owned railways from competition. In *Vizzard's Case*, decided the next year, the question at issue concerned a New South Wales Act much more clearly aimed at restricting competition with the railways. The Commonwealth intervened to support the State, and in the course of argument its counsel, Robert Garran, suggested that the Court should over-rule *McArthur's Case* and read S.92 in the narrow sense of a prohibition against direct imposts on interstate trade, a prohibition binding Commonwealth and States equally: this would make possible both federal and State *regulation* of trade. A majority of the Bench held the challenged Act valid, but Dixon was joined in dissent by Starke, and the reasons of the majority varied widely. The Court, in effect, declined Garran's invitation to simplify the issue. It had already, in the *Peanut*

Board Case, heard shortly before *Vizzard*, applied, or perhaps extended, the Privy Council's ban on acquisition of a crop by a State as a means of regulating trade. By the end of 1934, therefore, the powers of the States where interstate trade was involved had virtually disappeared, and those of the Commonwealth were coming under attack from what can perhaps be called the 'Dixon doctrine'.

At this point that tireless defender of *laissez-faire*, James, again intervened. He challenged new regulations made by the Commonwealth under its Dried Fruits Act and in 1936 persuaded the Privy Council to accept the view that the Commonwealth was bound as much as the States not to interfere with trade between States in any way. This second *James* v. *Commonwealth* case thus overruled *McArthur's Case*. It, and subsequent cases in the High Court, simplified the situation a little: but the Privy Council put a wider interpretation on S.92 than Garran had argued for in 1934. This left Mr Justice Dixon free to continue his campaign to have the section interpreted in very wide terms, as a prohibition of any interference by either the Commonwealth or the States with the interstate activities of private enterprise. An attempt by the federal government to amend the Constitution so as to exempt Commonwealth marketing laws from the operation of S.92 as now interpreted failed in 1937, when it was opposed not only by those who wanted freedom from governmental regulation of business but also by doctrinaire States-righters and by Labor supporters, who wanted a more radical amendment, one which would also make possible federal control of monopolies. The Dixon doctrine therefore survived, to have, after World War II, serious consequences for *all* Australian governments.

While the changes which took place between the wars in the interpretation of S.92 did not so much exalt Commonwealth over State authority as end by imposing restrictions on both, developments in the field of industrial arbitration transferred power from the State parliaments to a body virtually independent of both them and the federal Parliament, the Commonwealth Court of Conciliation and Arbitration. If the very narrow interpretation of the original justices of the High Court concerning the arbitration power had been accepted by their successors this could hardly have happened. The ruling of 1910, mentioned in Chapter Six, that the Arbitration Court could not make a 'common rule' for an industry but only settle actual disputes, and another of 1912, which prevented it from dealing with a 'paper dispute' (the mere serving and rejection of a 'log of claims') restricted its powers greatly; but these rulings did not stand. In 1913 in the *Felt Hatter's Case* the Bench reversed its attitude to paper disputes; the next year the justices greatly widened the scope of federal arbitration by accepting any dispute where workers in two or more States made common cause against their various employers as 'extending beyond the limits of any one State'; then in 1920 they ruled that any matter arising within the 'ambit' of a previous award of the Arbitration Court came under that Court's jurisdiction even if it concerned workers in only one State; and in 1923 they widened the definition of 'industrial' to cover such activities as banking and insurance. By the middle of the 1920s, therefore, the theoretical restriction of the federal arbitration power to *disputes* which are both *industrial* and *interstate* had ceased to have much real importance, and the temptation for unions to make the ambit of a particular dispute wide enough to cover all eventualities was greatly increasing the influence of the federal Court on Australian economic life.

The growth of the power of the Court up to 1926 was mainly at the expense of State tribunals and wages boards, but in that year the High Court exalted it over even the parliaments of the States by ruling in *Cowburn's Case* (see p. 171) that an award providing for a working week longer than forty-four hours would supersede State forty-four-hour legislation. Although the federal government subsequently failed to have accepted a constitutional amendment which would have given the Commonwealth plenary powers over industrial matters, the influence of the Arbitration Court steadily grew. State tribunals found themselves forced to follow its lead, because men covered by their awards frequently worked beside men covered by its; and by the early 1930s the federal basic wage, first determined in 1907, had become the foundation of a national uniform standard of living. This knitted the country together economically and so further weakened the importance of the States as units. When World War II began their decline was already obvious. The war was to accelerate it greatly.

Uniform Taxation and other Wartime Developments

As during World War I, the Commonwealth was able to use the defence power to expand its influence. The High Court Bench, now without such committed nationalists as Isaacs and Higgins, and therefore inclined to be guided by what Sir Owen Dixon was to call, when he became Chief Justice in 1952, 'a strict and complete legalism', required the Commonwealth to demonstrate a definite connection between a challenged regulation and the needs of defence: it invalidated regulations on such matters as industrial lighting standards, the admission of students to universities, and the right of State public servants to a particular holiday; but on the other hand it ruled that all industrial unrest in wartime, not simply those interstate disputes which came under the arbitration power and disputes covered by S.51(i) — 'Trade and commerce with other countries and among the States' — could be dealt with by the Commonwealth, and it authorized the imposition of industrial conscription. The apparently temporary expansion of federal powers thus sanctioned, again as in the earlier war, led to the development of public attitudes which were of permanent effect. But by far the most important decision of the war years was one in which the main lines of reasoning did not depend on the defence power, that in the *Uniform Tax Case* of 1942.

One of the irritations and inconveniences of a federal system is the existence of a complicated tax structure, and when the 1927 Financial Agreement was being negotiated there were people, such as the economist Professor R.C. Mills, who advocated including provision for uniform income and inheritance taxes to replace the mixture of standard federal and differing State imposts. This seemed to Mills to be a way of raising revenue more equitably than it could be raised while the Commonwealth had a monopoly of non-progressive, indirect taxes, and those taxes which could be levied progressively varied widely from State to State. With the outbreak of war there arose questions more serious than convenience or even equity: by 1942 the survival of Australia seemed to depend upon raising money in unprecedented amounts, and the existing income-tax structure, with its enormous variations in rates and patterns in the different States, made it impossible for the Commonwealth to exploit fully the taxable capacity of the country without either discriminating between the States in the incidence of federal taxation (which was forbidden by the Constitution) or imposing rates which would cripple some taxpayers in some States. The government's solution to the problem was a scheme which would transfer all income-taxing power to the Commonwealth.

Parliament passed two Acts providing for the staff, equipment, buildings and records of State income-tax departments to be transferred to the Commonwealth for the duration of the war and six months afterwards; an Income Tax Assessment Act fixing rates so high that they could hardly be paid by people who also had to pay State taxes, and giving the Commonwealth priority of collection; and another Act providing, again until six months after the war, for the payment to the States of sums roughly equal to their existing income-tax revenue, on condition that they ceased their own collections. Four States unsuccessfully challenged the scheme. The Court in the *Uniform Tax Case* accepted the validity of the Acts providing for the acquisition of the State machinery, the only part of the scheme which depended on the defence power, by a bare majority, but the crux of the scheme, the imposition of high rates of federal tax with priority of collection, was upheld unanimously as an exercise of the Commonwealth's taxation power. On the question of the conditional grants Mr Justice Starke dissented from the opinion of the other four justices who sat on the case, objecting that to uphold them would be to give the Commonwealth the right to destroy completely the financial powers of the States. But his objection involved ignoring the very specific words of S.96, which authorizes 'financial assistance to any State *on such terms and conditions as the Parliament thinks fit*', and falling back on ideas about the nature of federalism which had been unfashionable since 1920. The Chief Justice, Sir John Latham, pointed out that, even if S.96 were not held to cover such a stringent condition as the Commonwealth now sought to impose, there would be nothing to prevent the federal government from letting it be known unofficially that no grant would be made to a State which tried to collect its own income tax. He agreed with Starke that the Commonwealth could, by the same methods as used in this scheme, strip the States of all independent revenue: but he insisted that the power to prevent this did not reside in the High Court. As has been seen, Isaacs had argued in the *Engineers' Case* judgement that 'The extravagant use of the granted powers in the actual working of the Constitution is a matter to be guarded against by the constituencies and not by the courts'. Latham, and his brethren Rich, McTiernan and Williams, agreed. And it soon became clear that the constituencies had no interest whatever in protecting the right of the States to impose income tax.

Professor K.H. Bailey, who was later to become the Commonwealth solicitor-general, commented at the time that 'the logic of the Uniform Tax Plan is that the States should eventually move, with a simplified political structure, into the position primarily of administrative agencies, the main lines of policy in all major matters being nationally determined'. The simplification of political structure has not eventuated, but the rest of Bailey's logic is impeccable. The pressures of war organization contributed to the process he predicted. The States accepted the role of agents for such Commonwealth activities as manpower and price control and their status as agents had a psychological effect which outlived the war: the people got used to accepting Commonwealth initiative and State executive agency as normal in a range of fields which widened rather than contracted with the end of the war and the appearance of problems of reconstruction. Professor Sawer has suggested that 'perhaps only an emergency as great as that produced by the Japanese attack in 1941-42 could have produced an atmosphere in which so fundamental a change in the balance of financial power [as uniform taxation] was upheld by the courts'. But once the change occurred there was little chance of reversing it. 'The clock will not go backwards'. When the Prime Minister, J.B. Chifley, told the Premiers in 1946 that he intended to continue the uniform-tax system and they raised objections, it is said that he described their attitude as 'so much damned nonsense'. If he did he fairly stated the facts as far as the future was concerned.

The government to the leadership of which he had succeeded the previous year was not, however, satisfied with a *de facto* extension of federal authority through the operation of uniform taxation and wartime psychology. As early as September 1942 a Bill was introduced to initiate a constitutional amendment which would give the

Commonwealth complete control over what H.V. Evatt (who had left the High Court to enter Parliament and was now attorney-general) called 'economic security and social justice, including security of employment and the provision of useful occupation for all the people'. The proposed amendment had one feature which marked it off from all previous attempts to amend the Constitution: it aimed to protect the powers sought from the process of judicial review. 'I desire to make it perfectly clear', Evatt told the House of Representatives, 'that the amendment I propose will give the decision to Parliament itself, and no person will be able to challenge the validity of Parliament's decision'. But the government apparently changed its mind about this extraordinary plan: a week after Evatt had spoken the Bill was stood over, and in November it was referred, without the provision for making the opinion of Parliament conclusive on the question of what legislation might be covered by the phrase 'economic security and social justice', to a committee consisting of six government and six opposition members of federal Parliament and the Premier. and Leader of the Opposition in each State. This 'Constitutional Convention' examined the scheme and agreed that the States should pass, and 'entrench' (render unchangeable without referendum), legislation to transfer to the Commonwealth various powers needed to facilitate post-war reconstruction. A Bill drafted by the 'Convention' was subsequently passed by the Parliaments of New South Wales and Queensland and, subject to its passage by the other Parliaments before proclamation, by that of Victoria; but the Upper Houses of South Australia and Western Australia forced heavy amendment, and the measure was not passed at all in Tasmania.

The federal government, prompted by the Labor Party conference of December 1943, therefore reverted to the idea of amendment by referendum. In 1944 it asked the electors to sanction the transfer to the Commonwealth, for five years after the war, of power over fourteen specific matters which were at the time being controlled under the defence power. Before the end of the five years, the electors were informed, a full overhaul of the Constitution would be undertaken. There was some opposition sympathy for many of the proposed amendments, but others of them were open to suspicion of 'socialist' intent. Moreover the opposition leader, R.G. Menzies, believed that the recently reinforced financial authority of the Commonwealth gave it sufficient hold over the policies of the States to enable it to control the process of reconstruction. His party therefore urged a 'no' vote at the referendum. As the number of powers sought gave considerable scope for confusion of issues, and as growing antipathy to wartime 'controls' and 'bureaucracy' aroused suspicion of the kind of 'big government' which the powers seemed to promise, rejection was inevitable.

Evatt was perhaps less discouraged than some of his colleagues. He recognized that the verdict of the electors was by no means a clear expression of preference for a States'-rights view. And since 1936 he had placed great faith in the external affairs power as a means of using Commonwealth authority to by-pass the resistance of State Upper Houses to social change; his efforts, at the San Francisco Conference of 1945 and subsequently, to make the United Nations Organization a real force in the world are at least partly explicable in these terms. But the status in domestic law of United Nations resolutions, and even of the 1948 Universal Declaration of Human Rights, was to remain dubious, and the federal government had immediate practical problems when the war ended.

The most important of these concernèd welfare legislation. During the 1920s and 1930s various suggestions for simplifying and improving the complex systems of social security benefits in Australia on a basis of Commonwealth-State co-operation failed to bear fruit. There were two consequences: first, the introduction of adequate unemployment insurance was delayed; and secondly, when the war forced the Commonwealth to act alone in the field of social welfare its quite comprehensive legislation had no more permanent basis than the defence power. In 1945 a challenge to the validity of an Act providing for various pharmaceutical benefits brought the matter to a crisis. The High Court invalidated the Act, on the ground that it did not come under any specific head of S.51 and that it could not be covered, as the Commonwealth argued it could, by the general power given in S.81 to appropriate revenue. The *Pharmaceutical Benefits* judgement rather suggested that all Commonwealth social benefits—apart from old-age and invalid pensions, which are covered by S.51(xxiii)—were illegal. The next year, therefore, the government proposed a constitutional amendment which, after receiving majorities in all States at a referendum, became S.51 (xxiiiA): this gave the Commonwealth power to make laws for

> The provision of maternity allowances, widows' pensions, child endowment, unemployment, pharmaceutical, sickness and hospital benefits, medical and dental services (but not so as to authorize any form of civil conscription), benefits to students and family allowances.

At the same time two other proposals, one to give the Commonwealth power, untrammelled by S.92, to establish marketing organizations, and another to allow legislation 'on terms and conditions of employment in industry (but not so as to authorize any form of industrial conscription)', received small overall majorities, but failed because of adverse votes in Queensland, South Australia and Tasmania.

When, at another referendum in May 1948, the electors declined, by large majorities in each State, to give the Commonwealth permanently the power over rents and prices which the High Court had allowed it temporarily as part of the post-war 'unwinding' of the defence power,

Chifley's campaign for a redistribution of powers in the Australian federal system collapsed. The one formal change he had succeeded in making was less important than the informal changes which had taken place since 1939 in the way the system worked. In the next twenty years the Commonwealth was not going to have everything its own way, but all possibility of a revival of State power had disappeared.

The High Court and the Constitution 1946–71

Of course after the war there was a tendency for popular opinion, and even for the High Court, to react against the great centralization of power in Commonwealth hands which the war had produced. The need for a gradual transition from wartime controls to peacetime 'normality' led the Court to take upon itself a certain discretion about the rate at which the ambit of the defence power should be restricted in particular matters, and in exercising this discretion it at times appeared to be protecting the States against an attempt by a Commonwealth Labor government with a commitment to a centralist social policy to deprive them permanently of all significant power. But the most important decisions of the Court in the first decade after the war, beginning with the *Airlines Case* of 1945, in which it held invalid an Act and regulations designed to drive private airline operators out of business, had the effect not of protecting the States against the Commonwealth so much as protecting private enterprise against governments in general. Most of these decisions were based on the conversion of a majority of the Bench to the Dixonian view of S.92.

Before it became perfectly clear that the *Airlines Case* betokened such a conversion, the Court, again largely under Dixon's influence, based on other grounds a judgement with the same effect. Dixon had long been uneasy about Isaacs' view that the courts had no duty at all to prevent the implications of the *Engineers' Case* from destroying the States: at the time of the *Uniform Tax Case* he had been on leave from the Bench, acting as Australian minister in Washington, and was so unable to join Starke in dissent. But when *City of Melbourne* v. *Commonwealth* (the 'State Banking Case') came before the High Court in 1947 he was back and the issues were clearer. The Banking Act of 1947, which was mainly concerned with strengthening the Commonwealth Bank as a central bank, contained a section aimed at weakening the competitive position of private trading banks by prohibiting them from accepting the accounts of State governments or instrumentalities. Over the lone dissent of McTiernan the Bench held the clause invalid because neither the federal government nor the government of a State might 'destroy the other nor curtail in any substantial manner the exercise of its powers'. On the face of it this looked like a re-statement of implied immunity. Actually the justices stopped well short of reviving this doctrine in its pre-1920 form: in general they were prepared to agree that the right of the federal Parliament to legislate with regard to a particular subject matter, in this case banking, does include a right to bind the States and their instrumentalities, but they were not prepared to see the power to apply federal law to State bodies stretched to include a power to impose on those bodies rules that could not be imposed on individuals. The effect of the judgement was to protect the business of the banks, rather than the rights of the States.

That this is what the Bench intended became obvious when the Commonwealth tried to get round the decision with an Act to nationalize the banks and was immediately challenged, by the banks themselves and three State governments. The argument of the States, that the Act infringed an implied immunity which they should be held to enjoy, was rejected; but the Court, by a four-two majority, held the Act invalid on other grounds. The most important—the only one which could not have been overcome by amendment of details—was that it infringed S.92 of the Constitution. When the government, with some sacrifice of political consistency, appealed, the Privy Council found that the decision on this point was inseparable from other points which raised *inter se* issues (see p. 118) and that the High Court ruling was therefore final; but it added a comment implying that it agreed with this ruling. When the High Court's decision was handed down in 1949 Professor Geoffrey Sawer remarked that the 'extreme ambiguity' of S.92 was forcing the Court 'to perform the function of an administrative tribunal administering not law but a very broadly stated policy'. Inevitably that policy was being interpreted in the light of current ideas. Until a few years before the war there had been, shifts of emphasis and the dissent of Dixon notwithstanding, a fairly general tendency to see the section, at least as it affected the Commonwealth, as an embodiment of the traditional idea of 'free trade'. Now, with the socialist inclinations of the federal government apparently becoming unpopular in the country, the Court was tending to the Dixonian view. In doing so it attracted a great deal of work. During the first half-century of the Commonwealth's history S.92 had been at issue in fewer than forty cases; in the two decades after the *Bank Nationalization Case* it was to be raised in more than sixty.

The most serious of them concerned interstate road transport. In the early 1950s most of the States, faced with growing competition for their railways, passed laws to license and tax hauliers. Licences could generally be issued or withheld at discretion and the taxes imposed were overtly discriminatory. Despite the fact that the Commonwealth, the government of which was now strongly anti-socialist, and State administrations of every complexion supported this type of legislation, it was struck down in 1954 in *Hughes and Vale* v. *New South Wales*. Appeals to the Privy Council and minor amendments of the various laws produced more cases but the same result. Eventually the States had to be content with taxes and licensing systems which, as far as *bona fide* interstate journeys were concerned, went no further than requiring reasonable contributions to road maintenance and reasonable standards of safe operation. By 1957, when such limited attempts at regulation were approved in *Armstrong* v. *Victoria*, the Dixon doctrine had destroyed a policy on which the Commonwealth and the States were agreed: it had led the High Court (and the Privy Council) beyond the limits of operation of even an 'administrative tribunal'. Perhaps some uneasiness was beginning to develop on the Bench. In 1966 a margarine firm appealed against a conviction in a lower court for exceeding a production quota imposed by a New South Wales law. It claimed that batches in excess of its quota had been specifically manufactured for interstate sale and that the conviction therefore violated S.92, but the High Court rejected this argument and dismissed the appeal. Since this case (*Beal* v. *Marrickville Margarine*) the 'little bit of layman's language' has been before the courts rather less frequently. It is perhaps a coincidence that Dixon retired in 1964. There is no reason to believe that his successor, Sir Garfield Barwick—or most of Barwick's brethren for that matter—would be anxious to restrict the value of S.92 to free enterprise in any marked degree.

What is certain is that even in the years between the *State Banking Case* and Dixon's retirement the Court did not take a really restrictive view of Commonwealth powers *vis à vis* the States. In the *Pharmaceutical Benefits Case*, already mentioned, it gave a narrower meaning than the government wanted to the Commonwealth's appropriation power; and in the *Communist Party Case* (1951) it refused to allow the Commonwealth, in peace-time, to bring the defence power into operation against communists. But the Court was in this case not so much concerned with the scope of the defence power as unwilling to support the proposition that the Commonwealth could validly attach penalties to a mere executive opinion that the activities of certain persons are prejudicial to defence; and in the next year, in *Marcus Clark and Co.* v. *Commonwealth*, it upheld the government's right to control capital issues under a Defence Preparations Act, thus ruling, as a future justice, D.I. Menzies, wrote, 'that the defence power in time of peace is adequate to sustain legislation of a character that had hitherto not been regarded as within Commonwealth power except in time of war, or in a comparatively limited transitional period from war to peace'. This effective extension of federal powers was followed in 1954 by another. In *O'Sullivan* v. *Noarlunga Meat Ltd* the Court decided that the company could kill meat for export on the basis of a Commonwealth export permit although it did not have the licence required by State law: the external trade power was thus read as allowing a certain measure of federal control over industrial production. Then in the mid-1960s the judgements in *Airlines*

of New South Wales v. *New South Wales* gave a quite generous interpretation to the external affairs power—without, however, clearing up all
the ambiguities in the status of international conventions which had
existed since the case *ex parte Henry* of 1936.

The invasion of State fields through the Commonwealth's power over
defence, foreign trade and external affairs which was sanctioned in these
cases was more significant than the restrictions imposed by *Pharmaceutical
Benefits* and *Communist Party*. More significant still was the decision in a
second *Uniform Tax Case*. The original uniform taxation scheme had
been adopted only for the duration of the war and one year afterwards,
but, as has been seen, the High Court upheld its essentials even apart
from the defence power: so in 1946 the government was able to put it on
a permanent statutory basis. In 1952, in response to a certain amount of
grumbling by the larger States, the Prime Minister, R.G. Menzies,
offered to abandon the scheme, well aware that the smaller States did
not want their taxing powers back and that the inability of the
Commonwealth to impose different rates of taxation in different States
made practically impossible the return of these powers to some and not
to others. The 'offer' accordingly lapsed. Five years later Victoria took
the matter to court. The decision struck down the provisions of the
scheme for giving the Commonwealth priority of collection, but alone
this meant nothing more than that Victoria was free to impose heavier
taxes on its citizens in order to collect the same revenue, for the
Commonwealth could cut off grants to a State which levied its own
income tax. And what it could do for income tax it could do for any
other form of taxation, as in June 1968 another Prime Minister, J.G.
Gorton, reminded premiers who were endeavouring to supplement their
budgets with graduated stamp duties on wages and with various forms
of turnover tax.

The *Sydney Morning Herald* described Gorton's statement as 'dictatorial', but it was only an outspoken recognition of the fact of the financial subordination of the States, a subordination which became more
nearly absolute with every year's federal budget. The States, Professor
Crisp has remarked,

> were caught between rising popular demand for governmental action and
> expenditure within their fields ... and Commonwealth control of financial
> resources which section 96 empowered it to grant to the States upon con-
> ditions. They found the Commonwealth able and willing to influence—in
> some matters virtually to determine—policy objectives and standards to an
> ever increasing extent in one field after another within State constitutional
> jurisdiction.

Victoria, having failed to persuade the High Court to oppose this
process, tried in 1959 to stem it with a *reductio ad absurdum*: by applying,
along with Queensland, to join Western Australia, South Australia and

Tasmania as a 'claimant State' before the Grants Commission. The Commonwealth responded with a complex re-arrangement of its payments to the States: the *ad hoc* 'reimbursements' which had been made since 1952 were replaced by an agreement providing for a formula fixed for five or six years at a time and based on population and 'needs'. The new system improved the budgetary positions of the States, but tightened further the cords which bound them to 'the chariot wheels of the Commonwealth'. An extra knot was tied in 1962 when the federal government began the practice of adding to the loan programme approved by the Loan Council special non-repayable capital grants, apportioned and allocated at its own discretion. Since the early 1960s the States have been dependent upon the Commonwealth for about two-thirds of their income. Only an average of some fifteen per cent has been specifically 'earmarked' for such matters as roads, special development projects and disaster relief, but there is a tendency for this proportion to grow and, particularly since 1972, for the Commonwealth to tighten the conditions under which grants are made—and S.96 of the Constitution leaves the Commonwealth with general freedom of action.

The Commonwealth has, moreover, another means of financial influence. It has already been pointed out that the operation of the 1927 Financial Agreement subjected State budgets during the Great Depression to a measure of control by the then independent Commonwealth Bank Board. The Labor government's Banking Act of 1945 brought the policy of the bank under the direct control of the federal Treasurer, and although that government's opponents were critical of this they found when they came to power in 1949 that in the new economic milieu an independent central bank was an anachronism. Their legislation, passed in 1951, changed the situation more in form than in substance. Liberal and Country Party treasurers found it necessary, working through what was to become the Reserve Bank of Australia, to 'manage' both the private and public sectors of the economy—to manipulate the expenditure not only of firms and individuals but also of State instrumentalities. The States had to be tied to the chariot wheels or they would have got in the way of the reins.

Three-quarters of a century after the first federal government took office there were few, if any, people in Australia who would contest the proposition that its successor should hold those reins. The extent to which its grip had been strengthened in recent years was obvious from both its economic dominance and the willingness of the High Court to give a generally liberal scope to its specific powers. Only one of the forty sub-sections of S.51 had been interpreted in a remarkably narrow sense: this was S.51(xx), which gives power over 'Foreign corporations, and trading or financial corporations formed within the limits of the Commonwealth'. This failed, in *Huddart Parker* v. *Moorehead* in 1909, to provide a basis for national regulation of monopolistic practices. A reversal of opinion by the Court on this matter would virtually put the coping stone on the edifice of federal authority. Such a reversal came in 1971 in the *Rocla Pipes Case*. In 1970 the attorney-general launched a prosecution charging three manufacturers of concrete pipes with having made price-fixing agreements outlawed by the Trade Practices Act of 1965. The companies had already, under threat of action, terminated a nation-wide agreement and made separate compacts covering each of the six States, so as to prevent the use of the interstate trade power, S.51 (i) against them. The Commonwealth, therefore, when one of them appealed against the conviction, had to rely on the corporations power and ask the High Court to over-rule *Huddart Parker*. The Court found for the company, but only because the Act purported to apply to all restrictive agreements whether between companies or individuals: it accepted the proposition that *Huddart Parker* should be over-ruled and that S.51 (xx) should be read as giving the Commonwealth power to restrict the activities of corporations, even their intra-State activities. An amendment to the act to apply it only to companies—which, of course, were the real target of the government's policy—was all that was necessary. The long-term effect of the decision was to open the way for the Commonwealth to a whole, large field—including securities and exchange, consumer protection and consumer credit, and perhaps, though lawyers differ on the point, other aspects of company law—which had been closed to it for two generations. And it was not slow to exploit the opening: the new Trade Practices Act passed in 1974 is a most detailed piece of legislation. The *Rocla Pipes Case* of 1971 ranks with the *Engineers' Case* as a landmark of Australian constitutional development.

Co-operation and Uniformity

This chapter has been concerned with a fundamental change in Australia's 'working constitution'. The discussion has centred on the growth of federal power and the decline of the financial position of the States. But there is another side to the process which has made the States, as individual entities, less important than they were in 1919, when one of the 'Founding Fathers', Sir John Quick, described them as retaining 'the right of controlling . . . the springs of national life, domestic, social, industrial and commercial'. Not only has the regulation of many of those springs been taken over by the Commonwealth in the way so far described; their control has been affected also by the growth of co-operation between federal and State authorities and by an increasing tendency for the States to agree among themselves about uniform methods of regulation.

The most obvious gap in the Commonwealth Constitution was, perhaps, the absence of any specific provision for co-operation among the States, but that gap was to be filled by convention. As has been seen, the Premiers' Conference appeared early and had become a significant if informal element in Australian federalism long before it attracted Commonwealth interest in the 1920s and made its contribution towards dealing with the Depression in the 1930s. And apart from the Premiers' Conference and its *alter ego*, the Loan Council, there have been several other means of federal-State co-operation that deserve comment.

One of these is the use by the Commonwealth of State institutions and instrumentalities as agents of federal activity. From the beginning the Commonwealth, while carefully safeguarding the primary authority of the High Court, used existing State courts in many matters arising under federal law rather than constructing, on the United States pattern, a whole infrastructure of its own tribunals. It also used State administrative, and even executive, machinery—very cautiously at first, but during World War II to an extent which included the delegation to State authorities of legislative-order powers under the National Security Act. The States have also been prepared to employ federal services on occasions.

A second, and since 1945 an increasingly significant, form of co-operation has been the establishment of joint agencies. The most obvious early example is the River Murray Commission. This was set up in 1915, by a Commonwealth Act and supplementary legislation in New South Wales, Victoria and South Australia, after a great drought had virtually caused the stream to disappear. Four commissioners, one appointed by each party, were authorized to regulate the use of water, to report on proposals for conservation works and—in the early years while some people still clung to the illusion that navigation was economical—to maintain locks. The Commission has, despite many difficulties, been very successful. The operating authority of the Snowy Mountains Scheme was consequently designed on similar lines in 1959. In the meantime other joint authorities appeared. During the 1930s some of the constitutional difficulties over the marketing of primary produce were met by the establishment of boards endowed with both federal and State authority; after World War II there were Commonwealth-State housing agreements and land-settlement schemes (the latter not as successful as hoped in avoiding constitutional traps); and in 1947 the Joint Coal Board became something of a model for future joint ventures. It was established by Acts of the Commonwealth and New South Wales, passed in the same form except, in the words of its first report, 'that the powers granted to the Board to control collieries and compulsorily to requisition and resume land, buildings, plant, machinery and equipment were contained only in the New South Wales Act'. This enabled the federal government's powers over interstate commerce, and its ability to find the money needed to rehabilitate a vital but run-down industry, to be employed jointly with the State's competency in matters of intra-State trade, mines regulation, health, and social welfare. It also enabled both the powers which the New South Wales Industrial Commission could alone exercise over intra-State disputes and the powers of the Commonwealth Arbitration Court to be vested in a special Coal Industry Tribunal.

Attempts to pool legislative resources in other ways have been of some significance. The States, as already noted (p. 120), have been less than enthusiastic about surrendering powers under the terms of S.51 (xxxvii) of the Constitution. New South Wales handed over certain powers in 1915 for the duration of the war; between 1920 and 1937 the Commonwealth enjoyed the right to control air transport in four States; in 1949 three States temporarily surrendered the power necessary for the Commonwealth to continue petrol rationing after the High Court ruled that it was no longer covered by the defence power; and later Tasmania and Queensland again surrendered air navigation powers. But, as has been seen, the transfers made during World War II were vitiated by lack of uniformity. Some States, rather than make a transfer of authority, have preferred to adopt by statute regulations made by the Commonwealth for its territories: three States continued petrol rationing by this means in 1949–50, and both New South Wales and Queensland employed the method to apply certain federal air rules in the 1930s.

Executive co-operation has been as important as legislative, and often indeed a precursor of it. Out of the precedents set by the Loan Council other regular ministerial conferences grew. The first was the Australian Agricultural Council. Originating in 1934 as a meeting of State ministers for agriculture, it eventually became a twice-yearly conference attended also by federal ministers with responsibility for trade, primary industry and the federal territories, and designed 'to provide a basis for continuous consultation amongst Australian governments on economic aspects of primary production and marketing of primary products'. Its pattern was closely followed when the Transport Advisory Council was established in 1946, and within a few years similar ministerial committees on such matters as immigration, education, development and law were contributing to the emergence of a system of 'co-operative federalism'. At the same time there grew up systems of conferences attended by State ministers or senior officials without federal representatives. The result was a great deal of standard, or even uniform legislation.

No attempt has ever been made to establish in Australia any equivalent of the American Bar Association's Commission on Uniform State Laws, which since 1892 has done much to standardize American legal principles, but Australian State laws have always been fairly similar, partly because of a tendency to copy relevant British statutes and partly because the small number of States has made possible a high degree of knowledge of one State's practices among the legislators of another. The first attempt at exact uniformity was in 1937 when, after the *ex parte Henry* case, all the States passed a law in the same form to cover air transport. It remained the only one for twenty years, but in 1957 the growth of hire-purchase persuaded them that they should consider co-operative regulation. The result was a uniform Hire Purchase Act passed two years later by all States, and by the Commonwealth for its territories. This provided the inspiration for a much more ambitious project which produced a uniform Companies Act in 1963. By that time a great deal of uniformity had also been achieved at the level of regulations and administrative orders, in matters as widely different as plant quarantine and traffic rules.

Co-operative federalism, like so many of the facts of Australian political life since the Second World War, has enhanced the importance of the Commonwealth. Where uniform laws have been a direct result of federal leadership, as, for example, in the case of those fostered by the Australian Agricultural Council, one must agree with Crisp and 'describe these developments as part of the steady movement towards national leadership in the ever-increasing complex of functions for which the unfolding sense of nationhood requires national standards and national provision of resources'. Even where the States have acted together without such leadership, the effect has been to reduce their importance as individual political units, to put further practical limits on their freedom of action, to support the opinion expressed by S.J. Butlin in 1954 that they 'have no future except as administrative agents'.

Epilogue: the End of Federalism?

The fundamental shifts in power which have marked the history of Australian federalism despite the consistent failure of attempts to add to federal authority by formal change in the Constitution have persuaded many people that the document should be thoroughly overhauled. As early as 1921 W.M. Hughes unsuccessfully proposed the establishment of a constitutional convention for this purpose. He was thinking of a body partly of men elected on a basis proportional to the States' representation in the federal Lower House, and partly of nominees, in equal numbers from each State, chosen by the State Parliaments. In 1927 a Royal Commission on the Constitution was appointed, but its report, delivered two years later, was shelved. Then there was the 'convention' of 1942. And from 1956 to 1959 an all-party parliamentary committee laboured on the problem with results no more fruitful than those of the Royal Commission. In the early 1970s the States decided to try again. The 'Constitutional Convention' which met in Sydney for a week in 1973 included in its large membership the Prime Minister, the Premiers

and many of their senior colleagues, and was described by one newspaper as 'the first major review of the Australian Constitution since it
took effect in 1901'; but it did little more than emphasize what has been
clear for years, that the Commonwealth and the States have very different views of what an ideal constitution would provide. It canvassed
the obvious issues but reached no substantive decisions. At another brief
session three years later it endorsed the federal government's decision to
support the principle of giving Territory residents votes in referendums.
Having no power beyond that of advising the federal government, it
seems hardly likely to have any great impact. There have been many
suggestions for the election of a convention with powers comparable to
those of the conventions of the 1890s, but such suggestions seem utopian.
The process of organic growth that has been going on for so long is
hardly likely ever to be reversed, but a radical re-writing of the
Constitution seems highly improbable to say the least.

The return at the end of 1972 of a Labor government after twenty-
three years of rule by parties with whom the maintenance of the States
has been an article of faith—if not, by any means, a principle of
action—was in itself a guarantee that the erosion of State power would
continue. Mr Whitlam and his colleagues, radical nationalists who were
inclined to see the federal system as an obstacle to their economic and
social policies, embarked on their government with the doctrinaire fervour natural to prophets newly emerged from the wilderness. In their
first two years they put to referendum, with predictable lack of success,
six proposals to amend the Constitution. As has been seen, they ham-
mered through a hostile Senate, by means of the country's third double
dissolution and first joint sitting, some of their most cherished policies,
including a Bill to assert Commonwealth control over the sea bed off the
States' coasts, with all its marine and mineral resources; and they stirred
up a teacup storm about the imaginary survival of British governmental
influence in Australia.

After 1972 the pressure on the States was increased in many ways.
Some of the attack was psychological: for example the Whitlam ministry
began immediately to describe itself as 'the Australian' rather than 'the
Commonwealth' government and to use the same adjective for all its
departments, instrumentalities and publications. The attempt to abolish
all right of appeal to the Privy Coucil, even in matters of State law, must
be placed in a similar category . Other aspects of the pressure were more
direct. The new government showed a much more brutally-open willingness than its predecessors to use S.96 grants as a means of controlling
State policy; by taking over complete financial responsibility for
Australian universities, it effectively annexed control over future developments in higher education; by giving local government bodies direct grants, it extended its influence into a field hitherto exclusively the
preserve of the States. In June 1973 Whitlam told the Premiers that his

government was 'trying to open up new and fruitful fields of co-operation with the States', but he made clear to them that what he envisaged was not a co-operation between equals. He made this even clearer in 1975, when he suggested that they solve some of their financial problems by selling their railways to the Commonwealth.

The attitude of his successor was different in appearance rather than fact. At the opening of Parliament in February 1976 the Governor-General's speech promised that

> to re-establish a pattern of co-operation in national affairs and reverse the excessive centralizing of power in Australia, the Government proposes to make the most important reform of the Federal system since Federation. Its core will be the principle of tax sharing.

The scheme was to provide, initially, for the States to receive a specified percentage of Commonwealth receipts from income tax; at a later stage they would be empowered to place a State surcharge on income tax instead. But it gave much less than it appeared to give. The States would have no control over the basic tax rate upon which their share would depend; in the second stage they would be forced to accept the uncongenial duty of raising from their electors amounts they had become used to receiving from the Commonwealth; and they would be expected to take financial responsibility for several matters currently enjoying Commonwealth funding. At a Premiers' Conference held three months after the 'new federalism' was announced, Fraser was little less dictatorial than Whitlam had been the previous year.

Perhaps the only significant difference between the two in their attitude to the States has been that the Fraser government has been less determined to exploit fully its control over offshore resources. Its right to exercise, if it wishes, virtually absolute control in this field was established by the High Court's judgement in the *Seabed Case*, handed down in December 1975. This blow to the States was delivered by the Bench only two months after another, the *Territory Senators'* judgement. The Whitlam government had put through legislation to give seats in the Senate, with full voting rights, to the Northern Territory and the Australian Capital Territory. The law was challenged by four States, on the ground that it was incompatible with S.7 of the Constitution, which provides that 'The Senate shall be composed of senators for each *State*'. The Commonwealth government argued that S.122, which empowers the federal parliament to 'make laws for the government of any territory ... and ... allow the representation of such territory in either House of Parliament to the extent and on the terms which it thinks fit', validated its action, and a majority of the Court accepted this argument. The judgement, confirmed in another case argued on slightly different grounds in late 1977, did not directly affect the powers of the States, but it significantly affected their status as parties to a federal compact.

The process which has so markedly enhanced the Commonwealth's status and so greatly increased its share in the federal division of power has not given the federal government the plenary authority of the government of a unitary state. The activities of Australian State legislatures still impinge on the life of the citizen much more than do those of local government bodies in countries with unitary constitutions. J.D.B. Miller points out that 'as government institutions the States are more active than ever [because] Governments do more now than they used to, whether they operate in Federations or unified States', and there are many matters which remain under the control of State parliaments. The semi-autonomous position of Commonwealth industrial tribunals, moreover, and the powers they can exercise without any necessary deference to national economic and social policy, place a restriction on the authority of the federal government which is peculiar by the standards of the world at large. But the independence of industrial tribunals can at least be circumvented, and even those functions of the State governments which have come under no direct federal influence have to be carried out in the context of federal control of the economy. Professor Wheare has argued that

> What is necessary for the federal principle is not merely that the general government, like the regional governments, should operate directly on the people, but, further, that each government should be limited to its own sphere and, within that sphere, should be independent of the other.

There are other definitions of federalism, but to accept Wheare's is to accept that Australia has long since ceased to be a federation.

Chronology of Constitutional Milestones

1787	Phillip's commissions and 'first charter of justice'—first basis of Australian government
1814	'Second charter of justice' establishes New South Wales Supreme Court
1819–20	Bigge enquiry
1823	First Legislative Council established in New South Wales
1825	Separate Legislative Council established in Van Diemen's Land
1828	New South Wales Legislative Council expanded in size and authority
1833	Bourke's Jury Act
1837–38	Molesworth Committee on Transportation
1838	Durham's Report on the government of Canada
1842	'Mixed' Legislative Council established in New South Wales
1843	Government of South Australia Act
1848	The 'Golden Despatch' of Earl Grey
1849	The *Hashemy* crisis
1850	Australian Colonies Government Act sets up 'mixed' Councils in three more colonies
1852	Pakington implicitly concedes responsible government to Australian colonies
1853	End of transportation to eastern Australia
1855–56	New constitutions with responsible government come into force in four colonies
1859	Queensland becomes separate colony
1865	Colonial Laws Validity Act
1865–68	First and second Upper House crises in Victoria
1870	'Mixed' Legislative Council established in Western Australia
1876–77	Major dispute between Houses in South Australia
1877–78	Third Upper House crisis in Victoria
1883	Convention in Melbourne agrees to set up Federal Council
1885–86	Major dispute between Houses in Queensland
1889	New South Wales Legislative Council 'swamped' for first time
1890	Responsible government conceded to Western Australia
1891	First Federal Convention (Sydney)
1892	Standard instructions to governors radically altered
1895	Hobart Premiers' Conference discusses 'new start' on federation
1895–96	New South Wales Legislative Council coerced by government
1897–98	Second Federal Convention (Adelaide, Sydney and Melbourne)
1898	First federal referendum fails in New South Wales

1899   Second federal referendum: constitution accepted by all States except Western Australia
1900   Western Australia agrees to federate
1901   Commonwealth of Australia inaugurated
1903   High Court of Australia established
1904   The case *D'Emden* v. *Pedder*: first statement of 'implied immunities' doctrine
1907   Australian States Constitution Act
1908   *Wire Netting* and *Steel Rails* cases complicate problem of implied immunity and *Huddart Parker* v. *Moorehead* restricts Commonwealth power over trade
1910   First Commonwealth-State Financial Agreement
1916   *Farey* v. *Burvett*: Commonwealth's implied powers given wide interpretation
1920   *Engineers' Case* destroys the protection given to the States by 'implied immunity'
1922   Queensland Legislative Council abolished
1926   Balfour Report on status of dominions
1927   Second Commonwealth-State Financial Agreement sets up Loan Council
1931   Statute of Westminster passed
1932   Lang Government dismissed in New South Wales
1933   Commonwealth Grants Commission established
1936   The case *ex parte Henry* suggests wide scope of external affairs power
1942   Statute of Westminster adopted by Commonwealth Parliament
1942   The *Uniform Tax Case*
1946   The 'social service' amendment to Commonwealth Constitution
1947   The *State Banking Case*
1949   The *Bank Nationalization Case* judgement
1951   The *Communist Party Case*
1954–57   Series of cases on road transport involving S.92
1959   New Commonwealth-State financial agreement to base grants on population and 'needs'
1966   The case *Beal* v. *Marrickville Margarine* on S.92
1971   The *Rocla Pipes Case* over-rules *Huddart Parker* and greatly extends Commonwealth powers over trading and financial corporations
1975   Whitlam Federal Government dismissed by Governor-General
1975–76   The *Seabed* and *Territory Senators* Cases
1976   The Fraser Government announces its 'new Federalism' policy
1978   Reform of the New South Wales Legislative Council

Bibliographical Note

The historiography of Australian constitutional development is remarkably uneven. Some fields have been thoroughly covered by historians; in others very little has been done at all; in others still what exists is largely the work of lawyers and political scientists, to whom the things which interest the historian have, naturally enough, seemed secondary; in all, the quality of the work varies widely. The summary which is attempted here is far from exhaustive; the aim is simply to comment, under three broad headings, on some of the more obvious of the books and articles which are available to the student.

A. *From Settlement to Responsible Government, 1788–1855*

The standard, even classic, work is A.C.V. Melbourne's *Early Constitutional Development in Australia: New South Wales 1788–1856* (Oxford, 1934; 2nd ed., Brisbane, 1963). Though in most ways superseded by Melbourne, Edward Sweetman's *Australian Constitutional Development* (London, 1925) is useful in providing clear summaries of the various Acts. F.L.W. Wood, *The Constitutional Development of Australia* (Sydney, 1933) is briefer, but both scholarly and readable. The article by T.H. Irving, 'The Idea of Responsible Government in New South Wales before 1856' in *Historical Studies*, vol. 11, provides insights which Melbourne does not give into changes in public opinion in the colonies, and that by Enid Campbell, 'Prerogative Rule in New South Wales 1788–1823' in the *Royal Australian Historical Society Journal*, vol. 50, analyses thoroughly the legal ambiguities in the Governor's position in the early period.

The crises to which these ambiguities gave rise are well dealt with in Marion Phillips, *A Colonial Autocracy* (London, 1909). The treatment of Macquarie's opponents, however, is rather uncritical, and should be supplemented by M.H. Ellis's brilliant if allusive biography, *Lachlan Macquarie, His Life, Adventures and Times* (Sydney, 1947). Among the many other relevant biographical works, two by C.H. Currey, *Sir Francis Forbes* and *The Brothers Bent* (both Sydney, 1968), Melbourne's sketch, *William Charles Wentworth* (Brisbane, 1934), which argues persuasively that Wentworth was really always a conservative, and the article by N. D. McLachlan in *Historical Studies*, vol. 10, 'Edward Eagar (1787–1866): a Colonial Spokesman in Sydney and London', deserve particular mention. The Bigge Reports are examined in John Ritchie, *Punishment and Profit* (Melbourne, 1970) and T.G. Parsons, 'Does the Bigge Report Follow from the Evidence?', *Historical Studies*, vol. 15.

The Australian Colonies Government Act and the 1855–56 constitutions are dealt with in impressive detail by J.M. Ward in *Earl Grey and the Australian Colonies 1846–1857* (Melbourne, 1958). Three of the essays in the New South Wales Legislative Council's commemorative volume, *Autocracy to Parliament 1824–1856* (Sydney, 1976) are relevant. They are: 'The "Blended" Legislative Council in New South Wales' by Ward; 'The Concession of Responsible

Government in New South Wales' by S.G. Foster; and the present author's 'Government and the Land Problem in New South Wales'. Ward's researches on the 'blended' councils and on the responsible government debates in the Australian colonies are presented fully in his *Colonial Self-Government, the British Experience* (London, 1976) which is also the first book to examine the development of colonial self-government in the light of constitutional change in Britain. Some differences in detail between two of the Constitutions are explained in J.M. Main, 'Making Constitutions in New South Wales and Victoria 1853–1854', *Historical Studies*, vol.7. Geoffrey Serle, *The Golden Age* (Melbourne, 1963) gives an excellent account of the early problems of responsible government in Victoria, and D.H. Pike, *Paradise of Dissent: South Australia 1829–57* (London, 1957) examines the process in the colony which liked to pride itself on its difference. There is information on Western Australia in F.K. Crowley's compendious *Australia's Western Third* (London, 1960). W.A. Townsley's *Struggle for Self-Government in Tasmania 1842–1856* (Hobart, 1951) gives valuable details of the issues which complicated the constitutional struggles. The most gravely complicating issue, in both Van Diemen's Land and New South Wales, was, of course, convictism. A.G.L. Shaw's *Convicts and the Colonies* (London, 1966) contains a particularly valuable section on the relationship of the convict system to the pattern of constitutional development.

A large number of the many books on British colonial policy in the first half of the nineteenth century are relevant. They include H.E. Egerton, *A Short History of British Colonial Policy* (12th ed., London, 1950); W.P. Morrell, *British Colonial Policy in the Age of Peel and Russell* (London, 1960), which provides a sympathetic interpretation of the views of the much criticized Grey; and Helen Taft Manning, *British Colonial Government after the American Revolution* (New Haven, 1933). This book, despite some howling inaccuracies about Australia, can help the reader to an understanding of the attitudes of the ministers responsible for its government before 1823. There are interesting comparisons in T.R. Recse, 'Colonial America and Early New South Wales', *Historical Studies*, vol. 9, and useful background in D.M. Young, *The Colonial Office in the Early Nineteenth Century* (London, 1961). More specifically concerned with the Australian aspects of British policy is J.J. Eddy, *Britain and the Australian Colonies 1818–1831* (Oxford, 1969), a scholarly but rather involved analysis of a critical period. G. Martin, *The Durham Report and British Policy: A Critical Essay* (London, 1972) argues that Durham's importance to the development of colonial policy has been consistently exaggerated.

The Report itself exists in many editions. The standard one is that edited by C.P. Lucas (Oxford, 1907); the best recent one is that of R. Coupland (Oxford, 1946). Outstanding among collections of documents is *Select Documents on British Colonial Policy 1830–1860* edited by K.N. Bell and W.P. Morrell (Oxford, 1928). C.M.H. Clark's *Select Documents in Australian History* (2 vols, Sydney, 1950–55) contains much of the relevant material. The largest collection is in the 33 volumes of the *Historical Records of Australia*. Wentworth's highly coloured account of colonial grievances, *A Statistical, Historical and Political Description of the Colony of New South Wales* (London, 1819—2nd ed., 1824) is worth reading, as is James Macarthur's *New South Wales, Its Present State and Future Prospects* (London, 1837).

B.   *The Operation and Evolution of Responsible Government since 1855*

A.B. Keith, *Responsible Government in the Dominions* (2nd ed., Oxford, 1928) has for long been a basic text on the evolution of colonial and dominion self-government up to the time of the Balfour Report. It remains valuable despite its author's bias and idiosyncracy. Its predecessor, and for many years the hand-book of colonial governors, Alpheus Todd, *Parliamentary Government in the British Colonies* (2nd ed., London, 1894) still has its uses: in particular it contains detailed factual accounts of the various *causes célèbres* of the period 1856–1890. Excellent brief surveys are in two chapters of vol. VII of the *Cambridge History of the British Empire* (Cambridge, 1933): K.H. Bailey, 'Self-Government in Australia 1860–1900', and F.W. Eggleston, 'Australia and the Empire 1855–1921'. D.B. Swinfen's *Imperial Control of Colonial Legislation 1813–1865* (Oxford, 1970) is an exhaustive analysis of the background to the Colonial Laws Validity Act from the imperial point of view.

Detailed examinations of the difficulties encountered when responsible government had to be made to work are rare. Serle's treatment of Victoria in *The Golden Age* has been mentioned. P. Loveday and A.W. Martin, *Parliament, Factions and Parties* (Melbourne, 1966) provides some insights into the problems of New South Wales, as does a rather discursive article by W.J.V. Windeyer, 'Responsible Government—Highlights, Sidelights and Reflections', in the *Royal Australian Historical Society Journal*, vol. 42. A previously unpublished draft in-cluded as an appendix to the second edition of Melbourne's book deals with Queensland, and there is a far-from-disinterested account of another colony in B.T. Finniss, *The Constitutional History of South Australia* (Adelaide, 1886).

The Victorian Legislative Council crises have been dealt with in a number of works. The commemorative volume, *Victoria, The First Century* (Melbourne, 1934), gives a concise but not always perfectly accurate account. H.G. Turner, *A History of the Colony of Victoria* (London, 1904) gives the conservative point of view. E.E. Morris, in his *Memoir of George Higinbotham* (London, 1895), naturally takes the other side; he prints some of Higinbotham's major speeches and memoranda. The Council's general record is unsympathetically examined by Geoffrey Serle in 'The Victorian Legislative Council 1856–1950', *Historical Studies*, vol. 6. A contrastingly sympathetic view of the New South Wales Upper House is taken in C.H. Currey's 'The Legislative Council of New South Wales 1843–1943' in the *Royal Australian Historical Society Journal*, vol. 29. C.A. Bernays, *Queensland Politics during Sixty Years 1859–1919* (Brisbane, n.d.) is rather chatty in style but gives a reasonable background to the final struggle between the Queensland houses.

The centenary of responsible government produced a number of works of uneven quality. G.D. Combe, *Responsible Government in South Australia* (Adelaide, 1957) is little more than a chronicle. On the other hand, *A Century of Responsible Government 1856–1956* edited by F.C. Green (Hobart, n.d.) contains useful chap-ters by W.A. Townsley on Tasmanian problems, and *One Hundred Years of Responsible Government in Victoria* (Melbourne, 1957) includes an 'Historical Survey of the Victorian Constitution' by Zelman Cowen.

Among works which deal with particular problems, by far the most significant is H.V. Evatt, *The King and his Dominion Governors* (London, 1936). This is an examination of the reserve powers of the Crown as they appeared to exist in the mid-1930s, in the light of the dismissal of J.T. Lang. It is essentially a plea for the exact definition of those powers, and as such it tends to exaggerate the problems caused by lack of definition; but it provides a good counterbalance to the prejudices of A.B.Keith. That the vagueness which worried Evatt was not fully dispelled two decades later is attested by a short anonymous article entitled 'The Australian States and Dominion Status' in the *Australian Law Journal*, vol. 31, which comments on the 1956 Tasmanian crisis. The Balfour Report is dealt with in J.G. Latham, *Australia and the British Commonwealth* (London, 1929). The analysis is careful, if a little euphoric, and the text of the Report is contained in an appendix. K.C. Wheare, *The Statute of Westminster and Dominion Status* (London, 1938) is thorough and scholarly. A.B. Keith's *The Dominions as Sovereign States* (London, 1938) provides a different view.

Among other books which contain valuable material is *The Government of the Australian States*, edited by S.R. Davis (Sydney, 1960). The introductory chapter and the chapter on New South Wales are relevant. R.D. Lumb, *The Constitutions of the Australian States* (4th ed., Brisbane, 1977) makes some interesting points; and S. Encel, *Cabinet Government in Australia* (Melbourne, 1962) examines some important constitutional issues in the light of 'differences in political character' between Australian government and its British prototype. G.N. Hawker, *The Parliament of New South Wales 1856–1965* (Sydney, 1971) is a useful comprehensive survey.

There are relevant documents in Todd's *Parliamentary Government in the British Dominions*, in Clark's second volume, and in A.B. Keith, *Selected Speeches and Documents on British Colonial Policy* (London, 1933). K.R. Cramp, *The State and Federal Constitutions of Australia* (Sydney, 1913) is still useful for comparison of the texts, though thoroughly uncritical.

C. *The Establishment and Development of the Federal System*

For many years the federation movement tended to be neglected by Australian historians, and students were forced to rely on the accounts of participants. Up to the time of the Second World War the best of these was the 'Historical Introduction' to J. Quick and R.R. Garran, *The Annotated Constitution of the Australian Commonwealth* (Sydney, 1901) and the second best Garran's chapter 'The Federation Movement and the Founding of the Commonwealth', in vol. VII of the *Cambridge History of the British Empire*. B.R. Wise, *The Making of the Australian Commonwealth* (London, 1913), though a full account, was spoiled by partisanship and self-justification. Much better is Alfred Deakin, *The Federal Story*, edited by Herbert Broookes (Melbourne, 1944). A revised edition was subsequently brought out by Deakin's biographer, J.A. La Nauze (Melbourne, 1963). In the early period a number of specialized monographs appeared. They included C.D. Allin, *The Early Federation Movement of Australia* (Kingston, Ont., 1907); E.M. Hunt, *American Precedents in Australian Federation* (New York, 1930); and H.L. Hall, *Victoria's Part in the Australian Federal Movement* (London, 1931).

Since the late 1950s much more scholarly work has been done. Ward's *Earl Grey and the Australian Colonies*, already cited, includes a painstaking treatment of the early federal proposals. *Essays in Australian Federation* edited by A.W. Martin (Melbourne, 1969) contains a number of important contributions. They include a long article by Geoffrey Serle, 'The Victorian Government's Campaign for Federation 1883–1889'; a detailed examination of the origins of S.92 by J.A. La Nauze, 'A Little Bit of Lawyer's Language: the History of "Absolutely Free" 1890–1900'; and a valuable article by B.K. de Garis, 'The Colonial Office and the Commonwealth Constitution Bill'. J.A. La Nauze, *The Making of the Australian Constitution* (Melbourne, 1972) is a definitive treatment of the process of federal negotiation, and R. Norris, *The Emergent Commonwealth* (Melbourne, 1975) compares the expectations of federalists and the achievements of the first federal decade. Three useful articles on the motives of federalists are A.W. Martin, 'Economic Influences on the "New Federation Movement"', *Historical Studies*, vol. 6; T.G. Parsons, 'New Caledonian Convicts in New South Wales', *Royal Australian Historical Society Journal*, vol. 52; and G.D. Patterson, 'The Murray River Border Customs Dispute 1853–1880', *Business Archives and History*, vol. 2. The present author has attempted to explain the role of G.H. Reid in two papers, 'George Reid and Federation: the Origin of the "Yes-No Policy"', *Historical Studies*, vol. 10; and 'G.H. Reid and Federation: the Case for the Defence', *Royal Australian Historical Society Journal*, vol. 49. Other relevant works are listed in La Nauze's book. Scott Bennett, *The Making of the Commonwealth* (Melbourne, 1971) is a collection of readings from primary sources, with perceptive commentary and a useful bibliography.

The development of the federal Constitution has always attracted more attention than its origins and drafting. A student might well begin with K.C. Wheare, *Federal Government* (4th ed., London, 1963). This comparative treatment of the United States, Switzerland, Canada and Australia has become, since its first edition appeared in 1946, a standard handbook. There are some criticisms of its views as applied to Australia in S.R. Davis, 'Co-operative Federalism in Retrospect', *Historical Studies*, vol. 5. But the leading authority on Australian federalism is undoubtedly Geoffrey Sawer. His *Australian Federal Politics and Law*, vol. I, 1900–1929; vol. II, 1929–1949 (Melbourne, 1956 and 1963) is both a compendium and an analysis of constitutional as well as political development; his *Australian Federalism in the Courts* is the clearest available treatment of the record of judicial review; and his *Modern Federalism* (2nd ed., Melbourne, 1976) is a sophisticated analysis of the basic principles of federalism which contains some views on the decline of State powers in Australia different from those expressed in this book. He has also contributed to many symposia. Among these are *Federalism: an Australian Jubilee Survey* (Melbourne, 1952), of which he was editor, and *The Commonwealth of Australia: the Development of its Laws and Constitution*, edited by G.W. Paton (London, 1952). Although the former is mainly concerned with policy, it contains very useful historical papers by Sawer, Sir Douglas Copland and P.H. Partridge. Sawer's *Australian Government Today* (11th ed., Melbourne, 1973) is an excellent and clearly written brief handbook. Leslie Zines, 'The Australian Constitution 1951–76', *Federal Law Review*, vol. 7, deals clearly with the constitutional issues which came before the High Court in the third quarter-century of Australian federation.

Two standard political science texts are invaluable. L.F. Crisp, *Australian National Government* (2nd ed., Melbourne, 1972) has four relevant chapters, and J.D.B. Miller, *Australian Government and Politics* (2nd ed., London, 1959) has three. P.E. Joske, *Australian Federal Government* (Sydney, 1967) covers ground well trodden by Sawer as well as by Crisp, but from a highly conservative angle and

in a rather quaint manner. Three of the many excellent books primarily intended for lawyers are worth special mention. P.H. Lane, *Some Principles and
Sources of Australian Constitutional Law* (Sydney, 1964) can help to clarify some
historical points; H.S. Nicholas, *The Australian Constitution, an Analysis* (2nd ed.,
Sydney, 1952) is useful for reference; Christopher Enright, *Constitutional Law*
(Sydney, 1977) is an excellent handbook. *Essays on the Australian Constitution*
edited by R. Else-Mitchell (Sydney, 1952) also contains material of interest to
historians, as does the standard legal treatise on the division of powers between
Commonwealth and States: W.A. Wynes, *Legislative, Executive and Judicial Powers
in Australia* (4th ed., Sydney, 1970).

Several particular problems have been thoroughly discussed. G.V. Portus
(ed.), *Studies in the Australian Constitution* (Sydney, 1933) contains contemporary
analyses of the Financial Agreement. R.H. Leach, *Interstate Relations in Australia*
(Lexington, 1965), though primarily concerned with public administration,
makes some interesting points about uniform legislation. A detailed, if not
always perfectly accurate examination of the most ambitious attempts to amend
the Constitution before the end of the Second World War is C. Joyner, *Holman
versus Hughes: Extension of Australian Commonwealth Powers* (Gainesville, Fla.,
1961). There is a serious, though not necessarily unprejudiced treatment of the
1944 referendum in P.M.C. Hasluck, *The Government and the People 1942–45*
(Canberra, 1970). A.H. Birch, *Federalism, Finance and Social Legislation in Canada,
Australia and the United States* (Oxford, 1958) provides a comparative analysis of
two vital aspects of modern federalism and also some general comment on
Wheare's views. D.I. Wright, *Shadow of Dispute* (Canberra, 1970) is a very clear
and detailed treatment of some of the early problems faced by the
Commonwealth in its relations with the States. It is supplemented by a number
of articles by the same author, of which 'The Political Significance of "Implied
Immunities" 1901–1910', *Royal Australian Historical Society Journal*, vol. 55 is
particularly important. A contemporary treatment, from a lawyer's point of
view, of the early period is W.H. Moore, *The Constitution of the Commonwealth of
Australia* (2nd ed., Melbourne, 1910). Moore also wrote the chapter, 'The
Constitution and its Working' in vol. VII of the *Cambridge History of the British
Empire*.

Some of the many tendentious works on the Constitution that have been
published can be helpful to the student. The various contributions to the
Australian Institute of Political Science's symposium, *Federalism in Australia*
(Melbourne, 1949) are among these. F.A. Bland (ed.), *Changing the Constitution*
(Sydney, 1949) is an extreme States'-rights criticism of the evolution of the
Constitution in its first fifty years. The opposite view is given in Gordon
Greenwood, *The Future of Australian Federalism* (Melbourne, 1946). T.C.
Brennan, *Interpreting the Constitution* (Melbourne, 1935) argues that a con-
sequence of the judgement in the *Engineers' Case* was to make trade unions
dangerously powerful.

The 1975 crisis produced a flood of more or less tendentious literature.
Geoffrey Sawer's *Federation under Strain* (Melbourne, 1977), though not without
its own point of view, is by far the most balanced. Also less polemical than most
is G. Evans (ed.), *Labor and the Constitution* (Melbourne, 1977).

The student can best approach the primary sources of the history of
Australian federalism through Geoffrey Sawer's *Cases on the Constitution of the*

Commonwealth of Australia (Sydney, 1957). The text of the Constitution (before its amendment in 1977) is printed with a very thorough commentary in R.D. Lumb and K.W. Ryan, *The Constitution of the Commonwealth of Australia Annotated* (Melbourne, 1977). There are readings of constitutional relevance in F.A. Bland, *Government in Australia* (2nd ed., Sydney, 1944).

Index

207

DATE DUE

SEP 2 3 1998		
APR 2 5 2002		